INDIANS IN CHINA
1800-1949

INDIANS IN CHINA
1800-1949

MADHAVI·THAMPI

MANOHAR
2005

First published 2005

© Madhavi Thampi, 2005

ISBN 81-7304-615-8

Published by
Ajay Kumar Jain for
Manohar Publishers & Distributors
4753/23 Ansari Road, Daryaganj
New Delhi 110002

Typeset by
A J Software Publishing Co. Pvt. Ltd.
New Delhi 110005

Printed at
Lordson Publishers Pvt. Ltd.
Delhi 110007

Distributed in South Asia by
FOUNDATION
BOOKS
4381/4 Ansari Road,
Daryaganj, New Delhi 110 002
and its branches at Mumbai, Hyderabad,
Bangalore, Chennai, Kolkata

For
my Father and Mother

Contents

Acknowledgements

Following the trail of the Indians who lived in China in the nine-teenth and twentieth centuries has taken me to a number of different cities, libraries and archives. One of the pleasures of this work was getting to know and interact with many people who gave generously of their time and assistance, and who showed enthusiasm about the project. I thank all of them: listing their names below is an inadequate way of expressing my appreciation for all their help.

This volume has emerged out of the work towards a doctoral degree at the University of Delhi. To Dr Sreemati Chakrabarti, for her cheerful encouragement and support at all times as my dissertation adviser and friend, and to Professor V.P. Dutt, under whose guidance this work was first begun and who gave the draft a thorough reading, I express my deepest gratitude. I would also like to thank my other colleagues in the Department of Chinese and Japanese Studies of Delhi University for their coop-eration and encouragement, and particularly my senior col-league, Mrs. Huang I-shu, for carefully checking my translations of Chinese language materials. Professor Manoranjan Mohanty encouraged and assisted me at various stages of the work.

For taking the time to read through the draft manuscript and giving me very valuable suggestions, my deep appreciation to Dr Shivashankar Menon and to Professor Prasenjit Duara. I am also most grateful to Dr Asiya Siddiqi and the Rev. Carl T. Smith for sharing with me their deep knowledge on Bombay's China trade and of Indians in Hong Kong and Macao. In China, I greatly benefited from the discussions I had with, and the exceptional kindness of scholars I met in China, including Professors Lin Chengjie, Wang Shuying, Zhang Haipeng, Zhang Zhenkun, Liu Xinru, Wang Dehua, Zhang Jiazhe, Yuan Chuanwei and Duan Shaobo.

Various institutions and people made possible and facilitated the trips I made to China and Hong Kong to collect research materials. For their assistance in this connection, I would like to thank the University of Delhi, the Rajiv Gandhi Foundation, the China Association for International Friendly Contact (CAIFC), the Centre of Asian Studies at the University of Hong Kong and Coonoor Kripalani-Thadani in particular, and Betty Co and Bill Watkins of the Yale-China Association at Hong Kong. Ambassador and Mrs V.K. Nambiar, Consul-General Biren Nanda, and the staff of the Indian Embassy at Beijing and the Indian Consulate at Shanghai, also provided timely assistance and hospitality.

T.C.A. Rangachari of the Ministry of External Affairs, helped me with the knotty problem of trying to gain access to classified materials vital to my research in the National Archives at New Delhi. My deep gratitude as well to R.D. Sathe for taking the trouble to write down for me his memories of the last days of the Indian Consulate at Kashgar. My thanks also go to Ruby Master, U.S. Chellaram and Jafferbhoy Ebrahim for willingly sharing with me their memories and knowledge of pre-1949 Hong Kong. The task of collecting research materials was facilitated by the staff of a number of libraries and archives, but for their help beyond the call of duty, I would particularly like to thank Jaya Ravindran and P.K. Roy of the National Archives of India, and Zhu Xiaolan of the Beijing National Library.

Family and close friends responded willingly and enthusiastically to my calls for help and advice at various stages of my work. It would be true to say that I could not have accomplished whatever I did without their support. In Hong Kong, Santhanam was a most obliging guide. Sharmishtha Gupta Basant drew my attention to some valuable literature in Chinese and also helped me with translations. Prabhat, Srimant, Madhusudan, Srikant and Sujatha in Beijing and Dayawanti in Shanghai, helped me to find my way around and to make the most of my stay in China. My trips to different places to collect research materials were made possible because of the unstinting help and support given by my mother-in-law and other family members. Finally, I cannot thank enough Kannan, for his constant prodding as well as technical, logistical and moral support; Padma, for putting up with my repeated absences, and my parents, for the encouragement and support that they have always given me.

MADHAVI THAMPI

A note on Romanization and on the use of Abbreviations

Chinese names are transcribed in the now widely prevalent *pinyin* system of romanization, except where an alternative system of romanization has been used in a citation. Thus, for example, Sinkiang is referred to as Xinjiang, Tientsin as Tianjin, and so on. However, in a few cases where a name has come to be very well known, another system of romanization (as in the case of Sun Yat-sen, for example) would be difficult to recognize in its *pinyin* form by a reader not familiar with Chinese. In such cases, an alternative spelling has been used. This is particularly the case with Canton and Macao (instead of Guangzhou and Aomen) and with towns in Xinjiang, such as Kashgar, Yarkand, and Yangi Hissar.

The use of diacritical marks in transcribing the names of some Buddhist missionaries in Chapter 2 has been dispensed with.

The following are some of the abbreviations repeatedly used in the text:

NAI	National Archives of India
MSA	Maharashtra State Archives
CO 129	Great Britain Colonial Office—Hong Kong: Original Correspondence (microfilm)
JJP	Jamsetjee Jejeebhoy Papers
YWSM	Qingdai Chouban Yiwu Shimo
YPZZ	Yapian Zhanzheng Ziliao Congkan
MNI	Madras Native Infantry
BNI	Bengal Native Infantry
ByNI	Bombay Native Infantry

CHAPTER 1

Introduction

This study explores a relatively neglected phase of Sino-Indian relations—that of the nineteenth and early twentieth centuries. Moreover, it seeks to do so from a largely unexplored angle, that of the Indian community resident in China during this period. A quick look at the shelves of Indian libraries devoted to Sino-Indian relations would show that they are overwhelmingly preoccupied with the 1962 War, its immediate background, and the aftermath. Studies with a different focus largely tend to general descriptions expressing nostalgia for a golden age of Sino-Indian relations in the distant past, most of them written in or before the 1950s. The full complexity and continuity of Sino-Indian relations thus remain elusive. One could be misled into assuming that, between the golden era of relations based on Buddhism on the one hand, and the highs and lows of Sino-Indian relations in the post-colonial world on the other, these two great neighbours had practically nothing to do with each other.

Recent research has, however, shed light on certain aspects and phases of the Sino-Indian relationship. Studies on trade and diverse forms of cultural interaction between India and China in the pre-modern period, on the Indian mercantile network in pre-colonial and colonial times, and on the inter-connections between the nationalist and anti-imperialist movements of India and China, have gradually fleshed out the picture and helped to correct distorted perspectives. Liu Xinru, Haraprasad Ray, and Tansen Sen, in their work on the trade of China with various regions of India at different periods of time, have shown the wide-ranging nature and overall continuity of the commercial relationship between the two countries sustained through many political vicissitudes, and also helped to establish that the ties based on trade and those based on religion were closely interlinked.[1] Claude Markovits' work on the merchants of Hyderabad and Shikarpur in Sind, though not confined to their presence in China, illuminates important facets of the economic relationship between India and China in the colonial period, as does Asiya Siddiqi's study of the prominent China trader, Jamsetjee Jejeebhoy.[2] At another level, Lin Chengjie's general survey of Sino-Indian relations from 1851 to 1949 is without doubt the pioneering attempt to focus attention on the 'dark century' in Sino-Indian relations.[3]

The present study was undertaken with the conviction that an understanding of what happened between India and China in the colonial era is crucial to our understanding of how the Sino-Indian relationship has taken its present shape. My work was motivated by the belief that a study of the small community of Indians living in China in that era could throw light on the nature and evolution of Sino-Indian relations in modern times. When I first began research on this community, what struck me more than anything else was its 'invisibility'. It undoubtedly existed. Yet, except for passing references, it was by and large ignored, not only by contemporary observers, but by even those scholars and officials concerned most directly with Sino-Indian relations. As a Chinese scholar has recently noted,

'Parsi' is a name that has long been neglected, but Parsi merchants have played an important role in many developments in China's modern history. These developments—such as the opium trade, the Opium War, etc.,—have been thoroughly researched by the Chinese and Western academic world; but the fact that Parsis have been participants (and even important participants) in them has been ignored by the Chinese academic world, while Western scholars also have not done systematic specialized research on it.[4]

What was more, even in the voluminous literature on overseas Indians there was little that had as its focus the Indian community in China. The sole exception was the study by K.N. Vaid of the Indian community in Hong Kong.[5] As my investigation progressed it became increasingly clear that the 'invisibility' of this particular group was not due just to its relatively small size in the Indian diaspora. It was equally a function of the prevailing historiography in India, China, Britain, and other Western countries which has equated the activities of the Indians in China in the colonial period with those of the British, on the assumption that the Indians, whether they were traders, or soldiers, or anything else, were 'imperial auxiliaries' and nothing more. It became important, to borrow the words from Claude Markovits, to 'restore the agency' of these Indians and to look more closely at the question of the extent to which they were in fact 'instrumentalized', that is, by investigating the factors motivating them to go to China and the nature of their activities there.[6]

In his work on the American community at Canton in the pre-Opium War period, Jacques Downs has remarked with some irony, 'A perspicacious reader might ask: "Why study any dead community at such length?"'[7] In the case of the Indian community in China in the colonial period, my answer would emphasize certain features that made Indian traders unique among all the diverse and far-flung Indian groups overseas. First of all, it was distinguished by the preponderance of men of the security services. While other overseas Indians consisted in the main of traders, shopkeepers, and also labourers, nearly half of the Indians in Hong Kong and eastern China were soldiers, policemen, and watchmen. One of the endeavours of the present study is to probe why this was the case, what factors impelled so many men from Punjab, in particular, to seek out a military career in China, and the implications of this phenomenon on Chinese perceptions of India and Indians. Secondly, the Indian community in China was also distinguished by the extent to which it served as an overseas base in the twentieth century for revolutionary nationalist movements and organizations fighting for the overthrow of British rule in India. It has been said that China was second in importance only to North America as an overseas base of radical nationalist activity among Indians.[8] This is particularly interesting when one considers that the Indian population there consisted of a high proportion of soldiers and policemen, the 'pillars' of British dominance in the Far East. There is a need to understand the reasons for the remarkable transformation of loyalties on the part of these Indians under the impact of nationalism and anti-imperialism, and on the ways in which this affected relations between Indians and Chinese.

Finally, the thoroughness of the dispersal of Indians from the Chinese mainland in the 1940s, and the manner of the dispersal, is also unique in the history of the Indian diaspora. Other Indian emigrant populations that emerged during the colonial era survived decolonization: what, then, were the reasons for the virtual disappearance of Indians from the Chinese mainland? And how did this phenomenon impact upon Sino-Indian relations in modern times?

Starting in the last decades of the eighteenth century, a steady trickle of Indian traders from the west coast of India began to land on the China coast. Their arrival marked the resumption of a particular pattern of Sino-Indian interaction—of Indians travelling to and residing in China—that appears to have altogether ceased after the fifteenth century. The trade carried on by these Indians eventually became a part of the larger triangular trade between Britain, China and India under the auspices of the British East India Company. Meanwhile, another pattern of trade established over many centuries brought other groups of Indian merchants from north-western India across some of the most formidable mountain terrain in the world into Western China.

Nearly half a century after Indian traders began to make their appearance at Macao and Canton, these very ports witnessed the arrival of an altogether separate contingent of Indians—sepoys of the British Indian armies, brought over to fight the battles of the British with the Chinese in the turbulent century that began with the first Opium War. The aftermath of the Opium Wars, and in particular the cession of Hong Kong to the British and the opening of foreign enclaves in the 'treaty ports', led to more Indian migrants arriving as garrison troops, policemen, and watchmen.

Together, the merchant on the one hand, and the soldier-policeman-watchman on the other, made up the basic profile of Indian immigrants in China in the nineteenth and the first half of the twentieth century. There were also others, including clerks, a small number of professionals, a handful of political exiles, and so on, but undoubtedly the most representative figures were the Sikh and other Punjabi policemen in Hong Kong and Shanghai and the other treaty ports; the Parsi, Ismaili, and Jewish traders in the same cities, followed later on by the Sindhi businessmen; and the Kashmiri and Hoshiarpuri traders and

Shikarpuri moneylenders in Xinjiang. All of them found commercial or other career opportunities in China attractive enough to make the arduous journey by ship or mule caravan, coupled with residence in an alien environment, seem worthwhile.

The Indians in China did not constitute a large community by any standard. A few hundred in Xinjiang, several hundreds in Shanghai, less than a couple of hundred in the other parts of eastern China put together, and a few thousand in Hong Kong, would be a reasonable estimate for most of the period under review. Except for some Indians in southern Xinjiang, the Indian presence in China was almost entirely urban in nature, confined to the areas of the foreign concessions within the treaty ports. A large proportion either returned to their homes in India at the end of their working lives, or else moved on to other countries, particularly in North America. Nevertheless, Indians seem to have found a fairly secure niche in China. From the end of the nineteenth century, the disproportionate number of adult males in the community began to be balanced out with an increasing number of Indian women and children. Some intermarriage between Indian settlers and Chinese women also took place. In the twentieth century, the number of Indians in China grew steadily until it peaked at about 10,000 in the 1930s. Yet just after attaining this peak, political turmoil and war, the end of colonial rule in India, and the communist-led revolution in China, caused that number to decline sharply. There was an officially-sponsored mass repatriation of Indians from China in the late 1940s. Barring Hong Kong, which developed in a separate orbit from the rest of China after 1949, this meant the virtual end of the century and a half of Indian presence in China.

Along with the physical dispersal of the Indian community from the Chinese mainland, public memory of it also seems to have been extinguished, and neither the scholarly nor the official establishment in India or China has cared to resurrect it. A clue as to why, can perhaps be found in the words of the Chinese poet Xu Zhimo, who wrote in a regretful vein in 1923: 'I dare say when we look at an Indian we do not pity him, we despise him. I think Indians are the most misunderstood people there are; although they are in Asia, too, most people think of them as the same as the red-turbaned Sikh policeman on the streets.' [9]

Xu Zhimo's perception may have been that of a small section of Chinese intellectuals, that too, those with experience of Shanghai or other treaty ports. Nevertheless, this was not an unimportant section of Chinese society, nor does this perception seem to have been atypical of the way Indians were regarded in this period. M.N. Roy, who had first-hand experience of China, wrote in 1926 that because of the large number of Indian troops and policemen in some of the Chinese cities, 'the rickshaw coolies and street urchins stand in greater fear of the Indians than of the English or other foreigners'.[10] In this connection, it would not be out of place to consider what would have been the Indian perception of the Chinese if, for instance, Chinese had for over a century policed or garrisoned cities like Bombay and Calcutta for the British, or if they had fought on the British side in Plassey and other such battles. What is more, there is probably nothing in the Indian experience that corresponds to the degradation and humiliation undergone by the Chinese on account of opium —a commodity which was for a long time the mainstay of the Indians trading with China.

It is perhaps for this reason that little attention, scholarly or otherwise, has been paid to the role played by Indians in China in this period. Apparently, it is in the interests of neither Indians nor Chinese today to recall things which can be painful or embarrassing. An India and a China that are striving to 'normalize' their relations with each other do not need to be reminded about the presence of Indian opium traders or Indian policemen in the foreign concessions in China in the last century. And so the story of those and other Indians in China has remained largely untold.

Yet there is always a danger in letting the imperatives of diplomacy intrude into the writing of history. Realities that are suppressed or thrust aside have an uncomfortable way of resurfacing and forcing themselves on one's attention. Indians and Chinese need to look at the entire experience of their relations in the era of colonialism and imperialism dispassionately, and to come to terms with it. After all, colonialism and imperialism transformed not only the different societies which came under their domination, but also affected the relations between those societies and peoples. The migration of Indians to China in the nineteenth and early twentieth centuries was one facet of the process of western colonial and imperial expansion, a process that profoundly affected both India and China, in comparable ways. Whereas it is true that Indian traders and policemen made a living as part of a system oppressive or injurious to the majority of Chinese, their individual motives and actions pale into insignificance when seen in the context of powerful historical forces at work at the time. This is not to justify what they did in China, but we need to see things in their historical context. At the same time, a closer examination of the lives of the Indians in China would modify the prevailing image of this community and its role in China.

In a very real sense, the relations between Indians and Chinese are still living down the legacy of bitterness, suspicion and confrontation left behind by the colonial period. One aspect of this legacy is eurocentrism, that is, the mindset that has led different peoples to regard only what came out of Europe or the West as really important, while giving a much lower priority to other societies, and to relations with those societies. For most Indians, China, although recognized as a big neighbour, is 'distant in the public mind'.[11] China does not impinge on the Indian consciousness; Indian views of China by and large lack flesh and blood, a sense of involvement or strong feelings. The fact that thousands of Indians, many within living memory, chose to go to China to make a living, to establish businesses and settle down there, that they spoke Chinese and had first-hand experience of China and the Chinese way of life, would come as a surprise to most Indians—and to most Chinese too, for that matter. This is the significance of this historical study.

In this study, the term 'Indians' is used to refer to people of pre-1947 India, specifically to those from the area of the former British Indian empire, excluding Burma. 'China' refers to the territory within the boundaries of the present-day People's Republic of China, excluding Tibet.

This is not a study of all Indians who were in China in the period from 1800 to 1949, but is about the two largest socio-economic groups—the merchants on the one hand, and the category of soldiers, policemen, and watchmen on the other hand. It aims to bring to light the factors that brought them to China and kept them there, their activities in China, the nature of their interaction with the Chinese and with the British in China, the problems and difficulties they faced, and the factors that eventually impelled them to leave China—in short, the broad range of their experience as aliens in the Chinese environment. Since the merchants in the western regions were quite distinct from their counterparts on the China coast and eastern China, they have been treated in a separate chapter. The political mobilization of the Indian community in the twentieth century has been deemed as significant enough to also merit a separate chapter. As a background to the main subject of this work, it was further felt that it would be useful to deal with the subject of Indians who made the passage to China in pre-modern times, as well as with the phenomenon of Indian migration to different corners of the world in the colonial era, which provided the immediate context for the development of this Indian community in China.

It is unfortunate that the Indians in China who belonged to the major groups which are the subject of this study by and large did not leave any records of their own which would have made it convenient for a historian to document their activities or understand their frame of mind. A noteable exception are the records left by the prominent early China trader, Sir Jamsetjee Jejeebhoy, housed in the library of the University of Mumbai, although these papers emanate from the period after he had left China. Therefore, following the trail of these Indians has been a challenging exercise, rather resembling the efforts to put together a jigsaw puzzle the pieces of which have been scattered over different cities and countries. My own quest took me to libraries and archives at New Delhi, Mumbai, Hong Kong, Beijing and Shanghai. The collection in the National Archives of India at New Delhi proved surprisingly fruitful, particularly with respect to Indians in western China. It is still a source of amazement to me that it has been possible to uncover in these places so much information about what I had assumed, at the outset of my research, were a mass of nameless and faceless people about whom little would have been recorded.

NOTES

1. Liu Xinru, *Ancient India and Ancient China: Trade and Religious Exchanges,* AD *1-600,* New Delhi: Oxford University Press, 1988; Haraprasad Ray, *Trade and Diplomacy in India-China Relations: A Study of Bengal during the*

Fifteenth Century, New Delhi: Radiant Publishers, 1993; Tansen Sen., 'Maritime Contacts between China and the Cola Kingdom (AD 850-1279)', in *Mariners, Merchants and Oceans*, ed. K.S. Mathew, New Delhi: Manohar, 1995, pp. 25-41. See also his 'Gautama Zhuan: an Indian astronomer at the Tang Court', in *China Report*, vol. 31, no. 2, Apr.-Jun. 1995, pp. 197-208.

2. Claude Markovits, *The Global World of Indian Merchants, 1750-1947: Traders of Sind from Bukhara to Panama*, Cambridge: Cambridge University Press, 2000; Asiya Siddiqi, 'The Business World of Jamsetjee Jejeebhoy', *Indian Economic and Social History Review*, vol. 19, nos. 3-4, July-Dec. 1982, pp. 301-24.

3. Lin Chengjie, *Zhongyin Renmin Youhao Guanxi Shi 1851-1949* (The history of friendly relations between the Chinese and Indian peoples), Beijing: Beijing University Press, 1979.

4. Guo Deyan, 'Qingdai Guangzhoude Pasi Shangren' (The Parsee Merchants in Canton during Qing Period), unpublished Ph.D. thesis, Zhongshan University, Guangzhou, China, 2001, p. 6.

5. K.N. Vaid, *The Overseas Indian Community in Hong Kong*, Hong Kong: Centre of Asian Studies, University of Hong Kong, 1972. A more recent work, also focusing on the Indians in present-day Hong Kong, is Barbara-Sue White, *Turbans and Traders: Hong Kong's Indian Communities*, New York: Oxford University Press, 1994. The new millenium has thrown up two significant studies dealing in whole or in part with the Indian community in China. One is by Guo Deyan, based on a painstaking combing through of the Chinese sources. The other is an article by Claude Markovits, 'Indian communities in China, 1842-1949', in *New Frontiers: Imperialism's New Communities in East Asia, 1842-1953*, ed. Robert Bickers and Christian Henriot, Manchester: Manchester University Press, 2000, pp. 55-74.

6. Markovits, *The Global World*, p. 24, and 'Indian communities in China', p. 71.

7. Jacques M. Downs, *The Golden Ghetto: the American Commercial Community at Canton and the Shaping of American China Policy, 1784-1844*, Bethlehem: Lehigh University Press, 1997, p. 321.

8. Don Dignan, *The Indian Revolutionary Problem in British Diplomacy, 1914-1919*, New Delhi: Allied Publishers, 1983, pp. 32-3.

9. Cited in Stephen N. Hay, *Asian Ideas of East and West: Tagore and his Critics in Japan, China and India*, Cambridge, Mass: Harvard University Press, 1970, p. 241.

10. Sibanarayan Ray, ed., *Selected Works of M.N. Roy*, Vol. II (1927-37), New Delhi: Oxford University Press, 1988, p. 574.

11. Amba Bai, *Indian Views of China before the Communist Revolution*, Cambridge, Mass: M.I.T. Centre for International Studies, 1955, p. 35.

CHAPTER 2

Early Indian Travellers to China

This chapter explores the direct relations that existed between Indians and Chinese in the pre-colonial period. In particular, it is concerned with the role of those Indians who travelled to China. Although India and China are neighbours in a geographical sense, passage between the two has not been easy because of the formidable natural barriers between them. Consequently traffic between the two countries, as well as the exchange of material and spiritual values, has to a great extent had to pass through other areas such as Central and South-East Asia and through intermediaries from these and other regions.[1] Did Indians and Chinese have direct contacts with each other despite these constraints in the pre-modern period? If so, how extensive were these contacts and what impact did they have? Who were the Indians who travelled to China, where did they come from and what motivated them? These are some of the questions which will be explored in this chapter.

THE IMAGE

The predominant image of the early Indian traveller to China is that of a saintly individual in pursuit of lofty spiritual goals. The following lyrical description by Rabindranath Tagore captures the image eloquently.

I thought of that great pilgrimage, of those noble heroes, who, for the sake of their faith, their idea of the liberation of self that leads to the perfect love which unites all beings, risked life and accepted banishment from home and all that was familiar to them. Many perished and left no trace behind. A few were spared to tell their story, a story not of adventurers and trespassers whose heroism has provided a mere romantic excuse for careers of unchecked brigandage, but a story of pilgrims who came to offer their gifts of love and wisdom, a story indelibly recorded in the cultural memory of their hosts.[2]

In this passage, the early traveller from India to China is identified clearly with the Buddhist missionary. Tagore's idyllic perception of early travellers between India and China, as well as his understanding of early Sino-Indian relations as being uniquely problem-free, has been shared by a number of historians, officials, statesmen and others from both countries, and has not been substantially altered by the bitterness that has cropped up in Sino-Indian relations in more recent history. Writing in a similar vein to that of Tagore, Ting Hsi-lin has commented:

difficulties and dangers could not deter our Chinese and Indian forefathers from journeying to each other's country . . . their aim was not profit but the acquirement of knowledge. They absorbed new ideas and techniques at the same time that they made their own contribution. Such were the lofty ideals and selflessness that enriched the civilizations of both countries and fostered their mutual friendship. A frontier thousands of *li* long stretched between China and India, and their contacts date back thousands of years; yet not a single war has ever been waged between them. This miracle in international relations is due to high motives and admirable conduct.[3]

To a great extent, this 'golden age' portrayal of early Sino-Indian contacts, though not without historical basis, has derived from the comparison of these relations with the kind of relationship thrust upon China and India separately by the Western powers in modern times. A shared anti-colonialism has coloured the perception of this relationship on both sides. Apart from this, there is a discernible tendency, attributable to present-day diplomatic or political compulsions, to highlight the 'good' and downplay the other side in studies of the Sino-Indian relationship. This attitude, however, has come in for criticism in recent times. Warning against the dangers of taking a myopic view of the Sino-Indian relationship, Haraprasad Ray has commented: 'In assessing the significance of age-old India-China relations, the Indian mind is generally pre-occupied with the nostalgia for the golden period of its cultural exchange verging on obsession. The euphoria raised by the over-emphasis on Indianization of China through Buddhism sometimes blurs the view. . . .'

Ray specifically underscores how, in the course of this relationship, 'the zeal of the pious monk gave place to the initiative of the profit-seeking traders'.[4]

Early Sino-Indian relations in fact covered a wide spectrum of activity, religious and cultural, political and commercial. Interactions between the two peoples had their vicissitudes, ranging from the extraordinary warmth characteristic of the comings and goings of Buddhist missionaries and pilgrims, to long periods of minimal contacts bordering on what Tagore elsewhere called the 'accumulated dust of indifference',[5] although they were rarely coloured by hostility. A constant feature, however, was the intrepid character of those individuals who braved the rigours of travel through inhospitable terrain and unknown dangers of all kinds to make the journey to an unfamiliar land.

THE ROUTES

'Our way lay through an interminable sandy desert, with neither water nor grass. My companions gazed upon each other, not knowing when they must perish. . . . We looked around in bewilderment, having lost our bearings completely. We did not know whether to advance or to retreat. . . . So we travelled for several years.' In these piteous words did the Buddhist monk Dharmagupta describe the hazards of the journey he undertook to China towards the end of the sixth century AD.[6]

The passage from India to the major political, religious and commercial centres of China in the pre-modern period was by and large extraordinarily difficult, often necessitating a journey of several years through some of the most daunting terrain in the world. Apart from the sandy wasteland described by Dharmagupta above, the towering ranges of the Himalaya, Karakoram, and Pamir and Kunlun mountains, loomed large over the traveller. Those who took the route through Assam and Burma, avoiding these high mountain passes, nevertheless had to contend with virtually impenetrable forests. When the sea routes were opened, these too were not without dangers. Even among those who were fortunate to eventually reach their destination, many had to pass months adrift at sea, terror-stricken, with only the most rudimentary navigational aids to guide their ships. Bearing an uncanny resemblance to Dharmagupta's description of his overland journey is the following account by the Chinese pilgrim Fa Xian of his journey by sea back home from India in the fifth century: 'In the darkness of the night only the great waves were to be seen, breaking on one another, emitting a brightness like that of fire, with huge turtles and other monsters of the deep (all about). The merchants were full of terror, not knowing where they were going.'[7]

Broadly speaking, there were six routes between India and China, four by land and two by sea. Of these, by far the most important, prior to the eighth century, were the two that passed through Central Asia and which formed part of the famed Silk Route between the Roman Empire and China. Both these, starting from north-western India, crossed the Pamirs and emerged in the plains at Kashgar. From here the two routes diverged, one following the northern edge of the formidable Taklamakan Desert, bordering the Tian Shan mountains. The other took a southerly course, following the strip between the southern edge of the desert and the Kunlun mountains.

The mountain and desert landscape did indeed make the journey physically arduous. Nevertheless, from the time they came into existence, these routes were dotted with flourishing city-states or oases which had sprung up along the rivers that dried up in the desert. The Greeks who invaded northern India after the fall of the Mauryan Empire, as well as the Saka people and the Yue-zhi who established the Kushan Empire, succeeded to a great extent in culturally as well as politically linking these areas with India. In a parallel development starting in the second century BC, these areas also came to be connected with the Chinese empire. In an effort to contain the threat from the nomadic Xiongnu on their north-western frontier, the Han emperors launched an active policy of seeking alliances with and control of the principalities in the western region. Regular commerce followed, thereby opening up relatively safe routes for traders and other travellers between this region and the heartland of China.

The spread of Buddhism had a profound impact on the development of contacts between India and China. The welcome that Buddhist missionaries from India received in these regions encouraged and sustained them in their quest for the great empire to the east. Some of these oases, such as Kashgar, Khotan, Kucha, and Karashahar, in fact, became centres of Buddhist learning that attracted devout Buddhists, not only as convenient wayside stations en route to China or India, but as places to stay and learn. It was not uncommon for monks travelling from India to China to spend years on the way, out of choice, in these Central Asian oases. The monk Narendrayasas, for example, who travelled to China in the Tang period, is stated to have taken forty years passing through fifty kingdoms, covering a distance of 50,000 miles on foot![8] At the same time, the shifting political situation in this region, and the animosities and rivalries between the different states en route also posed dangers for travellers. Dharmaksema, who set out from northern India in the fifth century, was forcibly detained by a local chieftain in the western region of China. He worked zealously at translating Buddhist texts there for eighteen years, but was denied permission after that to return to India, lest he go to some rival principality in that region. When he defied the prohibition and set out on his return journey, he was murdered by his hosts.[9] Despite such hazards, the presence of culturally sympathetic and civilized centres along the way made the Central Asian routes the preferred routes for travellers between India and China until political turbulence in the later seventh century, and again in the tenth century, reduced their importance.

The other two overland routes were via Assam-Burma-Yunnan and Tibet. One school of thought considers the Assam-Burma route to be the earliest known route of passage between India and China. The foundation of this theory is the reference in the *Historical Records (Shi Ji)* of the great historian Sima Qian to the expedition by the Han envoy Zhang Qian to the western region from 138-126 BC. According to this reference, Zhang Qian, on his return to the Chinese court, reported that he had found bamboo and cotton cloth from Sichuan in Daxia (Bactria) which had supposedly been brought there by Indian merchants. This has been taken as indirect evidence of the existence of a south-western China–India route which antedates the routes through

Central Asia. This theory has, however, been disputed on the grounds that there exists no other substantial evidence of trade or intercourse along this route as early as this.[10] Nevertheless, despite the doubts about its antiquity and the fact that it was never as significant as the Central Asian or the sea routes, the Assam-Yunnan route was definitely used, perhaps mainly by the people of those regions.[11]

The route via Tibet developed relatively late, mainly after the seventh century, when Tibet developed closer relations with Tang China, although by some accounts some travellers between India and China had passed over it as early as the fourth or fifth centuries.[12] The conversion of a Tibetan king in the seventh century to Buddhism also facilitated passage through Tibet. The disruption of the Central Asian routes from the eighth century and, later on, the growing hold of Islam over Central Asia, increased the importance of this route, particularly in fostering relations based on Buddhism. But, like the Assam-Burma route, it was never a major channel of intercourse between India and China, the natural obstacles on this route perhaps proving to be a major deterrent.

For sea-borne traffic, the principal ports of embarkation for travellers on the Indian side were Bharukaccha, Surparaka, Kalyana, Quilon, Cochin, etc., on the western coast. On the eastern side, Kaveripattanam in the south and Tamralipti at the mouth of the Ganga were the most important. Initially, Tonkin in Annam was the port where ships bound for China unloaded their passengers and cargo. Later, Canton and Quanzhou became the major ports of disembarkation, with developed port facilities and flourishing colonies of foreign traders. Less frequently, ships offloaded further north, at Shandong. One route that was followed from India was via the open sea, with halts in Ceylon and Java. But, particularly in the days of unsophisticated navigational techniques, a more cautious route that hugged the coast of the Bay of Bengal and the Malay peninsula was also followed.

The sea routes developed in the early centuries of the present era. Various factors accounted for their increasing importance. As in Central Asia, the rise of strong, prosperous states along the route, which were influenced by Hindu and Buddhist culture and at the same time had cordial links with China, increased the attractiveness of the sea routes. The states of Funan, Kambuja, and Champa on the Indochinese peninsula, as well as Srivijaya (part of Sumatra and the Malay peninsula) and Java, played an important role in the interaction between Indians and Chinese. With the development of navigational and shipbuilding techniques, and particularly with the use of the compass from the twelfth century, these routes considerably cut down the travelling time between India and China. Furthermore, from the later part of the seventh century, the Silk Route was subjected to frequent disruption on account of the repeated political troubles the Chinese Empire faced from different nomadic peoples. For many centuries, the overland and the sea routes were used simultaneously, with many travellers, such as the famous Chinese pilgrim Fa Xian, choosing to travel by land one way and by sea on the return. At different times, one was more important than the other. But from the fourteenth century, after the death of the Mongol Kubilai Khan, the Central Asian route fell into disuse and the sea routes became virtually the exclusive route of traffic between India and China.[13] Although the links based on Buddhism were no longer important in this period, and although political and diplomatic links between India and China dwindled to nothing by the end of the fifteenth century, commercial contacts along this route were still being maintained when the Portuguese arrived in these waters.

BUDDHIST MISSIONARIES

Although there were various facets to the relations between India and China in ancient times, the transmission of Buddhism from India to China via the painstaking labours of missionaries and pilgrims from both sides certainly constitutes one of the most remarkable chapters of this history. Present-day Asian scholars, searching eagerly for some evidence of pan-Asian solidarity in the remote past, have highlighted the role of Buddhism as the most important factor which culturally unified the diverse Asian peoples, and that too in an altogether peaceful and voluntary manner. The historian and diplomat K.M. Panikkar undoubtedly had this in mind when he wrote that 'the thousand years of contact between India and China constitute one of the central facts of Asian history' and indeed 'the major factor in the shaping of the Asian mind.'[14] Indian historians have taken special pride in the fact that India was the fountainhead of Buddhism which transformed the cultural history of Asia. Chinese historians too, while being at pains to stress that Sino-Indian relations were not one-sided, acknowledge that China acquired much in terms of spiritual and cultural values from India.[15]

The 'Buddhist brotherhood' between India and China formed a discrete chapter in Sino-Indian relations. It commenced around the first century of this era and was more or less complete by the end of the eleventh. Thereafter Buddhism in India went into irreversible decline, and Chinese Buddhism, still flourishing despite the revival of Confucianism, nevertheless did not gain infusions of vitality from outside as it had done earlier.

For nearly ten centuries starting in the first century AD, a steady stream of Indians made their way by land and sea to China with the goal of propagating Buddhism. Unlike the merchants and traders, who are largely anonymous in the historical record, the identity of a large number of these individuals are known, their biographies having been carefully recorded in the Chinese sources. Indeed, the respect accorded them by their Chinese hosts was such that many of them have larger than life personalities: in all likelihood most of them were men of extraordinary capacity and determination.

Not all the Buddhist missionaries who came to China were from India. Several of the Central Asian city-states came under Buddhist influence, and became major centres of Buddhist learning, and produced scholars of eminence. The famous Kumarajiva, who revolutionized the process of translating Buddhist texts into Chinese, was himself from Kucha. He had his early training as a Buddhist scholar there, and went to Kashmir for further study.

Nevertheless, Kasyapa Matanga and Dharmaraksa, the first two Buddhist monks known to have arrived in China in AD 65, were from central India. As the well-known story about them goes, they arrived as a consequence of the expedition despatched by the Emperor Han Mingdi, after he had seen a dream to find out more about the Buddha and his teachings.[16] So well received were they that a monastery was built solely for the purpose of enabling them to stay and work, which was named the White Horse Monastery after the animal that had accompanied them on their journey. Apart from this account of the arrival of the first Indian missionaries in Luoyang, there is also evidence around the same time of Buddhist missionaries in south China (possibly arriving via the Assam-Burma route) being received by Prince Ying of Chu.[17]

Until the development of Nalanda as a great centre of Buddhism in the fifth century, Kashmir was the most important centre of Buddhist learning, the seat of the Sarvastivada sect. Many Indian scholars who travelled to China came from there, among whom were Sanghabhuti and Gautama Sanghadeva (in the later fourth century), as well as Punyatrata, Dharmayasas, Buddhayasas, Buddhajiva, Gunavarman and Dharmamitra (in the fifth century). However, the Buddhist missionaries went from virtually all parts of India to China. Dharmaksema, the ill-fated monk mentioned earlier, was from central India. Paramartha, who went in response to an invitation extended by the Emperor Wudi in the sixth century, was from Ujjain. From Jalalabad went Buddhabhadra, to whom even the great Kumarajiva considered himself inferior. Buddhabhadra, despite coming from the extreme north-west, is believed to have undertaken a difficult journey on foot via Burma, eventually reaching Tonkin. The monks Jnanabhadra, Jinayasas and Yasogupta came from the eastern region, Assam-Bengal. Dharmagupta, one of the few Indians to have recorded his impressions of his journey, came from Kathiawar. From southern India, one of the best known monks to go to China was Bodhidharma, the inspirer of the Chan school of contemplation, and a popular and mystical figure in Chinese Buddhist folklore. There was also Bodhiruci, who was invited by the Chinese envoy to what was in all probability the Chalukya court in AD 692.[18] Vajrabodhi, the last of the great Indian teachers who went to China, and who introduced a form of Tantric Buddhism there, was supposed to originally have been a Brahmin from Kerala. Some of these scholars belonged to the ruling elite: Gunavarman came from the royal family of Kashmir, Prabhakaramitra from one of the royal families of central India, and Vimoksasena from the Sakya royal family itself.

In China, the most significant work of these missionaries lay in bringing from India and translating into Chinese the various Buddhist scriptures. Their painstaking labours turned out to be of immense importance, not only from the point of view of transmitting Buddhism into China, but also in terms of preserving the core of the Buddhist canon. For most extant Buddhist scriptures are those that were rendered into Chinese. The difficulties of translation into Chinese were stupendous, not only because of the dissimilarities of language but also because of the gap in the philosophical concepts of the Chinese and Indian traditions. In fact, the work compiled by the earliest missionary, Kasyapa Matanga, entitled the 'Sutra of Forty-Two Sections', was not a translation of the scriptures at all, but an original work aiming to acquaint the Chinese with basic features of Buddhism.[19] Kumarajiva is acknowledged to have been the genius who made a real breakthrough in the process of translation in the fourth century, thereby facilitating the translation by others after him of the major part of the Buddhist scriptures, especially of the Mahayana school. Later, monks headed entire teams of Indian and Chinese translators at the monasteries where they were established, and some were responsible for translating more than a hundred volumes each. The prodigious output of Bodhiruci was supposed to have filled an entire room![20]

Indian monks were no doubt motivated to travel to China, in spite of the difficulties of their journeys and the slim likelihood of ever returning to their homeland, because of the respect and warmth with which they were received in China. From all accounts, the Indian missionaries to China were highly appreciated by their patrons, the Chinese emperors and princes, as well as other sections of society. The twelfth-century work, the *Zhufanzhi*, describes the reception accorded to a tenth-century priest called 'Lo-hu-na', who set up a Buddhist shrine called Baolinyuan in the trading port of Quanzhou. The traders, he said, 'vied with each other in presenting him gold, silks, jewels and precious stones, but the priest had no use for them himself'.[21]

The Chinese rulers extended special invitations to Indian monks, provided them with every facility for their stay and work, including the building of several monasteries, and lavished presents on them. On occasion, as in the case of Gunavarman who reached Nanjing in 431, the monarch even went out personally to receive his revered guest. At least a couple of the monks, such as Buddhayasas and Buddhabhadra, were confident and high-minded enough to refuse imperial gifts and to even refuse to pay their respects to the emperors, but were nevertheless allowed to stay and work in peace. Even the unfortunate Dharmaksema's murder on the order of his host was due to the latter's fear of losing him to rival—a perverse form of appreciation.

Despite such forms of appreciation, life may not have been easy for these Buddhist monks even after their safe arrival in China. For one, many of them had the misfortune to arrive in China during particularly turbulent times. Chinese accounts not infrequently record that their work was interrupted by political troubles. Some of them were detained before they reached the places they had originally set out for. Some were compelled to shift residence and flee from trouble, especially when their patron monarchs were forced to flee. Others sought, successfully or unsuccessfully, to leave China for India, their life's work left incomplete. The insecure conditions of the later Tang were particularly discouraging, to no small extent because of the insecurity of the Central Asian routes. But even relatively peaceful conditions could pose dangers for the monks who, as aliens totally dependent on the favour of the ruling elite, were highly vulnerable to hostility from different quarters. Prabhakaramitra came to China on an invitation from a Chinese envoy and made a favourable impression on the emperor on his arrival at court in the early Tang period. But apparently he fell victim to a slander campaign orchestrated by Confucian officials, as a result of which he fell out of grace with the Emperor and died 'brokenhearted'.[22]

Yet perhaps, even for those who did not experience such troubles, their sojourn in China could have involved sacrifice of another kind. Kumarajiva himself, whom the Emperor sought so hard to please and on whom he lavished attention, described himself as 'a bird with clipped wings'. He is believed to have lamented that his scholarly abilities were wasted in China, 'where the well-learned men are scarce'.[23] Obviously, the usefulness of the function he performed in China as the translator par excellence sustained him in a situation where he was starved of the company of his intellectual equals, because he remained in China till his death. Nevertheless, it is possible that among the early Indian missionaries to China, there were not just one, but several 'birds with clipped wings'.

INDIAN SCIENTISTS, ARTISTS AND CRAFTSMEN

Several Indian monks were men who were learned not only in the Buddhist scriptures, but in various sciences. During the reign of the Emperor Ming of the Wei dynasty in the third century AD, two Indian monks in Changan translated a treatise on the Panchavaidya or the five branches of knowledge, comprising phonetics and grammar, medicine, technology, philosophy, and logic. Another monk, Dharmaruci, translated an Indian treatise on astronomy. Many others were experts in medicine. The emperors Tang Taizong and Tang Gaozong were supposed to have taken medicines prescribed by Indian doctors, and Gaozong was so impressed that he sent a mission to India to search for good doctors.[24]

Indians made a special contribution in the field of astronomy. Astronomy and astrology had a special significance to the Chinese rulers as essential for the preparation of the official calendars. Both the Sui and Tang dynasties had special departments for astronomical calculation in which several Indians served, whose names are preserved in the official histories. Among them were a whole family of Indian astronomers, some of whom rose to the highest positions in the hierarchy. The best known among them, Gautama Zhuan (AD 712-76), was Director of the Bureau of Astronomy at the Tang court.[25] His forefathers, who originally came from Varanasi, arrived in China during the Wei dynasty in the early sixth century and settled in Loyang. His father was also head of the Bureau of Astronomy, and his grandfather too was Director of Astronomy under the Tang. A significant fact is that this family had become Sinicized to such an extent that the Tang records do not even record them as being originally natives of India.[26]

Indian artisans, painters, sculptors, and musicians also travelled to China in this period. The high value placed on their skills was no doubt related to the fact that Indian aesthetic values were transmitted to China along with Buddhism. The three great Buddhist centres of Dunhuang, Longmen, and Yunkang show the profound influence wrought on Chinese painting, sculpture, and architecture by Indian traditions. Of the artists and craftsmen who worked at these and other places in China, a number were from India, of whom the names of at least three painters—

Sakyabuddha, Buddhakirti and Kumarabodhi—have been preserved. Indian builders and sculptors were particularly appreciated in the Yuan dynasty. A builder called 'A-ni-ko' was brought to the court of Kubilai Khan, who set him to work building and repairing statues. He rose high, and was eventually put in charge of all metal-working craftsmen and became Controller of Imperial Manufactures.[27]

The offical history of the Tang Dynasty[28] refers to the presence of performing artists from India, such as musicians and dancers as well as acrobats. Indian music had reached China initially through musicians from Kucha, and became such a rage that the first Sui Emperor had tried unsuccessfully to impose a ban on it.

Chin Keh-mu has summed up the impact of the Indian visual and performing artists saying, 'The artists from India exercised a great influence on Chinese painting, sculpture, architecture, music, dancing and acrobatics. With very few exceptions, however, they have left no records and no names behind them'.[29]

POLITICAL MISSIONS

Apart from the contacts in the spiritual and cultural domain, India and China also had direct political and diplomatic contacts from early times. These took the form of fairly elaborate missions to each others' courts. On the Indian side were such diverse places as Kashmir and Cochin, Kanchipuram and Bengal. The Chinese imperial histories were particularly careful to record these missions, their size, frequency, the nature of the gifts exchanged, and so on. This was because these matters had a direct bearing on the prestige of the Emperor during whose reign they took place.

It is no coincidence that it was during the reign of Han Wudi (140-87 BC) that we find reference to the earliest efforts of the rulers of the newly-established unified Chinese empire to open up political and diplomatic relations with India. Han Wudi inaugurated the policy of actively seeking alliances with different states, especially to the west of China, in order to counter the threat from the Xiongnu. *The History of the Former Han Dynasty* (*Qian Han Shu*) mentions that Han Wudi also had diplomatic relations with Kashmir, referred to as 'Ki-pin'. He also is said to have sent envoys to Bengal.[30] The later Han dynasty historian, Ban Gu, in addition records the arrival of embassies from 'Huangzhi', believed to be Kanchi in southern India. The usurper Wang Mang, whose reign came midway through the nearly 400 years of Han rule, was reported to have sent gifts to the King of Kanchi, with Chinese silk and gold being exchanged for 'shining pearls, rare gems and strange products'.[31] Thus, from the accounts preserved in the Chinese sources, China from a very early stage had relations with kingdoms in literally all the corners of India.

The lengthy period of disunion in China, after the fall of the Han Dynasty in the third century AD and until the Sui rulers re-established the unified empire in 589, far from interrupting the political ties between China and India, saw the further evolution of these ties. By this time, the prestige of Buddhism was on the rise in China, and many rulers were ardent Buddhists. Relations were sought with India, the land that gave birth to Buddhism. The Gupta kings are reported to have sent embassies to the Southern Dynasties in 428 and 502. The rulers of north China are also believed to have maintained diplomatic links with India.[32]

The heyday of political ties between China and India was in the seventh to eighth centuries. During this period, China is believed to have maintained ties with kingdoms such as Baltistan, Kapisa, Uddiyana, Gandhara, Magadha, Kashmir, and so on.[33] Chinese sources record the arrival of a mission from King Siladitya in 692. The Pallava king, Narasimha Varman Raja, also sent an embassy in 720.[34] However, probably the best known of these relationships was that between King Harsha and the Emperor Taizong. A mission was sent by Harsha from Kanauj to the Tang court at Changan in 641. There was a curious sequel to this mission. The Chinese emperor sent a return mission headed by his envoy Wang Xuance in 647. By that time, Harsha had died, and his successor, a usurper, received the Chinese envoy with hostility. Wang Xuance was no ordinary envoy, and by way of punishment, he launched a military campaign against him with the assistance of Nepal and Tibet, resulting in the defeat of the Indian ruler. The latter became Wang's prisoner and was transported back to China.[35] Perhaps this was the only instance of an armed conflict between the Chinese and an Indian ruler in the ancient period.

The Song dynasty, which succeeded the Tang after a fifty-year interregnum, continued the political links with India. However, the sustained pressure mounted against it from the nomads to the north and west compelled it to turn its attention seaward. Song ties were mainly with the Chola kings. The Cholas are known to have sent envoys to their court on at least four occasions. The first, sent by Rajaraja I, reached in May 1015 while the second arrived in February 1020. Rajendra Chola sent a mission which reached in November 1033. A fourth mission was despatched much later, in 1077.[36] The twelfth-century Chinese work, *Zhu-fanzhi* mentions that the Chola envoys were ranked with those of the small Central Asian principality of Kucha, indicating a not very high estimation of the Chola kingdom by the Chinese court.[37] Relations with India continued under the Mongol Yuan dynasty. One of the missions despatched in 1280 by the ruler of 'Maabar' (in the Madurai region), specifically sought the help of the Chinese Emperor against adversaries.[38]

The last phase of the political relations between the Chinese and Indian rulers in the pre-modern period was during the Ming dynasty (1368-1644). The early Ming rulers, especially the Yongle emperor,[39] actively sought to build relations with other states and to invoke admiration, respect, and awe for the Chinese empire. The exploits of his naval commander, Zheng He, who in the fifteenth-century, headed several expeditions as far as the east coast of Africa, are well known. Zheng He and some of the ships under his command touched various ports on the Indian coast. Even apart from these expeditions, diplomatic relations through the bilateral exchange of envoys were maintained between China and various Indian kingdoms.

While the Chinese sent four missions to Bengal, the rulers of Bengal sent as many as fourteen to the Chinese court between 1404 and 1439. Diplomatic ties are supposed to have developed shortly after the founding of the Ming dynasty and during the reign of Sultan Sikandar Shah of the Ilyas Shah family.[40] The frequency of the missions from Bengal in the early fifteenth century—at times, as often as once a year—suggests a regular, and mutually profitable interaction. Those of 1408, 1409, 1410, and 1411 were sent by Sultan Giasuddin Ajam Sah, with the one of 1409 consisting of a huge delegation of 230 persons. The *Ming History* (*Ming Shi*) records that the mission of 1412 notified the

Chinese about the death of Giasuddin, following which the Yongle Emperor sent an envoy to Bengal to pay his respects to the dead king and to invest his successor, Saifuddin, who carried on with the practice of sending missions. The 1412 Chinese mission also visited Jaunpur and Delhi. The *Ming History* explains the absence of missions from Jaunpur to China on the grounds that Jaunpur was too far from China. The 1420 mission from Bengal was sent by the Sultan Jalal al-Din Muhammad Shah, while the last two missions, in 1438 and 1439, were sent by Samsuddin Ahmad Sah. 'After that', notes the *Ming History*, 'they came no more'.[41]

Apart from Bengal, the Ming emperors also maintained diplomatic ties with the rulers of Calicut and Cochin. They sent ten missions to Calicut between 1402 and 1433, and the ruler of Calicut sent eleven to China. Chinese sources refer to the envoys from Calicut as 'Naina' and 'Gabumanduluya'. The envoy sent by the King of Cochin in 1405 was listed as 'Wanzhedar' and the one sent in 1433 as 'Jiabu Bilima'. According to Haraprasad Ray, the names suggest that these envoys were all Hindu, even though by that period the Arabs had come to dominate the coastal trade, and in spite of the general belief that Hindus were prohibited from undertaking overseas voyages.[42]

Not much, however, is known about the identity of those who were sent to China as envoys. The chief envoys of the four Chola missions to Song China were listed in Chinese sources as Sa (Po)-li-san-wen (1015), Pa-lan-de-ma-lie-di (1020), Pu Ya-to-li (1033) and Qi-lo-lo (1077).[43] The *Veritable Records of the Ming Dynasty* (*Ming Shi Lu*)[44] record the names of some of the Bengali envoys as Sai-i-ma-ha-mieh (Said Muhammad), Pa-i-chi and Pa-chi-i (most likely the same person named Bayazid), Wu-to-man (Osman), Hsia-er-ye-mei and Na-ting.[45] The most prominent among them all was Said Muhammad, who led several delegations and served under five successive monarchs. Writing about him and others like him, Ray has commented: 'Not all of these representatives were real envoys, but merchants who were generally accredited by their rulers in view of their prowess and usefulness in extending trade relations. Envoys from foreign countries were not always officially appointed, but because of the importance of gaining the goodwill of foreign countries, no close examination ever took place in China. So they were allowed to pass themselves off as envoys and well-treated.'[46] This draws attention to the intricate balance that existed between diplomatic relations and trade. Certainly, the Chinese emperors—some more than others—desired relations with states from faraway places like India for political reasons, in the sense that the much-heralded arrival and reception of foreign missions served to enchance their prestige. Yet it could not be said that such relations were vital for the security of the empire. Similarly, for the various Indian rulers who maintained diplomatic relations with China, it could not be said that these relations directly affected the security of their states or of their thrones. Then what prompted both sides to outfit lavish missions and send them with costly gifts on a journey of hundreds of miles? A mutually profitable trade would seem to be the answer. What the Chinese records inevitably referred to as 'tribute missions' from these states were for the most part vehicles for an exchange of commodities desired by both sides. The envoys from India, often none other than traders, were willing to abide by the regulations governing tribute missions for the sake of the favourable trading opportunities that these provided, and their kings were willing to despatch such missions for the sake of the precious goods that they received from China as outright gifts or otherwise.[47] It is significant that, particularly in the later centuries, the main states in India which maintained regular political relations with the Chinese empire, such as Bengal and Calicut, were ones whose flourishing economies relied on trade.

Despite the undoubted commercial underpinnings of the missions between India and China, some also had specific political objectives. Mention has already been made of the mission from 'Maabar' which sought help for its ruler against his enemies from the Chinese emperor. Chinese missions were also sent for the investiture or formal recognition of Saifuddin of Bengal and Manavikraman of Calicut, and from time to time, the emperors personally composed inscriptions to commemorate such occasions. On one occasion, the Chinese emperor was even called upon to mediate between two warring Indian states. The Bengali king Jalaluddin sent a mission headed by Said Muhammad to the court of the Yongle Emperor of the Ming dynasty, complaining about the aggressive activities of the King of Jaunpur,

Ibrahim Sharqi. Although the emperor did not intervene militarily, as had been done in similar cases in other countries, he despatched a mission to Jaunpur, advising that 'only through good neighbourliness can you protect your own territory'.[48] The position of 'big brother' which the Chinese empire seems to have had in its political relations with India, as seen in the accounts of the various missions in Chinese sources, could of course be chiefly attributed to the hyperbole in praise of the Emperor in which such accounts were traditionally couched. However, it could also have been a reflection of the actual equations between China and India in this period, when China was a strong, unified empire and India fragmented into a series of small kingdoms, some of them more flourishing commercial emporia than rival states.[49]

TRADERS

Direct relations between India and China began with trade, and it was trade that sustained this relationship when Buddhism lost its prominent role and when political relations also ceased. The famous story concerning Zhang Qian's discovery of how Indian merchants had transported Chinese cloth and bamboo to Bactria indicates a commercial relationship that may have gone back to the second century BC or earlier. Although the dating of these sources poses a problem for historians, there are references to *Cina*, as well as *Cinapatta* and numerous other products of an obviously Chinese origin, in the *Mahabharata*, the *Ramayana* and the *Manusmriti* as well as ancient Buddhist Sutras. According to one account, the Chinese Emperor Han Wudi tried to open a trade route to India through the southwest in order to evade the Xiongnu, but was frustrated by the local people who were suspicious of any attempt to undermine their own monopoly of the border trade.[50] Together, all these references add up to a picture of direct trade between India and China that antedated the beginning of the present era. The routes along which missionaries, pilgrims, and envoys were to travel in later centuries were essentially the routes marked out initially by enterprising traders.

During the reign of Emperor Han Mingdi (AD 58-75), Indians were living in what is presently the Baoshan county of Yunnan province, pointing to a regular trade between India and China through the southwestern route.[51] The Histories of both the Former Han and the Later Han Dynasties ennumerate a number of products from different parts of India, including precious stones, pearls, perfumes, spices, fine linen, copper, tin, and exotic animals such as the rhinoceros and peacock. Following the break-up of China after the fall of the Han Empire, some of the Southern Dynasties, cut off from the Central Asian sources of horses, which were a politically and militarily important com-modity, began to import horses from Kashmir. These were transported to Funan on the Indo-Chinese peninsula, and from there shipped to China via the sea route.[52]

The trade between India and China was vulnerable to fluctuating political conditions in the two countries and along the route, particularly in Central Asia. Once the sea route was opened up, trade tended to swing between the land and the sea routes, depending on relative security. At the same time the trade showed a remarkable resilience in the face of political vicissitudes and, much like a river, found the most convenient channel to carry on. One reason could have been that the trade, although it consisted mostly of luxury goods, was important to the economies of certain areas (such as fifteenth-century Bengal or the ports along the Kerala coast) or else, it was an important source of rare and exotic items desired by the Chinese court and nobility. A study by Liu Xinru highlights the role of religion, and specifically Buddhism, in sustaining the demand for certain types of commodities in the Sino-Indian trade during times of political instability and de-urbanization in parts of north India and China, and despite the disruption of trade routes.[53] Analysing the nature of the items traded during this period, Liu suggests that ideological change and increasing emphasis on donations as a way of gaining merit for the believer, played an important role in keeping up the demands for goods from India, such as precious stones, camphor, and incense. For his part Tansen Sen argues convincingly that in the period after Buddhism ceased to be a major factor in the exchanges between India and China, the trade between these two regions, far from declining, continued to flourish on a restructured basis.[54]

With the growing importance of the sea route, particularly

during the Song dynasty (tenth to twelfth centuries), the major port of trade became Canton, which housed the headquarters of the Superintendent of Maritime Trade (*Shiboshi*). The Mongols who established the Yuan dynasty in the thirteenth-century were also keen to facilitate overseas trade. Under them, Quanzhou (known elsewhere as Zaytun) became an even more important port, with its own large resident foreign merchant community and its offices supervising the maritime trade.

For the purposes of this study, an important question concerns the extent to which this Sino-Indian trade was actually carried on by traders from India. Records from Central Asia, including both Sogdian records as well as Chinese documents, indicate the presence of Indian traders and trading colonies in Chinese Central Asia from as early as the third century AD. Other Chinese records show that the presence of Indian traders on the Chinese coast dates back to as early as the fifth century AD.[55] The famous pilgrim, Fa Xian, for his passage from Java to Canton on his return from India, chose to board a large merchant ship belonging to the 'Po-lo-mon', a term used at that time for those from the west coast of India.[56] From early times, important Chinese cities contained distinct neighbourhoods reserved for foreigners and their trading activities. Both the Han capitals of Changan and Luoyang had such areas, and the Northern Wei kingdom also maintained one when Luoyang became their capital.[57]

It is well known that enterprising Persian and Arab traders gradually came to play a major role in the carrying trade in the Indian Ocean. Thus, Panikkar concludes that after the Arab takeover of this trade, there was no direct contact between the Indian and Chinese merchants.[58] This is belied by diverse evidence that indicates the presence of Indian traders in China at a later date. Zhao Rugua, writing in the twelfth century, mentions a certain 'Shi-lo-pa-chi-li-kan, father and son' from Malabar, who 'are now living in the southern suburb of the city of Ts'uan (chou-fu)'.[59] The fact that these were not isolated individuals, but members of organized guilds, is corroborated by the archaeological evidence showing that south Indian traders built Hindu temples decorated by Hindu craftsmen at Quanzhou and other places along the south China coast. The remains found at Quanzhou include among other things, an inscription in

Tamil, *lingams* and medallions on pillars with the images of Narasimha, Vishnu, Krishna, and other Hindu deities. This certainly indicates the presence of a not insignificant number of Indian traders resident there.[60] It has also been pointed out that sailors from Calicut plying the eastern route were known by the Persian slang term of *Chini-bachagan,* which could be interpreted as 'China boys' or 'sons of the Chinese'.[61] Some of the large number of Muslim traders known to have been present in Quanzhou could also have been connected with Bengal or the west coast of India, and not necessarily with the Persian Gulf region.

Apparently these Indian merchants trading with China were not small peddlers, but included a number of veritable 'merchant kings'. Chinese sources of the eighth century refer to the enormous size of the ships of the Hindu and Arab traders, which were apparently so large that ladders several tens of feet high were needed to board them.[62] It appears that in the late eleventh and early twelfth centuries, the commerce between India and China was predominantly by Indian ships. However, shortly thereafter, with the development of Song naval power, the improvements in Chinese shipbuilding and the discovery of the compass, the Chinese began to displace the Indians in this aspect of the trade.

For centuries after this, Indian traders continued to be extremely active in the Indian Ocean and in trading goods with their Chinese counterparts. Nevertheless, their meeting-point was not in the various Chinese ports, but in Malacca, which became the principal entrepot in the eastern trade. By this time, Cambay became the principal port of trade on the Indian side, and Gujarati traders the most active elements in this trade. The Portuguese occupation of Malacca in 1511 diverted Indian traders' attention away from the east to the Red Sea trade, but did not displace their maritime commercial activities altogether. There was a brief revival of Indian trade with South-East Asia and China in the end of the seventeenth century, with Indian ships even venturing into the China Sea. But the eighteenth century saw an absolute decline in Gujarati trade and shipping. It was only in the later eighteenth century that Indian maritime trade and shipping revived somewhat on the basis of the British-sponsored and Bombay-based China trade.

NOTES

1. From the eighth century AD, Arab and later Persian traders, became important intermediaries in the Sino-Indian sea-borne trade.
2. Inaugural address on the opening of Cheena Bhavan at Santiniketan. From Tan Chung, ed., *Indian Horizons Special Issue: India and China*, vol. 43, nos. 1-2, 1994, New Delhi: Indian Council for Cultural Relations, p. 68.
3. From the foreward to Chin Keh-mu, *A Short History of Sino-Indian Friendship*, Calcutta: New Book Centre, 1981, p. 1.
4. Haraprasad Ray, 'Nature of Trade and Diplomacy Between India and China during Ancient and Medieval Periods', *Journal of the Indian Congress of Asia-Pacific Studies*, vol. 1, no. 1, Jan. 1995, pp. 39-40.
5. Tagore, op. cit., p. 67.
6. Cited in Chin Keh-mu, *A Short History*, p. 1.
7. Cited in Frederick Hirth and W.W. Rockhill, *Chau Ju-kua: His Work on the Chinese and Arab Trade in the Twelfth and Thirteenth Centuries, Entitled Chu-fan-chi*, New York: Paragon Book Reprint Corp., 1966, p. 27.
8. Chin Keh-mu, *A Short History*, p. 98.
9. From P.C. Bagchi, *India and China: A Thousand Years of Cultural Relations*, Bombay: Hind Kitabs Ltd., second edition, 1950, p. 42.
10. Dilip K. Chakrabarti and Nayanjot Lahiri, 'The Assam-Burma Route to China', in *Man and Environment*, vol. 10, 1986, pp. 123-34.
11. Chin Keh-mu, *A Short History*, p. 14. A Chinese source of the late eighth-century AD, 'Passages to Foreign Countries from the Border Prefectures', by Jia Dan, clearly describes two routes starting from Chengdu in Sichuan to India via Yunnan and Myanmar. See Chakrabarti and Lahiri, 'The Assam-Burma Route', p. 125.
12. Chin Keh-mu, *A Short History*, p. 14.
13. See Ray, 'The Southern Silk Route from China to India—an Approach from India', *China Report*, vol. 31, no. 2, Apr.-Jun. 1995, p. 34.
14. K.M. Panikkar, *India and China*, Bombay: Asia Publishing House, 1957, pp. viii-ix.
15. An example is the article by the doyen of Indology in China, Ji Xianlin, entitled 'Endless Flow of Cross Cultural Currents Between India and China', *Indian Horizons*, op. cit., pp. 5-9. See also in the same volume, Jin Dinghan, 'Give and Take in Sino-Indian Cultural Interface', pp. 33-6.
16. There are believed to be more than a dozen versions of this story. See Panikkar, *India and China*, p. 26.
17. Bagchi, *India and China*, pp. 7-8.
18. Ibid., p. 15.
19. Panikkar, *India and China*, p. 26.

20. Chin Keh-mu, *A Short History*, p. 96.
21. Hirth and Rockhill, *Chau Ju-kua*, p. 111.
22. Bagchi, *India and China*, p. 50.
23. Panikkar, *India and China*, p. 31.
24. Chin Keh-mu, *A Short History*, pp. 20-5, 97.
25. For an account of Gautama Zhuan and his unique family, see Tansen Sen, 'Gautama Zhuan: An Indian Astronomer at the Tang Court', *China Report*, vol. 31, no. 2, Apr.-Jun. 1995, pp. 197-208.
26. Sen, 'Gautama Zhuan', p. 201.
27. See Bagchi, *India and China*, pp. 146-73.
28. The 'official histories' of the different dynasties, such as the *Tang History*, constitute a major source for the history of imperial China. The official history of a paticular dynasty was actually compiled by the historians of the succeeding dynasty, based on court records, daily chronicles and other sources. Although they were written in such a way as to justify the replacement of the earlier dynasty by the one succeeding it, the official histories are usually acknowledged to be reliable sources of information containing a wealth of detail on all aspects of life in the period they covered.
29. Chin Keh-mu, *A Short History*, p. 79.
30. Ray, 'Nature of Trade and Diplomacy', p. 32. See also Chin Keh-mu, *A Short History*, pp. 12-13.
31. Panikkar, *India and China*, p. 18.
32. Chin Keh-mu, *A Short History*, p. 46.
33. Bagchi, *India and China*, p. 78.
34. Panikkar, *India and China*, pp. 22-3.
35. Bagchi, *India and China*, pp. 74-5.
36. Ray, 'Nature of Trade and Diplomacy', p. 35.
37. Hirth and Rockhill, *Chau Ju-Kua*, pp. 96, 101. For a study of Chola-China contacts, see Tansea Sen, 'Maritime Contacts between China and the Cola Kingdom (A.D. 850-1279)', *Mariners, Merchants and Oceans: Studies in Maritime History*, K.M. Mathew, ed., New Delhi: Manohar, pp. 25-42.
38. Ray, 'Nature of Trade and Diplomacy', p. 35.
39. Yongle refers to the reign name of this particular Ming dynasty ruler. Chinese emperors were often identified by the name given to their reign period, rather than by their personal names. Hence, the correct reference is to 'the Yongle Emperor' rather than to 'Emperor Yongle'.
40. Tatsuro Yamamoto, 'International Relations Between China and Countries along the Ganga in the Early Ming Period', *The Indian Historical Review*, vol. 4, no. 1, 1 July 1977, p. 15.
41. Sujit Kumar Mukhopadhyaya and Hsiao Ling Wu, 'Political Intercourse Between Bengal and China (Translated from Chinese Records)', *Modern Review*, vol. 77, no. 3, March 1945, p. 122. See also Yamamoto, 'International Relations', pp. 17-18.

42. Haraprasad Ray, *Trade and Diplomacy in India-China Relations: A Study of Bengal During the Fifteenth Century*, New Delhi: Radiant Publishers, 1993, p. 125.

43. Tansen Sen, 'Maritime Contacts', pp. 28-9. The author argues that at least some of the Chola envoys seem to have been Arab traders who represented different states on different missions.

44. The 'Veritable Records' of a dynasty refer to the chronicle of events at court recorded daily by the official scribes. They constitute one of the main primary sources on which the offical histories and other historical works of imperial China are based.

45. Yamamoto, 'International Relations', p. 15.

46. Ray, *Trade and Diplomacy*, p. 125.

47. The nature of what has been called 'tributary trade' has been analyzed in some detail by Mark Mancall in his article, 'The Ch'ing Tribute System: An Interpretive Essay', in *The Chinese World Order*, ed. J.K. Fairbank, Cambridge, Mass: Harvard University Press, 1968, pp. 79-85.

48. Ray, 'Nature of Trade and Diplomancy', p. 36.

49. Ibid., p. 39.

50. Ibid., p. 32.

51. Ibid., p. 33.

52. Ibid., p. 33. See also Chin Keh-mu, *A Short History*, pp. 12-13, and Tansen Sen, *Buddhism, Diplomacy and Trade: The Realignment of Sino-Indian Relations, 600-1400*, Honolulu: Association for Asian Studies and University of Hawaii Press, 2003, p. 163.

53. Liu Xinru, *Ancient India and Ancient China: Trade and Religious Exchanges, A.D. 1-600*, New Delhi: Oxford University Press, 1994.

54. Sen, *Buddhism, Diplomacy and Trade*, pp. 240-3.

55. Ibid., pp. 162-3.

56. Hirth and Rockhill, *Chau Ju-Kua*, p. 7.

57. Liu Xinru, *Ancient India and Ancient China*, p. 47.

58. Panikkar, *India and China*, p. 23.

59. Hirth and Rockhill, *Chau Ju-kua*, p. 88.

60. Tansen Sen, 'Maritime Contacts', pp. 32-3. See also Chen Dasheng and Denys Lombard, 'Foreign Merchants in Maritime Trade in Quanzhou ("Zaitun"): 13th and 14th centuries', in *Asian Merchants and Businessmen in the Indian Ocean and the China Sea*, ed. Denys Lombard and Jean Aubin, New Delhi: Oxford University Press, 2000, pp. 20-1, and Simon Digby, 'The Maritime Trade of India,' in *The Cambridge Economic History of India*, vol.1, ed. T. Raychaudhuri and I. Habib, Cambridge: Cambridge University Press, pp. 407-33.

61. H.P. Ray, however, disputes this interpretation of the term *chini bachagan*, pointing out that in Malayalam the word *cina* refers to a 'large cargo boat' and hence *chinibachagan* would merely imply 'boatmen'. See

his 'An Enquiry into the Presence of the Chinese in South and South-East Asia after the Voyages of Zheng He in Early Fifteenth Century', in *Mariners, Merchants and Oceans,* ed. K.S. Mathew, op. cit., pp. 98-9.

62. Hirth and Rockhill, *Chau Ju-kua,* p. 9.

CHAPTER 3

Indian Emigration in the Modern Era

The migration of Indians to China in the nineteenth and twentieth centuries was a product of the conjunction of two phenomena. One was a search for better commercial opportunities on
the part of Indians from distinct business communities, which
led them to foreign lands. Some of them were temporary
sojourners, some settled down there. This was a very old phenomenon, accounting for the presence of Indians over many centuries
in a wide arc of states bordering the Indian Ocean as well as in
Central Asia, Russia and China. The term 'trade diaspora' has
been used to characterize this kind of a broad, if not voluminous,
dispersal of merchants in pre-modern times. The other phenomenon was the much more extensive emigration of Indian
people beginning in the nineteenth century, as a direct or
indirect product of British colonial expansion. Indians emigrated
to far-flung areas stretching from Europe to North and South
America and the Caribbean, as well as to the Pacific islands and
Australasia. For the first time, Indians went abroad not only in
their time-honoured role as merchants, but also as labourers and
as functionaries of the paramount power abroad, as clerks,
policemen, soldiers and so on.

True, too fine a distinction cannot be made between these
two phenomena. In a very real sense, they overlapped. The Parsi
traders involved in the China trade, for instance, could be viewed
both as free actors impelled by their own search for lucrative
profits as well as auxiliaries of the dominant British commercial
interests. On the other hand, the Punjabi youth who served in
the ranks of the British army deployed in other lands was not,

strictly speaking, a forced recruit, but had an eye on bettering his own economic prospects. Nevertheless, maintaining this distinction is useful to highlight that the migration of Indians to places like China in the nineteenth and twentieth centuries was both a continuation of a centuries-old process as well as a product of circumstances related to the altogether new British colonial presence in India.

THE INDIAN TRADE DIASPORA

In *Cross-Cultural Trade in World History* Philip Curtin has noted that 'trade diasporas are an old and widespread institution.'[1] Tracing the early history of cross-cultural trade, he observes that apart from merchants who moved back and forth along the trade routes, there arose the distinct phenomenon of trading settlements consisting of 'commercial specialists' from other countries. A series of such trading settlements formed a trade network or a trade diaspora.

In a parallel to Braudel's study of the Mediterranean, K.N. Chaudhuri has argued that the Indian Ocean region too has to be seen as having an underlying unity, represented by 'means of travel, movements of peoples, economic exchange, climate and historical forces'.[2] In the sustaining of the links binding the Indian Ocean region as well as its contiguous land mass of Central Asia, it can be argued that the Indian mercantile diaspora played no small role. Indian merchants went far and wide, disproving notions that religious considerations prevented them from doing so.[3] They were famed for their commercial ability and their staying power in the face of the difficulties frequently encountered in cross-cultural trade. A contemporary account of the role of Indians in East Africa in the mid-nineteenth century notes that 'the preponderating influence, if not monopoly of the Indian trader is equally great, as far as the Portuguese possessions extend to the south, and on the north-west coast of Madagascar. . . . Along some 6,000 miles of sea coast in Africa and its islands, and nearly the same extent in Asia, the Indian trader is, if not the monopolist, the most influential, permanent and all-pervading element of the commercial community.'[4] Stephen F. Dale has gone so far as to talk in terms of an 'Indian world economy' in the early modern era which, he claims, has not received adequate scholarly attention only because of a Eurocentric bias in historical scholarship in this field.[5]

For a long time, the image of the Asian, and hence Indian, trader in Western scholarship was dominated by Jacob Van Leur's portrayal of the peddlar hawking his luxury goods from market to market. This characterization is now generally considered to be inadequate. For apart from those who broadly conformed to the 'peddlar' type, there were a number of wealthy merchants and skilled professionals who commanded considerable capital and who used a variety of sophisticated trading mechanisms. Some accompanied their cargo themselves to and from foreign markets, while others deputed junior partners to oversee their business there, or else consigned their cargo to agents. Others stayed on for years in foreign locations, even marrying locally and playing a more diversified role in the commercial life of the areas where they resided. In some cases, the competition they offered to local businessmen was serious enough to arouse jealousy and suspicion against them.[6] Generally speaking, despite having virtually no political or material support from their home governments, Indian merchants abroad were able to prosper in varied foreign locations. One of their advantages was their propensity to rely on the family-based firm, with fewer managerial costs and greater stability and cohesion.

There seems to be broad agreement among scholars that the sixteenth to eighteenth centuries witnessed the heyday of overseas trade and commerce on the part of Indian merchants, whether it was maritime trade in the Indian Ocean or overland trade with Iran and Central Asia. Unlike the great European mercantile companies that began to penetrate the Indian Ocean trade in this period, the Indian merchants had very little by way of active political support from the government back home. Nevertheless, the success of their ventures abroad was not unrelated to the political conditions of the time. The Mughal milieu was not unfavourable to the development of commerce and was at the very least characterized by 'a quality of freedom' and willingness to leave the conduct of commerce to the merchants themselves, as long as the concerned officials received their dues and there was no major trouble.[7]

Under these conditions, Indian merchants carried on a flourishing trade in the Indian Ocean. Initially, they were particularly active on the route from Cambay, then the principal port on the west coast, to Malacca, the main entrepot in the eastern Indian Ocean. The Portuguese occupation of Malacca in 1511 diverted the main thrust of Indian commerce and shipping westwards, towards the Red Sea. Nevertheless, the direct trade with China from Surat, which replaced Cambay as the pre-eminent port in India of overseas trade on the west coast, revived from the last quarter of the seventeenth century. In this period, the major commodity sought from China seems to have been gold, along with some tea and porcelain, some of which was re-exported to the Red Sea region. The items exported from India to China were mainly silver, pepper, and sandalwood. It appears that for various reasons the profitability of this trade with China decreased after an initial spurt in its growth, but it nevertheless continued to prosper till about the middle of the eighteenth century.[8]

The entry of European traders, beginning with the Portuguese, did not itself disrupt or depress this trade. The Europeans initially participated in it without substantially altering its structure. Until the middle of the eighteenth century, the intra-Asian trade continued to be more important than the trade in the region which involved carrying goods between Asia and Europe.[9] Generally speaking, the Europeans, while adding an additional element of competition, were willing to 'play by the rules of the game'. In fact, by adding to the carrying capacity of this trade, they gave it an impetus. Indian traders, far from yielding in front of their new rivals, competed fiercely with them, especially in terms of defending their access to the Red Sea markets.[10]

In the early expansion of their economic activity in and from western India, the British were in fact vitally dependent on the long-established Indian trading community centred in Surat. Without access to the credit and financial facilities, as well as to the production and distribution network organized by the Gujarati traders, British trade in this region would have been greatly handicapped in a crucial phase of its development.[11] Many Indian merchants acted as brokers to the British, but not from the position of subservience that was to characterize later relations between Indian and British business. Ashin Das Gupta has discussed the inappropriateness of characterizing the Indian brokers of British trading firms in general and in all periods as 'compradors' and 'collaborators', pointing out that the principal could be as dependent on his broker as the broker on his principal. Talking about the Parsi partnership with the British in the China Trade, Claude Markovits has gone even further and argued that it would not be wrong to say that it was 'the Parsi network [that] contributed to shaping the specific form that British economic penetration took in China'.[12]

This relationship of relative equality or partnership initially characterized the dealings between British and Indian businessmen even in British-ruled Bombay. Hemmed in by the Maratha and Mysore powers, subject to pirate depredations and chronically short of revenue, the Bombay Presidency was the most vulnerable of all the major British possessions in India in the later part of the eighteenth century.[13] The Indians who were nevertheless attracted to Bombay and its growing trade were able to secure, under these conditions, largely favourable terms in their dealings with the British. Asiya Siddiqi finds that in this period, the Indian merchants, the European merchants, and the Bombay Government 'formed a remarkably close-knit oligarchy which governed both the island and its overseas trade'.[14]

With the decline of Surat as a trading centre from around the middle of the eighteenth century, various groups of Indian businessmen on the west coast began to shift their base of operations to Bombay. Of all of them, the Parsis were the most numerous. Before their establishment in Bombay and their association with the British, particularly in the China trade, the Parsis in western India had engaged in agriculture as well as in occupations such as spinning, weaving, carpentry, and so on, although a Dutch account of 1746 claimed that Parsis owned 10 per cent of Surat's total trading capital.[15] In 1735, Lowji Nussarwanji Wadia was invited to Bombay from Surat to become the East India Company's master shipbuilder. He built and repaired ships of the Royal British Navy and private traders as well as those of the Company. Another dominant personality from Bombay's China trade, Jamsetjee Jejeebhoy, was the son of a poor weaver of Navsari, who began earning his livelihood in Bombay participating in his uncle's bottle-selling business. By the 1780s, the early trickle of enterprising Parsis as well as others into Bombay had become a large-scale migration, contributing to Bombay's growing prosperity along with Surat's further eclipse.

It was, however, participation in the growing trade in bulk raw cotton exports and later, opium, to China from Bombay, that brought about 'a sharp turn to the fortunes' of the Parsis and other Indian traders.[16] Unlike the traditional overseas trade from India, including the traditional trade to China, the Bombay-based China trade was largely an outgrowth of the trade between Britain and China which, from the early seventeenth century, had been carried on exclusively by the East India Company on the British side. The Chinese market showed little capacity to absorb goods from Europe, and as the eighteenth century wore on, the Company found it increasingly difficult to secure the necessary amount of bullion with which to pay for its growing tea and silk purchases from China. There was, however, a sizeable market in China for the products of India, particularly raw cotton and opium. While Indian traders were debarred from participating in the trade between China and Britain, the prohibition did not apply to the trade in Asian waters. The Armenians were the first among the non-British private traders to take advantage of this, the so-called 'country trade' to China, since they had already been trading with China for a considerable length of time. But by the later eighteenth century, they were displaced by the Parsis. In 1756 Hirji Jivanji Readymoney visited China in an Armenian ship to explore the prospects for trade, and in 1775 the Readymoneys became the first Parsi family to commence trade with China in their own ships. Others followed in quick succession.[17] According to Asiya Siddiqi, a considerable part of the capital that had been accumulating in the hands of Indian traders at Surat and elsewhere in traditional trade and banking operations, and which needed an outlet particularly because of the overall decline in textile production as well as the decline in the trade to West Asia, was channelled into the China trade in this manner.[18]

Other indigenous commercial networks extended Indian economic influence in a northern and north-western direction over the high mountain ranges into Central Asia. When the Englishman Moorcroft visited Ladakh between 1820 and 1822, with the intention of finding out the prospects for opening up trade between British India and Central Asia, he found a system of trade already firmly established between Leh and Yarkand in Chinese Turkestan, which had existed for centuries.[19] This trade was dominated by a Kashmiri merchant network, formed between the fourteenth and seventeenth centuries, which extended into Tibet as well.[20] The distinctive features of this trade and its principal actors remained largely unchanged until it finally ended in the 1930s, despite the British political thrust into this area from the second half of the nineteenth century. Another such network was that of the Sindhi financiers of Shikarpur. They had risen to a position of importance in financing trade in Central Asia through their connections with the Durrani Empire in Afghanistan in the later eighteenth century, and were ubiquitous as moneylenders in Xinjiang in the later nineteenth and early twentieth centuries. They too, in the words of Claude Markovits, constituted a 'case of a network which developed independently of the British connection and was able to maintain this relative independence until the time of the Russian Revolution'.[21]

The age-old Indian trade diaspora thus did not actually come to an end with the advent of the British. However, by the nineteenth century, it had begun to undergo a substantial metamorphosis, not only changing its main thrust and area of operation (as it had done many times in the past), but also gradually becoming part of a larger trading network dominated by British and European economic power. Stephen Dale has commented that 'In the late nineteenth and early twentieth centuries, these diasporas became extensions or personifications not of Indian economic influence, but of a newly triumphant European world economy.'[22] Markovits however has a slightly different emphasis when he argues that 'from the point of view of the *longue duree*, the subordination of Indian merchants to European global interests can be seen as an interval in a longer history of intra-Asian trade of which Indian merchant networks were very much part.'[23]

INDIAN EMIGRATION IN THE COLONIAL PERIOD

The traditional Indian mercantile diaspora, however significant it may have been in terms of the history of cross-cultural trade, was never more than a trickle in terms of the numbers of persons involved. The merchants settled abroad and the travelling merchants were numbered in terms of hundreds, a few thousands at the most. By contrast, the migration of Indians abroad that began from the early nineteenth century was a virtual flood. It is estimated that the number of Indians leaving India between 1837 and 1937 amounted to about 31 million. Of course compared to the percentage of the population that emigrated from other countries in the same period, including the British Isles and various European countries, this did not amount to a significant exodus of the population of India. Nevertheless, the size of the migratory movement in the nineteenth and twentieth centuries makes it a qualitatively different phenomenon. Indian emigration to China in the nineteenth and early twentieth centuries, while never extensive, was also an integral part of this modern tide of migration that took Indians in large numbers to all the corners of the globe.

The spurt in Indian migration overseas between the 1830s and the 1930s was a product of British colonialism in two ways. First, the steady expansion of British overseas involvement required labour and services that could not be met adequately by relying on the British population alone. Second, within India, under the impact of British rule, changes were taking place in the economy and society that were uprooting people and compelling them to seek alternative means of livelihood. At the very least, it made them receptive to new prospects of employment.

Indian emigration in the nineteenth and early twentieth centuries is customarily identified with indentured labour: hundreds of thousands of destitute Indians did backbreaking labour in abominable conditions on plantations and mines in far-flung colonies, bonded to their employers until their period of contract had expired. The abolition of slavery in Britain in 1833 had put an end to a vital source of labour needed for the exploitation of land acquired in new territories in different parts of the globe. Initially, the British had experimented with the use of 'free native labour' in those colonies, but in parts of Africa, the Caribbean and the Pacific islands such labour was either unsuitable or unwilling to perform the kind of arduous and often degrading work required.[24]

The repeated and urgent requests made by British colonists overseas for Indian labour coincided with growing destitution and landlessness in India, particularly in those areas which had been longest under the rule of the East India Company. The decline of the traditional economy, especially of the traditional handicraft industry, the new land settlements with their fixed property rights in land and the onerous land tax systems, and repeated wars with their accompanying devastation, all combined to make rural areas of Bengal, Bihar and eastern UP good sources of readily available cheap labour. Starting in the late eighteenth century, famines occuring with regular periodicity also added to the desperation of the local population. Professional recruiters of labour fanned out into the countryside, making a point to visit those villages where there had recently been crop failure.

Indentured Indian labour was first sent overseas to Mauritius in 1836. From 1838, men began to be shipped out to the West Indies and to the Straits Settlements. The exodus to Ceylon had begun even earlier, while emigration to Burma began later, after the annexation of the Irrawady delta by the British in 1852. With the abolition of slavery in France in 1849, the French colonies also began to show interest in Indian labour, and the British government at this stage was willing to oblige. The Dutch also began to import Indian labour for Surinam on the north coast of Latin America.

Indian labourers, overwhelmingly male, were shipped out in vessels with frighteningly high mortality rates. Conditions out in the colonies were no better: the labourers had no right to change their employers for the duration of the five-year contract. Desperate though they were to have even gone out on contract in the first place, the hardship was too much for most of them to bear. A large number of those who returned home at the end of their contract refused to go back and also discouraged others from going. This resulted in a serious crisis for the plantation owners, as it led to an actual fall in the numbers of those going out for a while. Plantation owners began to resort to various means to prolong the period of stay for those already in their employ. This included punitive measures which virtually trapped the men into staying on, as well as inducements to stay permanently in the form of grants of small plots of land for homesteads. To some extent, these measures succeeded in establishing Indian communities in the West Indies, Surinam, Mauritius, Ceylon, Malaya, and Burma which remained in those territories even after the system of indentured labour was formally terminated in 1916.

The requirements of British imperial expansion, however,

included not only cheap labour but also the personnel to man the administration as well as military and police forces, part-icularly at the lower levels. For these requirement as well, the British found Indians suitable, though not usually Indians from the same regions or sections of society that provided the bulk of the indentured labour. British interests in China did not require the import of labour or a significant number of administrative personnel from India, but the British relied heavily on Indian army regiments and police. The first occasion when Indian troops were deployed in action was during the First Opium War in China.[25] Thereafter, they took part in practically every major military engagement of Britain in China and were also continuously involved in the garrisoning and policing of Hong Kong and of the foreign concessions in China's treaty ports in the nineteenth and twentieth centuries. It would not be an exaggeration to say that the most characteristic and well-recognized figure among Indians in China in the nineteenth and early twentieth centuries was the Sikh policeman wielding his baton and patrolling the streets of the foreign concessions in the treaty ports.

Britain's recruitment of Indian soldiers was facilitated by what has been called the existence of a 'military labour market' in India even before their arrival. In a period characterized by frequent wars between different Indian principalities, it was not uncommon for soldiers to move from one state to another or to transfer their loyalties from one ruler to another in pursuit of military service.[26] The military recruitment and organization policies adopted by the British in India changed according to the changing security needs of the expanding empire. Initially, the Company's forces were engaged in extending the areas of conquest within India. The near-completion of this process by the mid-nineteenth century and the shift to concern with internal stability and security, compounded by the scare caused by the Rebellion of 1857, led to a search for the most suitable policy. This resulted in the adoption of the territorial system of recruitment, whereby regiments were raised from all com-munities within a particular province and served within that province alone, being despatched outside only in case of emergencies. One of the objectives was to prevent that kind of fraternization among troops from different parts of India, that had nearly sounded the death-knell of the British Empire in 1857.[27]

The resurgence of concern with external security and expansion in the later nineteenth century, dominated by the perceived threat from Russia, led to another reconsideration of recruitment policies. The efficiency and battle-worthiness of troops against powerful and sophisticated enemies became the primary concern. This led to what was called the class system of recruitment, buttressed by the so-called 'martial races' theory. The emphasis was on carefully selecting homogeneous units composed of what the British authorities determined were the best available fighting material. Lord Roberts, the Commander-in-Chief of the Indian Army from 1885-93, argued that traditionally in India only certain groups bore arms and hence remained fit to bear arms.[28] The military authorities zeroed in on certain 'races', literally handpicking recruits from specified districts, villages, and even families. It was not surprising that the class system of recruitment and the promotion of the 'martial races' theory coincided with what has been called the 'Punjabization of the Indian Army'.[29] British military authorities were virtually unanimous in their praise for the bravery, reliability, and physique of Punjabi (particularly Jat Sikh) soldiers. Between 1862 and 1914, while the number of regiments from UP, Bengal, Bombay, and Madras actually decreased substantially, the number of Punjab regiments more than doubled (from twenty-eight to fifty-seven).

Similar considerations prevailed when the British were faced with the problem of policing the newly-acquired territory of Hong Kong after the First Opium War and the Malay States. For a number of years, the British experimented with a variety of policies, including recruiting Malays and West Indians. A few British personnel were also inducted into the police force, but on the whole were judged as easily dissatisfied and hard to control. Chinese were recruited too, but in both Hong Kong and the Malay States, the main law and order problem was the local Chinese population itself, and hence Chinese recruits were considered easily corruptible and untrustworthy. Indians were an obvious choice, but here again, it was found that south Indians, like the Malays, did not strike sufficient terror into the Chinese. Finally, in 1865-6, a Deputy Superintendent of the Hong Kong

Police, C.V. Creagh, who had had first-hand experience of India, recommended that Sikhs be recruited. The first batch of 100 Sikh policemen, personally selected by Creagh, arrived in June 1867 on a five-year contract. Apart from their physical qualities, Creagh selected his recruits on the basis of their clean record and lack of exposure to undesirable influences. These new policemen did indeed so successfully strike fear into the hearts of the local population that they began to be sent to the Straits Settlements from 1881. To balance the Sikhs in the Hong Kong police force, the British authorities also recruited Muslim Punjabis from Jhelum, Multan and Kamalpur districts.[30]

The British systematically went about the business of recruitment from the rural areas of Punjab. The months of July and August, as well as January and February, when there was less work to be done in the fields were judged to be the best seasons for recruitment. In general, those districts where agricultural prospects were relatively poor produced more and better recruits. However, this was not always the case, as some districts had a strong tradition of military service which overrode other factors. Sometimes, recruiters scouted for men in the seasonal fairs and melas held all over Punjab, but on the whole they preferred to recruit them from their own villages and in the presence of their relatives and neighbours as this generated a greater sense of responsibility on the part of the recruits. In fact the 'pull' exercised by an enthusiastic recruit on those close to him was considered to be so important, that some units organized local camps where the recruits were given their first couple of months' training, right near their own villages, so that others could see for themselves the benefits of military service.[31] This further reinforced the pattern of those enlisted in various army units coming from the same areas and villages.

While perhaps a majority of those deployed abroad by the British for military or police duties returned home at the end of their contract, a number stayed on in foreign locations, lured by the better prospects. It was but natural that, with their reputation as formidable fighters, Sikhs in East Asia found employment as watchmen and guards in private service as well. In this connection it is significant that those very districts that provided the largest number of recruits for the British Army were the ones from which originated the largest section of emigrants to the Far East.[32]

While migration of Punjabis outside Punjab had traditionally been confined largely to those from the commercial castes, especially the Khatris, the phase of Punjabi emigration that began in the middle of the nineteenth century has been characterized as 'a movement which largely derived from rural Punjab, which was initially based on police or military service, which offered hard work by generally unskilled labourers, and which assumed that the migrant would return to the Punjab after attaining the purpose for which he had left home'.[33] The reasons for this shift in the emigration pattern in Punjab are to found in the political as well as socio-economic conditions that came to prevail in the region in the nineteenth century.

With the end of the Anglo-Sikh Wars in 1849, one form of employment for young men in the form of military service in the Sikh armies was closed off. Initially, the British were hesitant to recruit the newly-vanquished Sikhs into their armies, even while they admired and respected their fighting prowess. This early suspicion, however, was quickly dissipated with the events of 1857, where the tottering British power was virtually saved by support from the regiments from Punjab, including those from the princely states of this region. Young Punjabi males, particularly those from the Malwa and Majha regions, once again found a career in military service which, in many cases, took them overseas.

Unlike those areas which supplied the bulk of indentured labour, Punjab was not a region of chronic poverty, even though famines did strike parts of Punjab in 1861 and again in 1869. Nor was it, following the end of the Anglo-Sikh wars, plagued by political instability. Nevertheless, various factors contributed to the vulnerability of rural families in Punjab from the later nineteenth century, which necessitated their seeking various means to supplement their incomes from the land.[34] The absence of primogeniture in land, for one, led to an increasing fragmentation, so that landholdings became uneconomic. Even the increasing productivity of agriculture and the growth of agricultural output in this period had adverse effects: as output increased, the prices of agricultural produce fell, and many cultivators did not have enough money to pay the taxes which, for the first time under the British, were fixed amounts to be paid in cash and not in kind.[35] Indebtedness and alienation of land began to be serious problems among rural households.

Under these circumstances, families who had at least one son to carry on the family line in the village, frequently took recourse to sending another son or sons to join the army or to go overseas, in order to supplement their income. The decision was usually a collective one on the part of the family as a whole, rather than a decision made by the individual migrant himself, and family considerations rather than individual betterment were the pre-dominant motivating factors.[36] Positive feedback received from earlier migrants was an important source of encouragement to go overseas. It was common for individual migrants to travel out-wards from Punjab in batches from the same village or area.

The remittances sent back by those who went abroad usually contributed significantly to preserving the landholdings of their families at home, for instance by paying off mortgages, and to expanding their landed property as well. Other beneficial outcomes were the ability to construct *pakka* houses and to bear the expense of the marriages of sisters. Apart from those who went abroad as part of the army or police services, others engaged in any kind of hard labour that would yield some earnings. After leading a life involving arduous work and much self-denial for a number of years, a good number of the migrants returned home. This corresponded to the general pattern of Indian emigration, in which as many as 90 per cent of those who went overseas came back sooner or later. Referring to this phenomenon Markovits says, 'Movements of people between South Asia and the rest of the world belong to the sphere of "circulation" more than to the sphere of "migration". This is a crucial point, which has often been lost sight of.'[37] 'Circulation' can explain much that was distinctive about Indians abroad, including their reluctance to shed many of their customs and traditions, their slowness to form links with the local population, and their close connection with developments back home, whether at the level of the family, community, locality, or even the country as a whole.

In the initial stages, because of the security needs of the expanding British Empire, the end destination of overseas emigration from Punjab was mainly the Far East and the Malay States. However, by the end of the nineteenth century, these areas came to be looked upon as stepping-stones to migration to more distant and reportedly more prosperous lands.[38] First Australia and New Zealand, then Fiji and the Pacific Islands, and then Canada and the United States of America, with their specific labour requirements for land clearance and the building of railroads, began to lure increasing numbers of migrants from Punjab. The prospects of employment were greater there and, unlike in China, held out the hope of the migrant being able to save enough to acquire land in the new country if he chose to settle there.

While for a few this dream became a reality, most had to contend with progressively discriminatory policies in those countries, which engendered much frustration and opened their eyes to their position as a people subservient to colonialism and imperialism. Australia was the first to close its doors to migrants from India in 1901, followed by Canada in 1914, the United States in 1917, New Zealand in 1920-1, and Fiji in the 1930s. Waves of discontent then began to travel back from the Indian emigrants particularly in North America, to India, giving strength to the incipient militant freedom movement. Thus it came to pass that China, which had been a stepping-stone for the migrants setting out to seek a livelihood on their journey outwards, became in the early decades of the twentieth century, an important base for returning soldiers and revolutionaries to overthrow British colonial rule and change the conditions that had propelled them to leave India in the first place. A chapter in the story of Indian migration abroad had come full circle.

NOTES

1. Philip D. Curtin, *Cross-Cultural Trade in World History*, Cambridge: Cambridge University Press, 1984, p. 3.
2. K.N. Chaudhuri, *Trade and Civilisation in the Indian Ocean: An Economic History from the Rise of Islam to 1750*, Cambridge: Cambridge University Press, 1985, p. 3.
3. An interesting study of a particular Indian merchant community abroad is the work on Indian merchants in Astrakhan by Stephen Frederick Dale, *Indian Merchants and Eurasian Trade, 1600-1750*, Cambridge: Cambridge University Press, 1994. Another is Surendra Gopal's *Indians in Russia in the 17th and 18th Centuries*, New Delhi: Indian Council of Historical Research, 1988.
4. Cited in Robert Gregory, *India and East Africa: A History of Race Relations within the British Empire, 1830-1949*, Oxford: Clarendon Press, 1971, p. 41.

5. Dale, *Indian Merchants*, p. 3.

6. Ibid., pp. 124-7.

7. See Ashin Das Gupta, 'Indian Merchants in the Age of Partnership, 1500-1800', in his *Merchants of Maritime India, 1500-1800*, U.K., Variorum, 1994. See also Dale, *Indian Merchants*, p. 4.

8. Indrani Ray, 'India in Asian Trade in the 1730s—an 18th Century Memoir', in *Essays in Medieval Indian Economic History*, ed., Satish Chandra, New Delhi: Indian History Congress Publication, 1987, pp. 244, 252. See also Ashin Das Gupta, *Indian Merchants and the Decline of Surat, 1700-1750*, New Delhi: Manohar, 1994, pp. 72-3, 137-8.

9. Indrani Ray, 'India in Asian Trade', p. 237.

10. Ashin Das Gupta has characterized the sixteenth to eighteenth centuries as 'the age of partnership' between the Indian and European traders in the Indian Ocean. He has developed this thesis in *Merchants of Maritime India*, op. cit.

11. Pamela Nightingale, *Trade and Empire in Western India, 1784-1806*, Cambridge: Cambridge University Press, 1970, pp. 20-1.

12. Claude Markovits, 'Indian communities in China, c. 1842-1949', in *New Frontiers: Imperialism's New Communities in East Asia, 1842-1953*, ed. Robert Bickers and Christian Henriot, Manchester: Manchester University Press, 2000, p. 71. See the elaboration of this idea also in Ashin Das Gupta, 'Indian Merchants in the Age of Partnership'.

13. Nightingale, *Trade and Empire*, pp. 12-13.

14. Asiya Siddiqi, 'The Business World of Jamsetjee Jejeebhoy', *Indian Economic and Social History Review*, vol. 19, 1982, p. 305.

15. Amalendu Guha, 'More About the Parsi Sheths: Their Roots, Entrepreneurship and Comprador Role, 1650-1918', in *Business Communities of India: A Historical Perspective*, ed. Dwijendra Tripathi, New Delhi: Manohar, 1984, p. 116.

16. Guha, 'More About the Parsi Sheths', p. 124.

17. The cemetery at Whampoa bears the names of Parsi traders going as far back as 1770. See K.N. Vaid, *The Overseas Indian Community in Hong Kong*, Hong Kong: Centre of Asian Studies, University of Hong Kong, 1972, p. 51.

18. Siddiqi, 'The Business World', op. cit., pp. 310, 312.

19. Janet Rizvi, 'The Trans-Karakoram Trade in the Nineteenth and Twentieth Centuries', *Indian Economic and Social History Review*, vol. 31, no. 1, 1994, pp. 27-8, 32-3.

20. Marc Gaborieau, 'Kashmiri Muslim Merchants in Tibet, Nepal and Northern India', in *Asian Merchants and Businessmen in the Indian Ocean and the China Sea*, ed. D. Lombard and J. Aubin, New Delhi: Oxford University Press, 2000, pp. 193-6.

21. See Claude Markovits, *The Global World of Indian Merchants, 1750-1947:*

Traders of Sind from Bukhara to Panama, Cambridge: Cambridge University Press, 2000, for a detailed discussion of this community. The citation is from p. 30.

22. Dale, *Indian Merchants,* p. 138.

23. Markovits, 'Indian communities', p. 71.

24. C. Kondapi, *Indians Overseas, 1830-1945,* New Delhi: Indian Council of World Affairs, 1951, pp. 2-4. Besides Kondapi, for comprehensive accounts of the indentured labour phase of Indian emigration, see also Hugh Tinker, *A New System of Slavery: the Export of Indian Labour Overseas, 1830-1920,* London and New York: Oxford University Press, 1974, as well as his *The Banyan Tree: Overseas Emigrants from India, Pakistan and Bangladesh,* New York: Oxford University Press, 1977.

25. Boris Mollo, *The Indian Army,* U.K: Blandford Press, 1981, p. 50. Interestingly, an earlier attempt to deploy Indian troops abroad appears to have been abortive. The 24th Bengal Infantry is recorded to have mutinied when faced with the prospect of having to go 'overseas' to fight in Burma. Tinker, *A New System of Slavery,* p. 46.

26. Ravindra K. Jain, *Indian Communities Abroad: Themes and Literature,* New Delhi: Manohar, 1993, pp. 1-2.

27. See Stephen P. Cohen, *The Indian Army: Its Contribution to the Development of a Nation,* Bombay: Oxford University Press, 1971, pp. 35-6, for an account of British military policies in India.

28. Cohen, *The Indian Army,* p. 46.

29. Ibid., p. 44.

30. The similarity between the circumstances under which Sikh policemen were recruited in both Hong Kong and the Malay States is remarkable. See Vaid, *The Overseas Indian Community,* pp. 37-8, and K.S. Sandhu, 'Sikh Immigration into Malaya During the Period of British Rule', in *Studies in the Social History of China and South East Asia,* ed. Jerome Ch'en and Nicholas Tarling, Cambridge: Cambridge University Press, 1970, pp. 336-40.

31. Major A.E. Barstow, *Handbooks for the Indian Army: Sikhs,* Government of India, 1899, rpt. 1940, pp. 195, 200-2.

32. Barstow, *Handbooks,* p. 33.

33. W.H. McLeod, 'The First Forty Years of Sikh Migration', in *The Sikh Diaspora: Migration and the Experience Beyond Punjab,* ed. N. Gerald Barrier and Verne A. Dusenbery, Delhi: Chanakya Publications, 1989, pp. 34-5.

34. The various factors underlying Punjabi migration in modern times have been thoroughly discussed by McLeod in the work cited above as well as *Punjabis in New Zealand: A History of Punjabi migration,* Amritsar: Guru Nanak Dev University, 1986, pp. 13-30. See also Tom G. Kessinger, *Vilayatpur, 1848-1968: Social And Economic Change in a North Indian*

Village, Berkeley, Calif: University of California Press, 1974, and Joyce Pettigrew, 'Socio-Economic Bacground to the Emigration of Sikhs from Doaba', in *Punjab Journal of Politics*, vol. 1, pp. 48-81.

35. G.S. Chhabra, *Social and Economic History of the Panjab (1848-1901)*, New Delhi: Sterling, 1962, p. 303.

36. This applied not just to military recruits, but also to those who travelled overseas on business.

37. Markovits, *The Global World*, p. 6. See also Pettigrew, 'Socio-Economic Background', p. 51, and Sandhu, 'Sikh Immigration', pp. 348, 352-3. Sandhu estimates that the return rate of Sikh emigrants to Malaya in the period from 1850 to 1959 was about 80 per cent.

38. For instance, of the little more than 300 Indian passengers who boarded the ill-fated *Komagata Maru* in 1914 in the hope of migrating to Canada, 73 boarded from Shanghai and 165 from Hong Kong. Hugh Johnston, *The Voyage of the Komagata Maru: The Sikh Challenge to Canada's Colour Bar*, New Delhi: Oxford University Press, 1979, p. 30.

CHAPTER 4

Indian Merchants and Entrepreneurs in Eastern China from the Eighteenth to the Twentieth Centuries

Indian traders from Bombay began to venture into Chinese waters from the middle of the eighteenth century. The pioneering voyage of Hirji Jivanji Readymoney in an Armenian ship in 1756 was an exploratory mission, but his brother Mancherji went on to establish a branch of his family's firm at Canton. The Readymoneys were followed by several other merchants from Bombay who were encouraged by the success of their ventures. Like the Readymoneys, almost all were Parsis. In that period, the laws of the Chinese empire permitted maritime trade with foreigners to be conducted from just one port in south China, Canton. Foreign traders were permitted to reside in Canton only for the duration of the three month trading season, and that too only in the vicinity of their warehouses (known as 'factories') on the riverfront. For the rest of the year, if they did not want to leave China's shores, they had to retreat downriver to the Portuguese-administered territory of Macao on the coast. Thus there emerged by the end of the eighteenth century a small group of Indian traders and their servants, based in Canton and Macao, who lived in close proximity with a few score other foreign merchants, mainly British, Europeans and Americans. Over the next two centuries, in spite of the many difficulties encountered and the turbulent political conditions in China, this group grew at a modest rate, and spread to other ports along the China coast and the Yangzi river. It survived into the middle of the twentieth century, even though the composition changed over time, with the near monopoly of the Parsis in the early phase giving way to the participation of other groups such as the Ismailis, Jews and Sindhis. But ultimately the complications arising from war and revolution in the twentieth century drove Indian traders and businessmen from the Chinese mainland. The present-day Indian business community in Hong Kong owes its origin to this group.

RAW COTTON AND OPIUM

The real spurt in the growth of the trade between India and China and, consequently, in the number of Indian merchants travelling to China in the modern period, began only after the 1770s. At that time, a famine in south China compelled peasants there to switch over from cultivating cotton to food crops. This led to a sudden increase in the Chinese demand for raw cotton— a commodity that was grown in plenty in the region of Gujarat in western India. Since the trade between India and the Asian region was not a monopoly of the East India Company, enterprising Indian traders from Bombay, along with private British agency houses, were quick to seize the opportunity to export raw cotton to China. A fleet of huge 'country ships' fitted out with spacious holds capable of carrying the bulky commodity, began to regularly set sail from Bombay for China. The spurt in the demand for Indian cotton coincided with the phenomenal increase in the sales of Chinese tea in Britain due to the reduction in the duty on the import of tea by an Act of Parliament in 1784. A snug arrangement was worked out whereby proceeds from the sale of Indian cotton at Canton were used to pay for the purchase of tea shipped to Britain by the East India Company, and in return, the Company gave the private traders bills of exchange on Calcutta or London. From just four ships that carrried raw cotton to China from Bombay in 1784, the number rose to seventeen just three years later.[1] Fortunes were made out of the export of 'the Great Staple', as it was called, and the prosperity of several of Bombay's leading merchant families, such as that of Jamsetjee Jejeebhoy, was based on it.

For various reasons, however, the demand for Indian raw

cotton in China began to drop off after the first decade of the nineteenth century. Cotton continued to be a major item of export from India to China for several decades more, but it no longer yielded the windfall profits that had made the China trade so attractive for Bombay merchants. In 1814, The *Bombay Courier* lamented that the market in China 'wore but a very sorry aspect, and must in a great measure damp the ardour of adventure to that country'.[2] The situation did not improve, and fifteen years later the *Canton Register*, the journal of the British trading community in Canton, complained about 'the long continued deplorable state of our Cotton market', and confirmed that 'the advices lately received from that quarter are all of a desponding cast'.[3]

Yet just when it seemed that the days of making fabulous profits from the China trade were over, another commodity produced in India was found for which the demand in China became even greater than that of cotton. This was opium. The export of opium from India to China was not something new. From the eighteenth century, Patna opium grown in eastern India was one of the commodities, along with Indian textiles, that was shipped by the English as well as Portuguese and Dutch traders to China to pay for tea and other commodities from that country exported to Europe. However, the scale of exports of Indian opium to China increased dramatically only in the nineteenth century. One reason was the growing demand in China for the other variety of opium grown in western India, known as Malwa opium. Malwa opium, although cheaper than the Patna variety, initially did not find a good market in China because of its inferior quality. However, a sharp rise in the price of Patna opium in 1816, provided the opportunity for increased sales of the Malwa drug. Being cheaper, it no doubt contributed to the spread of the opium-smoking habit among wider sections of society in China and consequently to the profits accruing from the trade. From under 5,000 chests of Malwa opium shipped in 1821, the number rose to over 9,000 ten years later. In 1831, British policies facilitating the export of Malwa from Bombay led to a jump in the number of chests exported to 14,007 chests in 1832-3. In 1835 and 1839, the number of chests climbed even more dramatically to over 20,000 and 40,000 respectively.[4] Traders from virtually every nationality operating at Canton were involved in the trade, although by far the greatest involvement was on the part of the British and Indian traders.

Although for the merchants the trade in opium seemed to be the answer to the gloom arising from the depression in the cotton market, it was in significant ways not in the same league as the cotton trade. In the first place, the addictive nature of the drug ensured a self-expanding market, once the scale of consumption had crossed a certain thresh-hold. It was also in every sense an illegal trade. The sale of opium within China had been banned by imperial edict as early as 1729. Its consumption was also prohibited in 1780. In 1796, the Emperor had banned its importation into China as well. These prohibitions were repeated at frequent intervals in subsequent years. Opium, swallowed raw as a form of medicine, had been used in China from as early as the eighth century, but its harmful and habit-forming effects came to the attention of the authorities only after the practice of smoking the opium extract was introduced in the seventeenth century. The problem for the Emperor and his officials was how to enforce the prohibitions, since the trade in the drug was carried on with the participation of a wide network of smugglers, dealers, retailers and others, and with the collusion of the authorities especially at the local level. Extraordinary ingenuity was exercised by the foreign traders and their Chinese accomplices to evade surveillance, bypass regulations and push ahead with the trade in spite of the risks. Until 1839, they appeared to be winning the contest. The Chinese government seemed powerless to prevent the spread of the opium menace.

Despite the fact that in the general literature on the opium trade in China, the Indian traders have on the whole received less attention than their British counterparts, there is no doubt that role of the Indian as a peddler of opium has influenced the Chinese perception of Indians as it has evolved in the modern era. This is something that Indians today cannot afford to overlook in trying to understand the development of their relations with China. Opium caused immense harm to the very fabric of Chinese society, apart from being a major symbol of China's economic and military humiliation at the hands of foreign powers in the nineteenth century. From the available evidence, the moral aspects of the accelerating trade in opium seemed to have troubled the Indian, or for that matter, other foreign traders very little. The regulations prohibiting the opium trade were regarded in much the same manner as other 'most vexatious' restrictions placed on their licence to trade by the Chinese Empire. Evading these restrictions in as clever a manner as possible was considered a challenge by the foreign merchants. While this is not altogether surprising, given the climate of those times in which the supreme virtues of 'free trade' were extolled above all else, it is a sobering thought that some of the most outstanding Indian businessmen of that era, renowned for their good works and philanthropy particularly in Bombay, were also among the leading opium traders of their time.

THE COUNTRY TRADE

The Indian merchants in China formed an essential part of the network of agency houses, agents, correspondents, brokers, shippers and procurers, which constituted the sinews of what was known as the 'country' trade between India and China in this period. Even while the East India Company retained its monopoly of the trade between Britain and India and between Britain and China, it was content to allow the trade between India and China to remain in private hands, both British and Indian, under its own licence. By and large, it was a mutually beneficial system that prevailed in the early decades. In terms of the working relationship between the Indian and European businessmen, the first half of the nineteenth century was a period of transition between what has been called an 'age of partnership'[5] as well as of fairly level competition on the one hand, and the 'clear-cut racial division of economic space' that emerged later on. Amalendu Guha has characterized it as a 'symbiotic patron-client relationship', in which the Parsi businessmen 'collaborated with the British agency houses, as brokers, junior partners or as both'.[6] Seen as a matter of individual traders or individual firms, it is arguable that in this period the British were as dependent on their Indian collaborators or partners as the latter were on them. In many cases, the same individual Indian merchant functioned both as broker and as partner, and sometimes even as competitor, to a British firm. Overall, however, the terms of trade were increasingly determined by the larger financial and commercial world centred in London.

The relationship between the Indian and British traders

operated within the framework of the consignment system of trade. In the era before the steamship and the telegraph made a more accurate exploitation of distant markets possible, private traders in Britain tended to pool their capital and goods and consign them to agency houses which had their branches overseas, and which did the buying and selling for them on a commission basis. In India, groups of traders like the Parsis on the west coast proved themselves indispensible to the European agency houses as brokers who procured and guaranteed contracts for the provision of goods for export. This became particularly true with the increasing importance of Malwa opium in the China market. Unlike in Bengal, where the Company was able to directly monopolize the cultivation and sale of opium, the production of and domestic trade in opium in the Malwa region remained firmly in Indian hands. The Parsi brokers, with their network of links with the inland traders, functioned as the vital link which secured the supply of opium for shipment abroad. Jamsetjee Jejeebhoy's firm was the major trading partner of the firm of Jardine, Matheson & Co. Heerjebhoy Rustomjee, another prominent Parsi trader, also was closely linked with Jardine Matheson. Cursetjee Framjee, on the other hand, of the Wadia family of shipbuilders, was an agent of the American Forbes & Co, one of Jardine Matheson's major rivals on the China coast.

The Parsi and other Indian merchants who participated in the China Trade also operated independently. Many were 'shippers' who purchased stocks of opium, cotton, etc., on their own account and consigned it to commission agents, both Indian and British, in Canton. The stocks remained their own property (and not that of the agents) until it was sold off. They also were a major source of credit to European firms, which at least in the early stages would have found it difficult to operate without their investment. In addition, the Parsis had a great hold on the shipbuilding business, and ran independent lines of shipping between India and the Far East. The family of Lowjee Wadia was particularly renowned in this respect. Framji Cowasji Banaji, who carried on an extensive trade with China, owned more than 40 sailing vessels at one time. Like the Wadias, his ships too were used by the British during the Opium War.[7] However, in the matter of military or political protection of their trade, the Indians came completely under the umbrella of the British power. That is probably why, in the literature on the Opium War and related events, the Indians rarely figured as independent actors, despite their relatively large number vis-a-vis the British and other Western traders in China.

A large and diverse body of Indian merchants was thus involved with the China trade in various capacities. This included not just merchants in port cities like Bombay, but those of the interior towns like Indore and Ratlam in the opium-growing region. For example, forty-three Indian China traders who sent a petition to the Governor of Bombay in 1829 included, besides twenty-six Parsis, one joint Hindu-Parsi firm, two Muslims, one Jew, one Maharashtrian Hindu and thirteen Gujarati Hindus or Jains.[8] Calcutta too was another pole of the India-China trade. The focus of this chapter, however, is not all those Indians who participated in the China trade, but specifically those who travelled to and spent some time in China. The Bengali Banians of Calcutta as well some other Indian business communities preferred for the most part, at least in the early stages, to conduct their business through agents rather than to deal directly with the Chinese.[9] The Parsi traders of Bombay, on the other hand, made it a point to send their sons to cut their teeth in the business in China. The common practice was to send sons and young male relatives to look after the family business in China for a few years, after an apprenticeship with a European firm. It was perhaps the direct presence of the Parsis in China, along with the special modus vivendi that they managed to establish with the British traders and authorities, that enabled them to take a commanding lead among the early Indian China traders.

INDIAN BUSINESS COMMUNITIES IN CHINA

In *Origins of the Modern Indian Business Class*, D.R. Gadgil has observed that because Indian society was characterized by a number of divisions based on region, religion and caste, with little mobility amongst the different sections, 'the history of the rise and development of modern business becomes, to a large extent, the history of the activities of members of certain groups'.[10] Other scholars, writing specifically about the Indian business class in China in the nineteenth and twentieth centuries, have also emphasized the diversity in its composition and of the need to speak of different communities rather than one single Indian community in China.[11] Migratory pulls which drew Indians to China operated with greater strength, as we have seen in the preceding chapter, on certain families, certain villages and localities, and certain communities. It would thus make sense to look at the history of the Indian business class in China in terms of the activities of the Parsis, Ismailis, Jews and Sindhis, in that order.

While doing so, however, it would be wrong to be rigid or to make too much of a fetish about these identities. The fragmentation among Indians in China that has so strongly struck scholars and observers could be attributed to caste, religion, language, geographical origin and occupation, and it is not at all clear which of these factors operated more strongly than others. For example, it is interesting that while the Parsis naturally maintained a separate burial ground from other Indians in China because of their religious beliefs, the tombstones of those buried in the nineteenth century in the Parsi cemetery at Hong Kong, after giving the names and dates of birth and death of the deceased, almost uniformly identify them with the single phrase, 'inhabitant and resident of *Bombay*'. That is to say, there is a clear identification with, above other things, the city in India from which they had embarked on their journey to China, despite the fact that the families of most of these Parsis would not then have lived in Bombay for more than two or three generations.

To speak of the Parsi, Ismaili, Jewish, and Sindhi merchants is also not to deny that there was a commonality to the experience undergone by these various Indian business groups in China. Their position in the hybrid society of pre-Opium War Canton, and the post-War treaty ports and Hong Kong was clearly defined, as separate and unequal vis-à-vis the Europeans, although individual wealthy Indian merchants may have had a more or less exalted status within this group. They faced similar if not identical difficulties in adapting to their new environment, maintaining their own traditions and carving out niches for themselves within the structures that emerged from the tussle between the Chinese and the dominant European powers (and later, the Japanese too).

A special problem that comes up in discussing in terms of these communities is the question whether some of them could be considered 'Indian' at all. The question is posed particularly in speaking of the Armenian, Parsi and Jewish traders, all of whom figured significantly in India's trade with China in the period under consideration. In one sense, all of these communities were exiles uprooted from their historical homelands outside India. In the case of the small number of Armenians who came to China from India—such as Paul Chater who was to make a huge mark as a tycoon in Hong Kong—it seems difficult to regard them as one of the 'Indian communities'. But the same cannot be said of the Parsis, who had migrated from their original homeland of Persia to India a thousand years earlier, even if they maintained a distinctive set of beliefs and customs in the intervening period. In the complex mosaic that made up Indian society, and particularly Bombay society, the Parsis did not stand out as particularly 'alien'. The case of the Jewish traders who were involved in the China trade from India, however, is more problematic. Unlike the other Jewish communities in India, the Jewish merchants in the China trade were predominantly Baghdadi Jews who had arrived in India only from about the 1830s. To differentiate themselves from the others, they tended to style themselves as 'Jewish merchants of Arabia, inhabitants and residents of Bombay'.[12] In the case of their most prominent family, the Sassoons, many of its members very rapidly adopted English culture and shifted their residence to England by the early twentieth century. Nevertheless, the fact remains that during the century from the 1830s until the 1930s, the headquarters of the Sassoon family—and especially that segment of it that had the maximum interests in the China Trade—was in Bombay. Any account of the links of the Bombay trading community with China, which leaves out the role of the Sassoons and other Baghdadi Jews operating out of India, would be incomplete.

THE PARSIS

The group that was dominant among the Indians in China for nearly a century were the Parsis. Following the lead of the Armenians, the Paris began arriving on the China coast as early as 1756. A perusal of the two-volume compendium of biographies of eminent Parsis, *Parsi Lustre on Indian Soil*,[13] reveals just how large was the number of Parsi families who had direct links with

China in this period. These included the Readymoneys, Banajees, Wadias, Dadyseths, Camas, Jejeebhoys, Petits, Patels, Tatas, Batlibois and others whose prosperity, built up in the China trade, has in many cases continued to this day.

The first among them was Hirji Jivanji Readymoney, who owed his last name to his family's reputation for promptness in making payments. His brother Mancherji established the family firm in China. Other early Parsi traders in China included Dorabjee Rustomjee Patel, who visited China three times before his death in 1804, and who simultaneously also traded with Bassein, Pegu, Rangoon and other places. Ardeshir Dady Dadyseth, 1765-1810, a wealthy merchant and public figure in Bombay, also carried on an extensive trade with China and the Far East.[14] The firm of Cowasjee Pallanjee & Co, a subsidiary of the Bombay-based Cursetjee Bomanjee & Co, was established in Canton in 1794.[15] The founder of the firm, Pestonjee Cowasjee Sethna, died at Macao in August 1842. The first recorded burial in the Parsi cemetery in Macao was that of Cursetjee Framjee of the Wadia family, who died in 1829. Another well-known family whose members spent much time in China was that of Banaji Limji who had established the family fortune in Bombay in the early eighteenth century. Among its members were the pioneering Readymoneys. Another of its prominent members, through another branch of the family, was Rustomjee Cowasjee, who spent three years in China between 1812 and 1820. His sons were Dadabhoy and Manockjee, who together operated a firm called D. and M. Rustomjee at Canton. The doyen of the Parsi China traders in the first half of the nineteenth century, Jamsetjee Jejeebhoy, himself made five voyages to China between 1799 and 1807, starting as a penniless apprentice to his cousin and ending as a wealthy and established merchant prince.[16]

At that time, sailing to China was a dangerous affair, because of the typhoons and squalls encountered, as well as raids by pirates who sailed the waters of the South China Sea. The voyages of Dadabhoy Rustomjee were particularly plagued with misfortune. He had to undergo the experience of being attacked by pirates as well as being swept off course by typhoons. On his debut voyage at the age of sixteen in his uncle Framjee Cursetjee's ship *Sullimany*, the storm was so severe that they ran off course and became dangerously short of provisions, and had to land at the first dry land in China they could find. At that time, the regulations of the Chinese empire were very severe about foreign traders being permitted to come only to Canton and nowhere else. Taken by surprise, the local officials and people made preparations to attack and forcibly boarded their ship. On being received by the captain and crew with great courtesy, however, the Chinese relaxed and allowed the ship to sail away after supplying provisions and water, though the passengers and crew were not allowed to disembark and were watched continuously for any suspicious movements.[17] That such difficulties did not deter the enterprising Parsis is shown by the fact that Dadabhoy made several more voyages and spent many years in China, becoming one of the most prominent Indian traders there at the time of the Opium War.

The outbreak of the Napoleonic Wars added to the dangers faced by the travelling merchants, as merchant vessels belonging to British subjects became fair game for French naval and pirate ships. A letter of 12 June 1800 to the Governor of Bombay from a group of Indian merchants requested British naval protection for their ships bound for China, as 'the Enemy's Privateers have lately made their appearance in the Straits of Malacca'.[18] During his second and fourth voyages, Jamsetjee Jejeebhoy found himself caught in a crossfire of Anglo-French hostilities. Within a few days of the commencement of his fourth voyage to China in 1805, the ship he was travelling on was intercepted by the French who hijacked it in a westerly direction, as far as the Cape of Good Hope! All his goods were confiscated. Eventually, he and some of his co-passengers managed with great difficulty to secure passage on a Danish ship which transported them to Calcutta, more than five months after they had set sail from Bombay.[19] Jamsetjee too was not deterred by the difficulties he faced on this journey, but went on to become the leading China trader of his time.

Yet perhaps nothing illustrates the persistence of the early Parsi traders, which enabled them to reap huge rewards from the China trade, as the career of Muncherjee Jamsetji Wadia. Muncherjee first formed a partnership in 1814 with a certain J.A. Pope and Hormusjee Dhunjee Patel to trade with China, but this firm dissolved in just eight years. Muncherjee then formed a partnership with a Portuguese named Fernandes, who disappeared together with ship and cargo worth over Rs. 40,000. Undaunted, he formed another partnership with Hormusjee Dhunjee Patel and one Captain Thomas Crawford. But Crawford too disappeared with both ship and cargo! Muncherjee was ruined and was compelled to become a selling agent for some Bombay merchants wanting to trade with China. In 1832 he left for Canton, and a year later brought his son over to join him. He made several trips to Bombay and back to China, and by 1834 had managed to recoup his fortunes. By 1834, the first Chamber of Commerce was founded in Canton by Muncherjee along with some others.[20]

A little recognized fact is that, numerically at least, the Parsis were more prominent than even the private English traders on the China coast in the period before the Opium Wars. According to one source, in 1809 there was only one private English trader resident in Canton as opposed to several Parsis. The corresponding figures for 1831 and 1835 were thirty-two English and forty-one Parsis, and thirty-five English as opposed to fifty-two Parsis, respectively.[21] In his major study of the Parsi merchants in Canton during the Qing period, Guo Deyan estimates that Parsi merchants formed one-third of the foreign merchant community in the pre-Opium War period.[22] Of twenty-nine large ships trading between Bombay and Canton in 1812-13, as many as twelve belonged to Parsis.[23] Even as late as the mid-1840s, one-quarter of the approximately one hundred foreign firms on the China coast belonged to Indians.[24]

A contemporary Western observer, Toogood Downing, described Parsis as striking figures in the streets of Canton in the area of the foreign factories, with their white, loose flowing clothes and caps which, he claimed, suited their surroundings much better than did the tight clothes and stiff hats of the Europeans.[25] In fact, on account of their clothing and in particular their white caps, the Parsi merchants came to be referred to by the Chinese, even in some official documents, as 'whiteheads' (*baitouren, baitouyi*).[26] Besides wearing their own kind of clothing, the Parsis, particularly during the early decades, seemed to have followed their own customs rather strictly, for instance, they would dine separately. Their strict rules about eating only their own kind of food may have accounted for the fact that the Parsis in Canton and Macao included a high proportion of servants.[27] During the siege of the factories in the crisis preceding the Opium War as well as earlier, during the Chinese standoff with the British representative Lord Napier, this proved useful to the foreigners as a whole, as the Parsis 'lent' their servants to the British when their Chinese employees were compelled by the Qing authorities to withdraw.

The Parsis, like other Indian traders on the China coast in the early period, were predominantly men without their families. Initially, the tendency was for them to be sent out to China by their firms to do relatively short tours of duty, and they could not be considered to have been anything more than temporary residents there. For instance, between 1844 and 1887, all but one of the eight sons of the famous trader David Sassoon were sent out to China, but few spent more than a few years there, following which they returned home.[28] Significantly, the Parsi cemeteries in Hong Kong record no burial of women till as late as 1906. Even as late as the 1920s, there seem to have been only a handful of Parsi women resident in Hong Kong.[29] A contemporary noted disapprovingly that 'in the absence of Parsee ladies a great evil is gaining ground in China. Parsees are associating with women of bad reputation and prostitutes'.[30] Apparently some Parsi men did enter into formal or informal relationships with Chinese women. A document in the Hong Kong Land Office from 1864, for instance, shows that a certain Jamsetjee Byramjee Colah leased out some property of his to a single Chinese woman named Tow Foo Kee for a token rent of just one dollar per year for the duration of her natural life.[31] The writer Zhang Ailing has also recalled an encounter in his student days in the 1930s with a Parsi named Banaji who got married to a Chinese woman who was herself the daughter of a Chinese mother and an Indian father.[32] Nevertheless, such integration of Parsis with Chinese society as did take place came slowly and was always limited.

ISMAILIS, JEWS AND SINDHIS

In the literature on the early decades of the China trade from India, the Ismaili Muslim traders from the west coast have in general received less attention than the Parsis. More low-profile than the Parsi and Jewish tycoons, they nevertheless formed an important segment of the Indian mercantile community in China from a fairly early stage. The strength of their presence on the China coast is seen in the fact that, out of twenty-eight Indian traders whom the Hong Kong Government listed in 1864 as due for compensation on account of opium surrendered before the Opium War, as many as fifteen were Ismailis. They were: Mohammedbhoy Dossabhoy, Ahmadbhoy Ramtoola, Ameroodin Jafferbhoy, Vully Mohammed Allobhoy, Abdoolally Ebrahim & Co., Solomon Ebrahim, Amerally Abdoolally, Habibbhoy Ebrahim Sons & Co., Ahmad Hadjee Essac, Hadjee Abdoola Nathan, Allarakia Adam, Cassumbhoy Nathabhoy, Hadjee Mohomed, M.M. Hossein and Alladinbhoy Habibbhoy.[33] Some of the Ismailis were brokers to Parsi firms, while others, like the Currimbhoys, were independent merchants. The Ismailis were a traditional trading community who took advantage of the new opportunities held out by the European penetration of Africa and Asia.[34] They were more famed for their commercial role on the east coast of Africa, but were almost as successful in the Far East. Currimbhoy Ebrahim was one of those who successfully shifted the focus of his commercial business from Zanzibar to the Far East.

When the role of the Jews in India's China trade is spoken of, the reference is for the most part overwhelmingly to the involvement of a single Jewish family (including their different branches), the Sassoons. The patriarch of the Sassoon family in Bombay, David Sassoon, was a refugee from Baghdad who arrived in Bombay at the age of forty in 1832, at a time when the lead of the Parsis in the China Trade seemed virtually unassailable. David Sassoon saw the opportunities that presented themselves in this trade, and although he himself never went to China, he made sure that most of his eight sons and younger male relatives did for varying lengths of time. Besides dealing in opium, the Sassoons also exported to China metals, muslins and cotton, and imported Chinese silk, tea, camphor, nankeen and other traditional items. They financed shipments, provided small-scale banking facilities and also acted as commission agents. Unlike most other Indian firms, the Sassoons bought their own warehouses and rented out space in them. However, it was on the basis of the opium trade that they established their commercial empire. Despite their late entry, they rapidly became frontrunners in the trade. An important factor in their success was their ability to cut costs by manipulating the sale price of opium at the Indian end in their favour. Among other things, they used to buy the unharvested crops directly from the cultivators. Their aggressive business practices paid off, in this case as well as in other lines of enterprise they were to enter thereafter. By 1871, the dominant position of Jardine, Matheson & Co. in the opium trade in China was taken over by the Sassoons in collaboration with other, predominantly Jewish, Indian agencies such as E. Gubbay & Co., E.D.I. Ezra & Co and S. Isaac.[35] By the time they pulled out of the opium trade, just before it ended in 1913, their average annual profits from it had registered a forty-fold increase.[36]

The Sassoons were instrumental in bringing out to China and training young Jewish men, and giving them profitable employment in their own concerns.[37] Some of these men then went on to found their own personal fortunes. Among them were Elly Kadoorie, whose commercial empire based in Hong Kong still flourishes, and the maverick Silas Hardoon.[38] Hardoon, whose family migrated to Bombay from Baghdad in 1856 when he was a boy, was employed by the Sassoons and sent out to China as a young man. He was rent-collector and godown watchman for the Sassoons in Shanghai from 1874, but left their employment in 1882 to strike out on his own as a cotton broker. When this failed he was re-employed by E.D. Sassoon & Co. as manager of their Shanghai branch, becoming a partner and general manager in the 1890s. In 1901, he branched out on his own again—this time with stupendous success, particularly in the field of real estate and in the opium trade, becoming one of the richest men in Shanghai at the time of his death. Yet despite the phenomenal wealth of the Sassoons, the Kadoories, Hardoon and a few others, Maisie Meyer avers that 'the great majority of the [Jewish] community were in fact poor with a mere handful of rich men and scarcely any middle class'. Most of the Jews were small-time independent merchants dealing in cotton, wool, silk and opium.[39]

Sindhi merchants from Hyderabad (as opposed to the other stream of Sindhi merchants from Shikarpur who travelled to western China)[40] began to arrive on the east coast of China from the late 1870s.[41] The 'Sindworkies', as they were sometimes known, had expanded their sphere of operations from small-time peddling of craft items from their home areas in Bombay, to selling curios and 'oriental' goods, not just from India, but from Japan, China and other regions around the world, to predominantly Western customers with a taste for such items. As Markovits has remarked, 'Why merchants of a medium-sized inland town in a province of British India found themselves particularly well placed to exploit these opportunities will always remain something of a mystery.'[42] But the fact is that the clientele for such goods greatly increased with the growth of foreign travel in the later nineteenth century, and the Sindhis, with their background in trade in craft items, were able to take on the role of 'global middlemen'.

The main centres of the trading network of these Sindhis lay along the major steamshipping routes of the time, and took them to far flung places such as Gibraltar, Panama, Hong Kong and Egypt. China was one of the places where they sourced, rather than sold, their goods. Initially concentrated in Canton and Hong Kong, they later set up branches in Shanghai, as well as in the northern cities of Tianjin, Qingdao and Port Arthur. The firm of Wassiamall Assomall was one of the first to make goods from the Far East their main focus. Other firms that had come to China by the late 1800s were those of Pohoomull Bros. and D. Chellaram. In contrast to the stereotyped image of the conservative Hindu merchant, the Hyderabadi Sindhi traders in the treaty ports of China and Hong Kong as well as elswhere were cosmopolitan in their lifestyles and attitudes. In Markovits' words again, 'there was a deliberate attempt on the part of the Sindwork merchants to appear different from the stereotypical "oriental" trader, so as to gain respectability and inspire confidence in a mostly European clientele full of racial prejudice. They made it a point to behave in as European a fashion as possible.'[43]

LIFE IN CHINA BEFORE THE OPIUM WAR

In the early decades of the China trade in Canton and Macao, the Indians necessarily lived in close proximity to the other foreign traders, since the Chinese authorities did not permit the foreigners to move beyond the area of the 'Thirteen Factories' on the waterfront of Canton. In this period the total number of foreigners was also not high, and there was not that same great difference in wealth and in class and occupational status between the majority of Indians and the Europeans as there was to be from the later nineteenth century. This meant that relations between the Indians and the Europeans, while not always amicable, were not yet characterized by that great aloofness and hierarchy that was so noticeable later on. With the Chinese, however, a different trend was noticeable. According to Guo Deyan, in the pre-Opium War period the Indians by and large had limited, purely business dealings with a relatively small number of Chinese merchants and shopkeepers (although Jamsetjee Jejeebhoy had a close personal friendship with the famous Chinese merchant Howqua), while later on they developed closer ties, including those of a more social character, with a wider circle of Chinese with whom they came into contact.[44]

In the period before the Opium War, the Indians, like the other foreign traders, were permitted to live in Canton only during the three-month trading season and, if they did not sail back home after that, they had to reside at Macao. Much to the discomfiture of the Select Committee of the East India Company at Canton, which was overall responsible for the activities of the British and Indian merchants there, enterprising Parsi merchants frequently contrived to stay on in Canton beyond the end of the trading season under some excuse or the other.[45] At Canton they were to be found largely in what was known as the 'Chow Chow' (*chaochao* or 'miscellaneous') Factory, also unofficially known as the 'Parsi factory'.[46] A contemporary, the American William Hunter, has described this factory as teeming with Indians, including 'Malwarees, Persians, Moors, Jews and Parsees'.[47] Obviously, however, the premises of the Chow Chow Factory were not enough to accommodate all the Indians there comfortably. Many chose to sublet rooms in other factories (or 'hongs' as they were called in Chinese) including the Dutch and French Hongs, the Fung Tai Hong and the Pao Shun Hong. However, this was not without its problems. Hunter records the case of an Indian Muslim who for a while occupied an empty quarters in the Dutch Hong, but promptly shifted out when its actual lessee, a Dutchman, began to charge him $100 per month as rent. He prudently decided to move into the Chow Chow Hong and sublet quarters from the firm of Dadabhoy and Manockjee Rustomjee for just Rs. 40 per month!

A more serious incident involving sharing living space between Indians and Europeans occurred in 1830. A Parsi merchant, Marvanjee Hormajee, had an agreement with a Dutchman to rent for two years building no. 3 in the Dutch Hong. It was agreed that both the front gate of the Hong, manned by a watchman, and the back gate would remain open until 10 p.m. However, a European named Bouvet who lived in the Dutch Hong took it upon himself to lock the back gate earlier than stipulated. Marvanjee, who apparently found it more convenient to return via the back gate, objected repeatedly, but to no avail. Finding the back gate locked when he returned one night, he instructed his servants to break the lock. He claimed that he himself then went out and eventually came back through the front gate. Meanwhile, when his servants tried to break the lock, Bouvet rushed out sword in hand. He apparently abused them and began to draw his sword. A friend of his, a Capt. McKenzie, rushed to his assistance, but during the ensuing scuffle, got a fatal wound to his head and died the next morning. The incident, which was witnessed by several persons from the neighbouring hongs as well, greatly excited the small foreign community and vexed the Chinese authorities. Although a European had been killed, the foreign community seems to have been united on not allowing the three Parsi servants to fall into the hands of the Qing judicial system. Eventually a compromise was worked out whereby the three Parsis were hastily sent back to India under custody to face proceedings there, following which the Chinese authorities made a formal but futile demand for their surrender.[48]

This particular incident highlights certain features of the Indians' situation in China at this time. In the first place, it confirms that the Indians did not live totally segregated from the other foreigners, but were to be found in Hongs belonging to other countries. It indicates that there was some history of tension and baiting of the Indians by the Europeans, but also that the Indians were not by any means submissive, evident more in the defiant act of breaking the lock than in the killing of McKenzie which appears to have been accidental. The Chinese, authorities however, apparently took this as further proof of the arrogant and troublesome nature of the Parsis, and complained that the Parsis were becoming 'daily more obstinate'.[49]

The Indians, and specifically the *baitouyi* (the Parsis), do not find much separate mention in the documents of the Qing authorities of that time, but when they did come in for comment, the image was by and large very unflattering. The general impression was that they used their connection with the British power as well as the strength of their numbers to bully not only the Chinese but also the other foreign merchants as well.[50] One of the most vexing things about the Parsis, as far as the authorities were concerned, was the role they played in the bankruptcy of a number of Chinese merchants. In the system of trade permitted by the Qing government at Canton in the pre-Opium War decades, the foreign traders were allowed to conduct their business only through a small number of licensed Chinese merchants, known as Hong merchants. However, many of these Hong merchants accumulated large debts to the foreign merchants, which they eventually found themselves unable to pay. Parsi traders were involved in several of these cases of bankruptcy which not only ruined individual merchants and their firms, but undermined the viability of the system as a whole.[51]

There were two main ways in which the Hong merchants became indebted to the foreign merchants. One was by taking imported goods on credit, on the expectation that a high price would be paid for them when sold in the market. Since the demand for and prices of goods like raw cotton fluctuated wildly, the more inexperienced Hong merchants in particular frequently found themselves with goods unsold and unable to repay their suppliers. Another way in which debts accumulated was through straightforward moneylending at high interest. Many Hong merchants for various reasons were chronically short of funds, and since moneylending was prohibited under the laws of the Qing dynasty, had no recourse but to turn to the foreign merchants. These in turn were more than willing to lend in most cases, especially because in the days before a safe system of remitting profits home had been established, many sought a profitable outlet for their funds in China itself, and moneylending seemed like an attractive proposition.

What irked both the Chinese authorities and the East India Company's Select Committee was that the Parsi traders appeared to actually strive to get the Hong merchants indebted to them.

They were accused of seeking out the most junior, inexperienced Hong merchants, and of urging them to take credit and loans from them.[52] Because interest rates were much higher in China than in India, it was said that the Parsis transferred funds in bulk from India specifically for the purpose of moneylending. Once the Hong merchants were hopelessly bankrupt, their Parsi creditors showed little patience or charity and troubled the authorities by vociferously petitioning for recovery of their funds. In the case of the 1838 bankruptcy of the Dongchang Hong which owed Dadabhoy Rustomjee and Heerjeebhoy Rustomjee 40,000 *yuan*, the Governor-General of Liangguang asked why the Parsis had allowed the debt to accumulate to such levels before complaining. Nevertheless, the authorities usually took action to punish the defaulting Hong merchants and to ensure that the foreigners recovered at least some of their money, even by making all the other Hong merchants together assume the liability.

Moneylending was by no means practised only by the Indians, but the fact remains that the Indians in particular were identified with it. 'The moneylending practices of the Parsi merchants are notorious to this day,' writes Guo Deyan in his doctoral dissertation. 'In Hong Kong, moneylenders are commonly refered to as *da er long* or "big earholes". This metaphor is connected with the Parsis. In the early days of the colony of Hong Kong, the moneylenders were Parsis or other Indian merchants. They wore big earrings, and because of this their ears had holes. From this the Chinese in Hong Kong began to refer to moneylenders as "big earholes".[53]

Like, the British private traders, the Indian merchants became increasingly restive with the Canton system of trade. On the one hand, they tried in various ways to circumvent the prescribed forms and structures of trade—for instance, by dealing with 'unofficial' merchants at Canton, and using Lintin island instead of Canton to unload their goods, especially opium. They also tried to bypass the Company's restrictions on their participation in the trade between China and Britain by exporting goods from China to Singapore, and then reloading the same goods in other vessels bound for Britain.[54] At the same time, they also articulated their grievances to the Chinese authorities as well as to the Select Committee. In 1829, they collectively petitioned the Governor-General of Liangguang about the problems they were facing with the trade, identifying three in particular: the difficulty of recovering debts owed to them by the Hong merchants; the fact that there were not enough licensed merchants with whom they could deal; and the lack of warehouses for them to store their goods, which meant that commodities they imported into China like raw cotton had to be sold off immediately upon arrival.[55] Forty-four Parsi merchants also petitioned the Select Committee along the same lines on 15 May 1829.[56]

In their fight with the East India Company and its monopoly, the Indian merchants by and large were on the same side as the private British traders. But from the time that the monopoly of the East India Company's trade with China was officially abolished in 1834, the dividing lines between the Indians and the British traders became sharper. Things came to a head during the standoff that year between the Chinese authorities and Lord Napier who arrived to replace the Select Committee as the authority responsible for Britain's trade at Canton. Egged on by the private British traders, Napier took an aggressive line towards the Qing authorities against various regulations deemed restrictive and demeaning to British prestige. The Qing authorities took an equally tough stand in response, and enforced a crippling boycott of the British and suspension of the trade. Recognizing that he did not have the power to press his cause further, Napier withdrew to Macao, and the Chinese reopened the trade. What embittered relations between the Indians and the British was that the Indians, just after Napier withdrew, separately petitioned the Chinese Governor-General to reopen the trade. In his reply to 'Dadabhoy Rustomjee and other merchants', the Governor-General presented the decision to reopen the trade as a gracious gesture by the Emperor to the foreigners' petition. Already frustrated by the failure of Napier's mission, the British mercantile community at Canton were stung at what they saw as an insult to their pride, and turned on the Parsi community, using fairly vituperative language to condemn them in their press. The Parsis responded in spirited fashion, challenging the journal to publish their response.[57] The Napier issue soon blew over, but the sourness in the relations between the Indian and British traders did not go away. Despite their tradition of making liberal donations for various causes, there were no Parsi subscribers for a monument raised by the British merchants to Napier, who died shortly after his arrival in Macao. Furthermore, on 12 Sept 1834, most of the Indian members of the newly established British Chamber of Commerce at Canton resigned en masse. In his letter of resignation Dadabhoy Rustomjee specifically gave as a reason the clause prohibiting Indians from voting for or contesting the posts of President and Vice-President. He and Framjee Pestonjee were later elected to the committee of a newly formed rival General Chamber of Commerce, that included, besides British and Parsis, Americans, Dutch and French merchants also.[58] Indian and British traders still lived and worked together, but the relationship became progressively uneasy.

THE OPIUM WAR

The tension between the British merchants at Canton and the Chinese authorities following the abolition of the East India Company's monopoly did not die down after the 'Napier affair', but continued to simmer. The rapid growth of opium smuggling in the following years strengthened the resolve of the Emperor and influential officials at court to crack down on the illicit trade. In 1839, a new Imperial Commissioner, Lin Zexu, arrived in Canton charged with the mission of stamping out the trade. Commissioner Lin took his duties extremely seriously, and within a short time after his arrival, enforced a series of measures to stop the sale and consumption of opium. He also insisted that foreign traders surrender their stocks of opium, and sign a bond pledging not to import any opium thereafter, before he would allow them to unload their goods. When the British refused, he did not hesitate to enforce a total boycott and siege of their factories. Unable to break the deadlock, and under mounting pressure, the British Superintendent of Trade at Canton, Charles Elliot, advised British and Indian traders to surrender their opium. A sizeable portion of the confiscated opium belonged to twenty-eight Indian firms. Of the 20,383 chests of opium surrendered at Canton, 5,315 belonged to Parsis, of which 1,000 belonged to Dadabhoy Rustomjee alone.[59] Among those detained during the siege of the factories at Canton were also a number of Indian traders.

The surrender of the opium provided Britain with the

opportunity it needed to launch a military offensive against the
Chinese Empire, the aim of which was not just to defend the
opium trade but to completely alter the traditional terms of trade
with China in its favour. In the Opium War, which began in 1840,
and was formally concluded by the Treaty of Nanjing in 1842,
China was completely humiliated. It was forced to sign several
treaties and had to agree, among other things, to open up four
other ports to foreign trade, end the earlier system of trade
through the Hong merchants, pay a huge indemnity, and accept
the British occupation of the island of Hong Kong. Interestingly,
the treaties made no mention of legalising the opium trade. But
with the position of the Qing government hopelessly weakened,
the opium traders knew they had nothing to fear.

The War affected the Indian merchants in China in two ways.
On the one hand, they benefitted from the altered terms of trade
imposed on China by the victorious powers at the end of the
War. On the other hand, many never recovered from the losses
they sustained through the destruction of their stocks and
accompanying disruption of the trade. Their losses were compounded by the lengthy delay in securing compensation from
the British Government. Even when the compensation was finally
received, about twenty years later, it amounted only to a portion
of the value of the stocks they had surrendered, despite the fact
that the British Government had demanded and secured from
the Chinese a hefty indemnity for damages at the end of the
War. '. . . You can have no idea of the ruin and misery which this
China War had brought to many families here and abroad', wrote
Jamsetjee Jejeebhoy from Bombay.[60] At least two Parsi traders
committed suicide because of the delay in compensating them
for their losses on account of the War.[61]

The experience of the Indian traders in the Opium War
highlighted the overall ambiguity of their position in China.
Although many of them continued to draw huge profits from
the China trade, the War had highlighted the great risks involved.
Moreover, the Indians' position vis-à-vis the British and other
Western traders became progressively uneasy, as the raw deal
they received at the end of the War showed. At the same time,
their relations with the Chinese remained compromised by their
association with the belligerent British and with the trade in
opium. Reacting to a memorial from his officials in Guangdong

after the commencement of hostilities, which had suggested that merchants from India be exempted from the prohibition on the foreigners trading, the Daoguang Emperor angrily replied: 'But that [India] is where the opium comes from! Whom do you think you are deceiving? It enrages me to read such a dispatch.'[62]

JAMSETJEE JEJEEBHOY

The conditions under which the Indian China trader functioned in the first half of the nineteenth century are best exemplified by the career of Jamsetjee Jejeebhoy. He was one of the only Indian merchants involved with the China trade who left records that give us a detailed picture of the nature of their activities in China and their attitude to the business. His records are valuable, not only because his career was in many respects the most outstanding of the early Indian China traders, but also because his letters give an insight into the actual working of the trade, the relationships among the British, Chinese, and Indian traders and officials, as well as the anxieties and difficulties faced by the Indians who took part in the trade.[63]

After his initial voyages to China in quick succession, Jamsetjee Jejeebhoy was content to direct his voluminous business with China from his headquarters in Bombay. Because of the contacts built up with many in China earlier on and his continuing intimacy with them, Jamsetjee retained a very lively interest in and understanding of developments in China and in the China trade as they unfolded. After an initial period when he, like many other Indian merchants, engaged in buying and selling for others on a commission basis, as well as in guarantee brokerage, Jamsetjee concentrated in the main on the shipping business. His firm was the major partner of the agency house of Jardine, Matheson & Co. in Canton, and tried to ensure that as much as possible of the opium leaving Bombay port for Canton was consigned to them. His firm joined Jardine, Matheson & Co. and Remington & Co. in an informal syndicate which sought to establish a monopoly of the market for Malwa opium at Canton. He had enough clout to bring the trade to a standstill whenever he chose.[64]

Many Indian merchants in western India who wanted to engage

.in the lucrative opium trade entrusted their stocks to him. 'With Jamsetjee acting as go-between,' observes Siddiqi, 'vast quantities of wealth accumulated in old time trade and banking were poured into the colonial mercantile network.'[65] Jamsetjee was accustomed to playing the role of advocate for his Indian friends in the trading world who frequently found themselves in distressing situations. His letters to his numerous English correspondents eloquently plead their case, whether on the matter of compensation for damages suffered during the Opium War, or of getting short-changed by the agency houses in China, or other matters.

Jamsetjee's letters also reveal a certain degree of sympathy for the plight of the Chinese after their military defeat at the hands of the British. He was of course effusive in his praise for the military action, insofar as it did away with certain activities of the 'most vexatious and harassing' Hong merchants. In one letter he also tried to reassure Matheson, who was uneasy that the opium question remained formally unresolved at the end of the War, saying that the Chinese 'had enough from us upon this matter and I am quite certain they will not interfere any more', and that he was sure that 'the [opium] consumption will be large and the price will be high'.[66] Yet Jamsetjee believed in avoiding further confrontation as far as possible. In another letter to Matheson in early 1843, he expressed strong reservations about resorting to hostilities once again. 'I think in my common sense that he [Sir Henry Pottinger] did right and wise of not allowing any force to go. What will be the consequence when the Emperor heard such row again take place, and how bitter would be the authority against us. But now keeping distance is far better than showing threat. They know very well now what we are and what is our force. This fear will do great good than by sending actual troops and destroy all the confidence among the Chinese. This is not now like former time that they were so much ignorant.'[67] Jamsetjee also wrote to Pottinger cautioning him against 'pressing too severely upon the Chinese, who in common with all other nations are entitled to have their prejudices respected and their self-love not too rudely disturbed'.[68]

Despite the enormous wealth and prestige he acquired, towards the end of his life, a note of dissatisfaction and pessimism began to creep into Jamsetjee's letters. As early as 1843, he wrote: 'The prospects of the shipping interests appear to be getting worse and worse instead of better, we have now in Bombay Harbour an immense fleet of free-traders who are willing to take cotton on to China for the very lowest freights, which it is impossible to sail in a country ship. Last year many of our fine Teak ships were laid up, and this season have gone on at miserably low freights.'[69] This theme became more insistent as the years passed. Writing to Donald Matheson in Edinburgh in 1851, he lamented that 'Our Trade with China which, even when you were in Hongkong was beginning to be on a reduced scale is now even more limited, and where there are so many competitors in the field it is hardly worthwhile pursuing it. In fact, times are very much changed here ever since you left and many new Houses have sprung up in China.'[70] Jamsetjee maintained generally cordial relations with his chief Indian competitors like David Sassoon, but was disturbed by their tendency to speculate in the opium market in India. He even had occasion to frequently complain about his long-time partners in China, Jardine, Matheson & Co., particularly after the departure of his old friend William Jardine in 1839. Both on his own behalf, as well on behalf of his friends in India who had consigned their stocks to the British agency house, he accused them of unnecessarily delaying the disposal of shipments, of selling them at low prices, and of other unfair practices which had led to 'heavy loss'.[71]

THE MID-CENTURY DIVIDE

The background to Jamsetjee's discontent, and to the increasingly strained relations between the Indian and British traders in China, was the changes taking place in the economy and trading patterns of Britain, India, and China. Already, the consignment system worked to the disadvantage of the shippers, who bore the entire risk of the venture, and to the advantage of the British agency houses which collected their commission irrespective of profit or loss. This inevitably led to complaints on the part of the traders and shippers regarding their being shortchanged by their agents in China. However, from around the mid-nineteenth century, the Indian merchants began to experience further difficulties. In the first place, they found it increasingly difficult to obtain the coveted bills of exchange so necessary to make their remittances from China. In the market for bills of exchange, they were unable to compete effectively with the flood of private British trading firms drawn to China following the abolition of the Company's monopoly in 1833, and which were able to command far more credit. On one occasion Jamsetjee tried to circumvent this problem of finding a way to get his funds out of China, by buying goods in China and shipping them to London. However, it turned out to be a costly misadventure, partly because of what Jamsetjee viewed as discrimination against his ships in the process of unloading in London.[72]

The older country traders from India were also at the receiving end of rate wars launched by European shipping firms with their new steamships. The huge country ships designed to accommodate bulk commodities like raw cotton could not profitably ship freight at the lowered rates offered by their competitors. In the midst of these troubles on the shipping front took place a series of mysterious fires in Bombay harbour which destroyed several of the fine old teak ships belonging to the Parsi merchants. Jamsetjee found himself left in possession of just one of his once proud fleet of sailing vessels. He was deeply troubled and embittered by what he considered were deliberate acts of sabotage. 'Without some effectual plan to prevent these disgraceful and most shocking occurrences can be hit upon, there will be no safety, for either owners, shippers or underwriters,' he wrote. But his laments were in vain. Jamsetjee himself died in 1859, and within a short time, the interests of his family firm in the China trade had lapsed.

According to Rajat Kanta Ray, Jamsetjee's career was an indication that 'after mid-century the international environment was no longer favourable to the growth of big Indian business in the country's ports and abroad'.[73] The early growth of Indian interests in the China trade was based on the export of two commodities from India, raw cotton and opium, on the Parsi domination of the shipowning business, and on the consignment system of trade. The trade in raw cotton entered a period of depression from which it never fully recovered by around 1820. The trade in opium, which had partially replaced raw cotton as the big money-spinner for the Bombay merchants, failed to take off as expected after the wars in the mid-century and peaked in the 1850s, though it continued to be profitable for some firms like that of the Sassoons for a number of decades thereafter. The growth of steam shipping sounded the death-knell of the old country ships and, together with the invention of the telegraph, rendered the consignment system of trade obsolete. The enhanced competition in China arising from a flood of eager private traders from Britain meant that those Indian firms that were unable to adapt to the new conditions rapidly enough could not survive. Not just Jamsetjee Jejeebhoy Sons & Co., but several old prestigious firms of India's pioneering China traders either collapsed or faded into oblivion. Others survived and remained in China, but turned from trading and entrepreneurial operations to income from rent and 'safe' investments, such as real estate or shares in big companies.[74]

THE DIVERSIFICATION OF INDIAN BUSINESS

What was remarkable, however, was that, despite the failure of some firms, the Indian mercantile presence in eastern China as a whole reinvented itself in the changed conditions. By diversifying their business interests and seeking out new opportunities in the expanding commercial life of the treaty ports and Hong Kong, the Indian business community in China managed to survive and grow into the twentieth century.

VERSATILE BUSINESSMEN:
THE TATAS AND THE SASSOONS

The Tatas were a family that exemplified the new trend. They, like the Sassoons, entered China on the second wave, and managed to sustain their interests there for a considerable length of time, even though they were beset by a fair share of troubles. In December 1859, Nusserwanji Tata, the founder of the family's fortunes, opened a firm called Jamsetji & Ardeshir in Hong Kong's Holywood Road, along with two partners, Kaliandas and Premchand Roychand. Initially they, like many other firms, engaged in the import of opium and cotton, and exported tea, silk, camphor, cinnamon, copper, brass, and Chinese gold.[75] In 1861, Nusserwanji sent his son, Jamsetji, to Hong Kong. After staying there a few months, Jamsetji went to Shanghai, where he set up another branch of the firm. In the two years that he spent in China, Jamsetji found the time to enrol in a British volunteer force and to acquire first-hand experience of combat in China.

In 1864, the trading community in Bombay was badly jolted by the great crash caused by the temporary boom in cotton exports to England on account of the American Civil War and the setback to this trade that followed when the War ended. Many firms involved in the China trade were among those that collapsed as a consequence of this crash, including those of the second Sir Jamsetji Jejeebhoy, K.J. Readymoney and K.N. Cama. The Tatas were particularly hit, since their partner Premchand Roychand was one of those most deeply involved. They were forced to discontinue their China business as a result. Nusserwanji, however, was not reconciled to the loss of his China interests and at the earliest opportunity sought to revive them in collaboration with his brothers-in-law Dadabhai and Sorabji, in the form of a new company called Tata & Co.

The new company went through various teething troubles, until it finally stabilized under the direction of Dadabhai's son in 1883.[76] The Tatas experimented with new lines of business in China. With one foot in industry in India, particularly the newly-established textile mills, they made the transition to exporting manufactured products to China. They also ventured, more adventurously, into steam shipping. Following the decline of Indian-owned country ships, Indian shipments of goods to China had been handicapped by the high freight rates they had to pay to the European shipping lines, which drove up the price of their goods in China. The European shipping lines jealously guarded their monopoly through the system of shipping 'conferences' set up with the aim of keeping out competitors. Challenging the established shipping lines like the P.&O., Jamsetji Tata set up his own, the Tata Line, in collaboration with the Japanese Nippon Yusen Kaisha. The rates offered by the Tata Line were less than two-thirds of the going rates.[77] However, Jamsetji's move predictably met with an outraged reaction on the part of his European rivals, backed by the British Government. A fierce 'freight war', accompanied by devastating propaganda against the Tata Line followed, eventually causing the Japanese firm to withdraw from the partnership and the Tata Line to fold up in

1895. Nevertheless, Tata Sons & Co. continued to remain active in business in Hong Kong, long after several other Parsi firms wound up their interests in China.

The Sassoon family also exemplified, and owed their lasting success to, the quality of flexibility and the ability to branch out into different spheres of business. They were not necessarily pioneers, but they knew how to make use of opportunities as they arose.[78]

Among the sons of David Sassoon who were despatched to China, the one who entrenched himself most deeply in the commercial life there was his second son Elias, or E.D. Sassoon. Elias arrived in Canton in 1844. However, he was quick to realize that Shanghai and Hongkong offered better opportunities in the post-Treaty of Nanjing scenario and he established offices in these places. After the death of his father in 1864, E.D. Sassoon decided to secede from the parent firm under his brother Albert, and to set up on his own. In 1872, he formed a new company with its headquarters at 5 Renji Road in Shanghai, called E.D.Sassoon & Sons, but which in popular parlance came to be known as the 'New Sassoon' firm as opposed to the 'Old Sassoon' company.

E.D. Sassoon and his son Jacob, who took over after his death, had a flourishing business in imported cloth from Manchester, Liverpool, and Glasgow, and counted the most prominent stores on Shanghai's Tianjin and Nanjing Roads among their customers.[79] The Sassoons at the same time continued with their penchant for seeking newer avenues for profitable investment. They engaged in the insurance business, acting as agents of the North British Fire and Marine Insurance Co. Ltd, as well as in shipping. One of their schemes was to invest in the China Steam Navigation Company. Later on, in the scramble to provide loans to the Chinese Government in the 1890s, the 'old' company, David Sassoon & Sons, offered sterling loans for railway construction. This particular scheme was aborted on account of the Sino-Japanese War. Taking advantage of the newly obtained concession that enabled foreigners to set up factories in China, both the Sassoon firms also set up spinning and weaving plants in China, as well as rice, paper and flour mills. Later, they even ventured into setting up breweries and laundries. The Sassoon firms employed several hundred Chinese workers, although their top-level managerial staff were practically all foreigners, especially English, brought to China from overseas, as well as some locally recruited non-Chinese, such as White Russians, Jews and Portuguese.[80]

Probably the shrewdest business move of the Sassoons was to enter the real estate business, particularly in Shanghai, in a big way. They began to acquire prime properties, especially along the waterfront, under the name of various companies such as the Hua Mao Real Estate Co., the Shanghai Real Estate Co., the Far East Real Estate Co., and so on. In the nineteenth century, their profits from real estate in Shanghai were estimated to be just about one-nineteenth of their profits from opium, but from the early 1920s, with the opium business at an end, real estate developed into the most profitable segment of their business empire. In addition, they invested in hotels, public utilities, and high-rise construction. In the 1920s and 1930s, Shanghai saw an influx of wealthy Chinese from other parts of the country due to the widespread conditions of insecurity prevailing in large parts of China at that time. The Sassoons took advantage of the situation to make even greater profits through the issue of shares and bonds. The devaluation of the currency in 1938, multiplied their profits from this source.[81]

It was the broad-based nature of the Sassoons' interests in China and their pragmatic outlook, as well as their aggressive attitude towards any competition, that enabled them to come through the most unscathed of all the Indian business houses in the face of competition, various crises and even the revolutionary upheavals that punctuated China's history in the twentieth century.

The Export of Cotton Yarn

With relative stagnation in the raw cotton and opium trade, some of the more enterprising China traders turned their attention to investment in industry in India itself. Following the success of the Bombay Spinning and Weaving Mill founded in 1851, Manockjee Nasarvanjee Petit from an old family of China Traders, founded the Oriental Spinning and Weaving Co. in 1858, and his son, Sir Dinshaw Manockjee Petit founded several more. Merwanji Framji Panday was another China trader who ventured into this business, along with the Tatas. After first watching and preparing the conditions, the Sassoons entered the cotton textile business in a big way in 1880, with the founding of the Alexandra Mill by E.D. Sassoon & Co. The Sassoons established seven such mills in total, employing over 15,000 workers.

The mill owners found that in the domestic market, their products could not compete with the import of manufactured cotton textiles from Britain. However, in the Chinese market, with which many of them already had the advantage of familiarity and long experience, there was a demand from the hand-weaving industry for the relatively coarse variety of cotton yarn which was produced by the Indian mills. Cotton yarn exports from India to China began in a big way from the 1870s. From just about 2,000 bales of cotton yarn per year in the period from 1875-9, exports rose to 452,000 bales in 1895-9.[82] By that time, they amounted to 16 per cent of the total value of Bombay's exports—more than the share of opium exports.[83] So important did cotton yarn become as a staple of Indian trade with China that Koh Sung-jae, in his comparative study of the cotton industry in Japan, India, China, and Korea, has emphasized that the 'vast and profitable export trade in cotton yarns with China was the main controlling factor in the development of the modern cotton industry of Bombay'.[84] However, at the turn of the century, the boom in cotton yarn exports began to reverse itself. By the second decade of the twentieth century, Japanese yarn imports into China had ousted Indian yarn from its dominant position, and later, by the late 1920s, Chinese manufactured yarn started to displace both Indian and Japanese yarn. Nevertheless, the importance of cotton yarn exports in sustaining India's China trade for more than three decades, at a time when the trade in the more traditional items faltered, should not be understimated.

The New Sindhi Firms

The more successful of the Sindhi firms also had to recast their business operations to some extent in the twentieth century. The disruption caused by the First World War led to a sharp falling off in the demand for their traditional items of trade, that is, curios, fine silk, and other luxury goods.[85] While this did not lead to the collapse of the old Sindhi firms, it did lead to the rise of several new firms that specialized in intra-Asian trade, especially the trade between Japan and the other countries of Asia, including China. Although the curios and luxury goods trade experienced a new upsurge in the post-War period, the Depression of 1930-3 again hit it very hard. As Markovits writes: 'In the long run the effect of the depression,' was to produce a shift in the orientation of the Sindwork merchants from an almost exclusive emphasis on goods which could be called 'semi-luxury', such as fairly fine silks and relatively expensive curios, to a wider range including cheaper textiles and tourist goods. Combined with the effects of the devaluation of the yen in 1931, this led to a growing specialization in the sale of Japanese goods. Sindhi firms often became agents in the commercial offensive of Japan on external markets, particularly those of the British colonial empire.'[86] However, this association with the Japanese placed some of the Sindhi firms in China in difficulties when hostilities broke out between the two countries in the 1930s, compelling some of them to close down their operations there. Nor did the Japanese connection help them particularly from an economic point of view when China's eastern cities and Hong Kong came under Japanese occupation. Nevertheless, despite these difficulties, the Sindhi firms are the ones that survived and grew most successfully in the twentieth century, entrenching themselves in particular in the retail, garment, and tailoring trades in Hong Kong.

THE DECLINE OF THE OPIUM TRADE

The opening years of the twentieth century were another watershed in the history of Indians and the China trade. The opium trade, the mainstay of this trade for nearly a century, had entered a period of irreversible decline leading to its total cessation in 1913. Before this, however, internal changes had been taking place on the Indian side. The balance of power had begun to shift in favour of the Marwaris and other upcountry opium merchants and dealers vis-à-vis the big shippers in the ports. As early as the mid-nineteenth century, the former, having had a taste of the profits to be garnered from the opium trade, had begun to bypass the shippers and transport opium stocks to China on their own account. They also began to exercise their leverage in the trade by holding back stocks as it suited them.[87]

The situation began to change only in the last five years of the opium trade. The Collector of Customs, Bombay, declared categorically that 'up to the year 1907, the export trade to China was entirely in the hands of the six large Bombay shipping firms who bought up all the export opium and shipped it themselves. No Marwaris were inclined then to trade at all.' By 1910, however, only 4,859 out of the total number of chests of Malwa opium for export belonged to the big Bombay shipping firms, whereas the remaining 6,394 belonged to thirty-seven Marwari opium dealers with their headquarters in the interior. The projection for 1911 was that the Bombay firms would corner only 34.1 per cent of the total share, while the Marwaris would get 65.9 per cent.[88]

Even before the formal termination of the opium trade, various measures on the Chinese side had placed constraints on the trade. Foremost among these was the encouragement given by the Chinese authorities to the domestic cultivation of opium. A report prepared by the Revenue Department of the Bombay Government in 1899, had noted that export of both Bengal and Malwa opium had declined in the preceding five years on account of the competition arising from Chinese-grown opium. The difficulties faced by Indian opium in the Chinese market were compounded by the rise in the exchange value of the Re following the currency legislation of June 1893.[89] Apart from this, sundry restrictions and assorted levies were placed on the imported opium by various provincial authorities in China.

In Britain itself, the clamour against the 'morally indefensible' trade in the drug had reached a high pitch.[90] Against this background, and with a view to putting an end to haphazard restrictions on the trade from the Chinese side, an opium agreement was concluded on 8 May 1911 between Sir J.N. Jordan, representing the British Government, and Zou Jialai, representing the Chinese foreign ministry, the *waiwubu*. This agreement stipulated that the Indian Government would decrease and ultimately stop the export of opium to China by 1917, if, and in the same proportion as, the Chinese Government curbed the production and consumption of home-grown opium.

The agreement did not spell the end of their problems for the

Indian opium traders. Meanwhile, the Imperial Government was overthrown in a revolution and a new Republic was declared. On 7 November 1911, the four big firms of David Sassoon & Co. Ltd, E.D. Sassoon & Co., Sassoon J. David & Co. and Currimbhoy Ebrahim & Co., hastily despatched a petition to the Government of India, stating: 'We, the undersigned opium shippers, respectfully beg to draw the attention of the Government of India to the present very serious political situation in China and to request that, as all business is at a standstill and as we already hold very heavy stocks of opium there, that Government will sanction an extension of time for the balance of opium for shipment from Bombay during this year.' The petition was rejected with the unsympathetic comment: 'The request is quite inadmissible; and if the exporters run some risk, it is a trifle to the profits they have made already.'[91]

Within just a few months, however, the Government of India appears to have woken up to the seriousness of the situation in China, as can be seen by their response to the following memorial from David Sassoon & Co. Ltd., dated 25 January 1912:

. . . owing to the revolution in China, the trade has been at a standstill for the past four months...at the end of last year the stocks in Hongkong and Shanghai were 13,850 chests of Bengal opium and 9,100 chests of Malwa opium, while 1,065 chests and 1606 and a half chests of Bengal and Malwa, respectively, were afloat. Of these huge quantities, fully 80% belonged to the Indian importing Houses . . . all advices indicate that the end of the revolution in China is far from being in sight...Under the circumstances it stands to reason that regular opium shippers cannot continue to invest their money in a commodity, the outlet for which is closed and the sale of which even before the revolution was greatly hampered by the Chinese officials, notwithstanding the agreement made as recently as May 8th last.

This time, the response from the authorities was: 'The memorialists have a good cause and their claim for relief should be admitted.'[92]

The actual end of the opium trade came much earlier than scheduled. In 1913, the Government of India was forced to suspend sales of Malwa opium to China and to purchase stocks to avoid distress to those involved in the trade. It announced that 'the Government of India have grave reasons for apprehending that the course of events in China may be such as not only to postpone the exports notified for 1913, but to preclude entirely and permanently the export from India of opium to China.' The end came, for all practical purposes, when the Government of Bombay followed this up with its own resolution of 26 August 1913, announcing the cessation of transactions at the Bombay Opium Warehouse from 31 December of that year and the closing down of the entire establishment.[93]

INDIAN BUSINESSMEN AND HONG KONG

Many of the early China coast traders from India were quick to realize the handsome business opportunities afforded by the establishment of Hong Kong as a British colony after the Treaty of Nanking. Several of them purchased land holdings in the earliest land auctions organized by the colonial authorities. Among those who purchased plots in the very first land sale of June 1841, were Dadabhoy Rustomjee (Marine Lots 5 and 20), Heerjebhoy Rustomjee (Marine Lot 24), Framjee Jamsetjee (Marine Lot 36) and Pestonjee Cowasjee (Marine Lot 7). About 346 Indian merchants set up base in Hong Kong in the first few years after its establishment. The first Indian firm to set itself up in Hong Kong, shortly after the Treaty of Nanking, was that of Cowasjee Pallanjee & Co. Cowasjee died at Macao in 1842, but his son Pestonjee Cowasjee carried on the import-export business in opium, spices and silk, and later, cotton yarn. F.M. Talati & Co. also shifted from Canton to Hongkong in 1842, and maintained its headquarters there until the 1920s (when it shifted to Surat). It dealt mainly in precious stones and jewels, silks, precious oils, and other luxury goods. Other early arrivals were Abdoolally Ebrahim & Co., Albert Sassoon and Rustomjee Dhunjee Shaw, the representative of F.F. Cama & Co. from Bombay.[94]

The colony had problems in its early days. Neither life nor property was secure for traders and small businessmen, as the frequent reports in the local newspapers of that time of robberies and murders involving Indians show. Of those Indian traders who bought land at the first sale, only one, Framjee Jamsetjee, stayed there for some time. Even he moved to Hong Kong from Macao in May 1844, only after he found that there were no takers for his plot which he had persistently tried to sell from January 1842. By 1854, he was ready to wind up his affairs in Hong Kong altogether, and issued a public notice which said that 'Mr. Framjee Jamsetjee, the oldest inhabitant of Hong Kong, being tired of the colony and obliged to leave at last, requests all accounts to be sent for liquidation.'[95]

By 1854, the number of Indian merchants in Hong Kong had actually dropped to 193.[96] While the unsettled conditions which prevailed in the colony in its infancy would have turned away many of the early arrivals, there was probably another reason too for the reduction in the number of Indian traders. Some of them appear to have moved to Hong Kong primarily to pursue their claims for compensation for opium surrendered to the authorities during the War. Since this turned out to be a protracted process, they made good use of their time in Hong Kong to engage in business of one kind or another. But when their claims were settled (most had been settled by around 1862) they packed up and returned to India.[97]

Nevertheless, once the initial problems had subsided, Hong Kong turned out to be not only a protected haven for the opium trade but, as a new and growing settlement with expanding needs, offered enterprising Indian businessmen a very broad field for their ventures in a way that even the other 'treaty ports' in China could not match. Many Indians came, attracted by the trade in opium and traditional items, but ended up with their main interests elsewhere. The conditions in Hong Kong spawned several Indian merchant princes or *taipans*, who came to be known not only for their wealth but for their charitable activities and their role in the development of Hong Kong itself.

H.N. Mody was one such person. He came to Hong Kong in 1861, to join the opium trading firm of S.A. Seth as a clerk, but branched out into real estate and share brokerage. He had the vision to invest substantially in real estate in Kowloon shortly after the territory was acquired by the British at the conclusion of the Second Opium War. He was eventually knighted by the British Government, primarily for his pioneering role in setting up the University of Hong Kong. At a time when the rest of the business community in Hong Kong saw little advantage in the colony having its own university, Mody offered a substantial sum towards the cost of erecting the main building of a university. Matching funds were not forthcoming for some time, and Mody had to keep extending and increasing his offer, but he persisted in soliciting support for the project. Ultimately the University of Hong Kong was inaugurated in 1910, one year before his death.[98]

Dorabji Naorojee, another prominent Hong Kong Indian personality, began his career as a stowaway aboard a ship to Hong Kong in 1852. He soon set up on his own, and by 1867 owned a flourishing bakery which won a contract to supply the army and navy. From there he branched out into the hotel business. The best hotels of the time—the Victoria, the King Edward and the Kowloon hotels—were all set up by him. He is usually credited with the establishment of the cross-harbour transport service which continues to play an important role in the life of Hong Kong as the 'Star Ferry', but according to the archives of the Hong Kong Urban Council, the first cross-harbour ferry was begun not by him but by the firm of Abdoolally Ebrahim & Co.[99]

Paul Catchik Chater, an Armenian from Calcutta, arrived in the colony in 1864, as a clerk in the Bank of Hindustan. He too went into share brokerage and real estate, purchasing and developing several important sites in the island's Central district.[100] He was instrumental in the development of Kowloon Harbour, through the Hong Kong and Kowloon Wharf and Godown Company which he set up in 1884, as well as of Kennedy Town on the north-western part of Hong Kong island. However, the project with which he was most notably associated was the Praya Reclamation scheme, which developed the central waterfront area on the island's northern shore. This was done through the agency of another company he formed, Hong Kong Land. Chater was also involved in the founding of the Hong Kong Electric Company. To sort out the problem of supplying enough fuel at relatively low cost for this company, he formed in collaboration with Mody a company to develop coal mines in Vietnam. For this he was awarded the French Legion d'Honneur.[101] When Chater died, on 26 May 1926, his estate was valued at a little under $5 million.

The Sassoons, including David Sassoon & Co., E.D. Sassoon & Co. and Sasson J. David & Co., were also prominent in the business life of Hong Kong, though they began to withdraw from around the turn of the century.[102] They were close associates of Chater. Two equally prominent businessmen from India of Jewish origin in Hong Kong were E.R. Belilios and Elly Kadoorie. Belilios began as a leading opium trader, before expanding into real estate and other interests. Kadoorie, who began as an associate of the Sassoons when he arrived in Hong Kong in the 1880s, later went on to build up one of the biggest commercial empires based in Hong Kong. Both were noted for their interest in setting up educational institutions. Belilios was the main force behind the founding of the first government school for Chinese girls in the colony, while Kadoorie established a school for Chinese boys in 1901, as well as one for Indian boys in 1916, both of which were named after him. Yet another prominent family were the Ruttonjees, who arrived in 1878. The Ruttonjees were also among those who invested in real estate. Besides, they carried on with import-export trade and also ventured into the liquor business. They showed keen interest and support for the establishment of an anti-tuberculosis sanatorium, on the site of the old Royal Naval Hospital, which was named after them.

Hong Kong's first bank, the Oriental Bank which opened in 1845, was an offshoot of a Calcutta bank. The Hong Kong and Shanghai Banking Corporation had an Indian Jew, Belilios, as its long-time chairman as well as three Parsis on the committee set up to establish it. Many other Hong Kong corporations had Indians on their boards of directors. In the 1880s, out of thirty-four members of the Chamber of Commerce, one was a Parsi, three were Indian Jews, and one was an Indian of Armenian descent.[103] Several of these Indians subsequently achieved a position of prominence in the colony's governing establishment. They became Justices of the Peace, Members of the Legislative Council and even unofficial Members of the Executive Council. Besides Belilios and Mody, personalities like Frederick Sassoon, Paul Chater and Robert Hormus Kotewall attained recognition in this manner from the British government of the Colony.

Despite their wealth, their substantial contributions to charity, and what has been described as 'an almost indecent enthusiasm for all things British',[104] these Indian tycoons in the period under consideration do not seem to have been completely accepted into the uppermost levels of society. Frederick Sassoon, for instance, never managed to join the exclusive Hong Kong Club. He was however a member of the Hong Kong Jockey Club, perhaps only because of the fact that the Sassoons were keen promoters of horse racing and themselves owned several race horses.

The Census of the Indian Population of Hong Kong taken on 20 May 1911, lists 233 Indian males as being engaged in the commercial sector. Of these, the bulk were described as Clerks (70), while others were General Merchants (34), Silk Dealers (22), Brokers (13), Shopkeepers and Shop Assistants (29 altogether), Drapers (33) and Tailors (23). The Report submitted by the Census Officer P.P.J. Wodehouse along with it notes: 'There is an important commercial community consisting almost entirely of Parsees and natives of Bombay and Scinde. Some of the business houses are of very old standing. The Indian shopkeepers are principally drapers and silk dealers.'[105] With the end of the opium trade, the complexion of the Indian mercantile community began to change. Many of the early Parsi, Ismaili, and Jewish family firms wound up their business, attracted more by business opportunities in India or other parts of the world. But the 1920s and 1930s saw an increasing influx of Sindhi businessmen in particular. These included P. Chellaram, the Harilelas, the Moorjanis, the Watumuls, O.K. Gidumul, and others.[106] Besides venturing into the area of retail trade, several of these businesses prospered through trade in garments and custom tailoring. The present-day fabulously wealthy Harilela Enterprises in Hong Kong, for example, took precisely this road to prosperity, after an initial stint in the trade in precious stones and artefacts based in Canton. Later, they branched out into the hotel and real estate business, as well as other ventures. Probably on account of the success of these Sindhis, Hong Kong became a favoured destination of many others who left Sindh after the partition of India and Pakistan in 1947.

FROM TRADERS TO BUSINESSMEN

As noted in an earlier chapter, a trade mainly in luxury items of small bulk had been maintained between India and China over centuries. The revival of the India-China trade from the later eighteenth century, which found Indian merchants once again journeying to China, was occasioned by the discovery of two items from India which were in demand in China, and which were bulk commodities, unlike in former times. These were raw cotton and opium. The trade in these two Indian items yielded profits on an unprecedented scale to the Indian merchants. Although they had to divide the profits with their European collaborators and rivals, they were never displaced by them.

Since the conditions of the early phase of this trade did not permit Indian or other foreign merchants and their families to settle down in China, virtually all the proceeds of the trade were shipped home—whether in the form of bullion, or commodities or bills of exchange. This contributed in a major way to the accumulation of wealth in the Indian ports and interior towns connected with the China trade, especially Bombay. In the days before Bombay emerged as the industrial and financial hub of India, the impact of this wealth on Bombay's growth must not be underestimated. Particularly significant for India's development was the investment of funds accumulated in the Chinese trade in the nascent modern textile industry. In the crucial early decades of this, the flagship industry of modern India, the Chinese market played a very important role in absorbing its products, especially cotton yarn.

The Opium Wars and the sustained pressure applied by the big powers on China to 'open doors', led in a general sense to an immense expansion of the opportunities to trade with China, compared to the relatively restrictive system in force earlier. Indian merchants were quick to take advantage of opportunities, both in China's treaty ports and in Hong Kong. Ironically, particularly from the last years of the nineteenth century, the import of products from India into China ceased to be their main concern. The bustling treaty ports and Hong Kong were a land of opportunity, a new economic frontier, where money could be made in a variety of ways by those enterprising or fortunate enough. Real estate, finance, share brokerage, manufacture, the garment business, retail trade, etc., all became fields of activity for the adaptable Indian businessmen. By becoming key factors in the growing intra-Asian trade from the twentieth century, they began to assume a new role as what Markovits has called 'global middlemen', 'using India as a resource base to raise capital and expertise, but trading in goods which were not produced in India itself'.[107]

In his panoramic study, *Cross-Cultural Trade in World History*, Philip Curtin has analysed the phenomenon whereby traders stayed on in foreign lands not to fulfill their original purpose of handling long-distance trade from their own countries, but to involve themselves in local business, such as wholesale or retail trade. These trading groups were examples of what he calls 'cultural minorities left over from a trade diaspora [who] were able to use their original commercial bent, and their community solidarity, to establish a partial monopoly over the commercial life of the host society.'[108] The Indian commercial community in China and particularly Hong Kong in the twentieth century provide a good example of this kind of transformation. In the economic sense, they were no longer a link between India and China. The India connection was only incidental to their presence in China, a reminder of their origin and nationality. The evolution from a travelling trader/merchant to migrant business-man/entrepreneur had taken place.

This partially explains why the 1949 revolution in China put an end to the presence of this community in mainland China, without even the necessity of a forced eviction. There were no more carefully protected treaty ports where any form of making money was considered legitimate and hence no avenue for business was left. The Indians fulfilled no special economic function that required their presence in China, they had no role to play in the refashioning of the Chinese economy that was to take place in subsequent years under the Communists. They saw the writing on the wall and, with very few exceptions, left China's shores even before the communist takeover was complete. In Hong Kong, however, where economic opportunities continued as before under British rule, and were even enhanced in the post-War scenario, the Indian business community stayed on and prospered.

NOTES

1. Anne Bulley, *The Bombay Country Ships*, Richmond, Surrey: The Curzon Press, 2000, p. 104.
2. Cited in ibid, p. 121.
3. *Canton Register*, vol. II, no. 11, 2 June 1829.
4. Michael Greenberg, *British Trade and the Opening of China*, Cambridge: Cambridge University Press, 1951, p. 221.
5. See Ashin Das Gupta, 'Indian Merchants in the Age of Partnership, 1500-1800', in *Business Communities of India: An Historical Perspective*,

ed. Dwijendra Tripathi, New Delhi: Manohar, 1984, for an elaboration of this thesis.

6. Guha, 'Parsi Seths as Entrepreneurs, 1750-1850', in *Economic and Political Weekly*, Aug. 1970, p. M-115.

7. S.H. Jhabvala, *Framji Cowasji Banaji: A Great Parsi*, Bombay, 1920, p. 5; Ruttonjee Ardeshir Wadia, *Scions of Lowjee Wadia*, Bombay, 1964, pp. 49-50.

8. Siddiqi, 'The Business World', p. 303.

9. Rajat Kanta Ray, ed., *Entrepreneurship and Industry in India, 1800-1947*, Delhi: Oxford University Press, 1992, p. 21.

10. D.R. Gadgil, *Origins of the Modern Indian Business Class: An Interim Report*, New York: Institute of Pacific Relations, 1959, p. 16.

11. Claude Markovits, 'Indian communities in China', pp. 55, 61. Barbara-Sue White has also emphasised this in the title of her book, *Turbans and Traders: Hong Kong's Indian Communities*, New York: Oxford University Press, 1994.

12. Maisie Meyer, 'The Sephardi Jewish Community of Shanghai and the Question of Identity', in *From Kaifeng . . . to Shanghai: Jews in China*, ed. Roman Malek, Nettetal: Steyler Verl., 2000, p. 349.

13. Darukhanawala, *Parsi Lustre*, 2 vols. Bombay: G. Claridge, 1939.

14. Ibid., vol. 1, pp. 496, 755-6.

15. Vaid, *The Overseas Indian Community*, p. 53. This particular firm was still in business in Hong Kong as late as 1914.

16. For a detailed chronology of his voyages, see the Appendix, pp. 163-7, in Jehangir R.P. Mody's *Jamsetjee Jejeebhoy: The First Indian Knight and Baronet (1783-1859)*, Bombay: the author, 1959.

17. W.H. Coates, *The Old Country Trade of the East Indies*, London, Corn Market Press, 1911, rpt. 1969, pp. 64-5.

18. No. 93 (1800), Secret and Political Diary, *Maharashtra State Archives* (hereafter referred to as *MSA*), pp. 3319-27.

19. Mody, *Jamsetjee Jejeebhoy*, pp. 21-8.

20. For the career of Muncherjee Jamsetjee Wadia, see Wadia, *Scions*, pp. 146-53. Anne Bulley also has done some investigation on the fluctuations in Muncherjee's fortunes in her book, *The Bombay Country Ships*, op. cit., 2000, pp. 198-9.

21. Guha, 'Parsi Seths', p. M-107.

22. Guo Deyan, 'Qingdai Guangzhoude Pasi Shangren' (The Parsi Merchants in Canton during Qing period), unpublished Ph.D. thesis, Zhongshan University, Guangzhou, 2001, pp. 44-5.

23. Amalendu Guha, 'More about the Parsi Sheths: their roots, entre-preneurship and comprador role, 1650-1918', in Tripathi (ed.), *Business Communities*, p. 125.

24. White, *Turbans and Traders*, p.12.

25. C. Toogood Downing, *The Fan-Qui in China in 1836-37*, 3 vols., London: Henry Colburn Publisher, 1838, vol. 2, p. 235.

26. Guo Deyan, op. cit., pp. 29-31.

27. The area in front of the American Factory directly on the waterfront was a popular hang-out of the Parsi servants. William C. Hunter, *The 'Fan-Kwae' at Canton before Treaty Days, 1825-44*, Shanghai: The Oriental Affairs, 1882, p. 72.

28. Carl T. Smith, *A Sense of History: Studies in the Social and Urban History of Hong Kong*, Hong Kong: Hong Kong Educational Publishing Co., 1995, pp. 408-9.

29. Conversation with Ms Ruby Master, of Pavri & Sons, originally established in Canton in 1910 (Hong Kong, April 1997). According to Ms. Master, when her mother first arrived in Hong Kong in 1926, there were only four other Parsi ladies there.

30. Quoted in Smith, *A Sense of History*, p. 397.

31. From the personal notes collection of the Rev. Carl T. Smith.

32. Guo Deyan, op. cit., pp. 87-9. The *Hong Kong Census for 1921* mentions that 'it is fairly common for Indians to marry Chinese especially as secondary wives', although it is not clear from the context to which particular sections of the Indian community this refers. *Hong Kong Census Reports, 1841-1941*, Hong Kong, 1965.

33. Vaid, *The Overseas Indian Community*, p. 10. Abdoolally Ebrahim & Co. is the oldest Indian firm to continue doing business on the China coast under its original name.

34. Markovits has categorised them as one of four groups of Indian traders who successfully adapted to the conditions of European domination of international trade and finance. See Markovits, *The Global World*, p. 23.

35. Colin N. Crisswell, *The Taipans: Hong Kong's Merchant Princes*, Hong Kong: Oxford University Press, 1981, pp. 135-7.

36. Zhang Zhongli and Chen Zengnian, *Shasun Jituan Zai Jiuzhongguo* (The Sassoon Group in Old China), Beijing: Renmin Chubanshe, 1985, p. 160.

37. Meyer, 'The Sephardi Jewish Community' p. 350.

38. For more on the colourful personality and career of Hardoon, see Chiara Betta, 'Myth and Memory: Chinese Portrayal of Silas Aaron Hardoon, Luo Jialing and the Aili Garden between 1924 and 1995', in Malek (ed.), *Jews in China*, op. cit.

39. Meyer, 'The Sephardi Jewish Community', pp. 351, 355.

40. See Chapter 5, for references to the Shikarpuri Sindhis.

41. This account of the Hyderabadi Sindhis draws mainly from Claude Markovits', *The Global World*, op. cit.

42. Markovits, *The Global World*, p. 120.

43. Ibid., p. 198.

44. See Guo Deyan, op. cit., pp. 86-92.

45. H.B. Morse, *Chronicles of the East India Company Trading to China*, 3 vols., Oxford: the Clarendon Press, 1926, vol. 2, pp. 103, 231.

46. See Guo Deyan, op. cit., pp. 37-48, for more on the 'Parsi factory'. In 1848, after the Opium War, the Parsi factory was shifted along with others to Changzhou island in the Whampoa area of Canton, despite some resistance from the local Chinese population. A new building was erected there in 1861.

47. Hunter, *The 'Fan-Kwae'*, pp. 33-5.

48. Details of this incident are found in the *Canton Register*, vol. 3, no. 20, 2/10/1830, and vol. 3, no. 22, 2/11/1830.

49. See Guo Deyan, op. cit., pp. 43-4, for the unfavourable impression left on the Chinese authorities by this incident.

50. This at least is the impression conveyed in Guo Deyan's study, pp. 43-4.

51. See Morse, *Chronicles*, vol. 2, pp. 44, 110-11, 149, 181, 273, 299, on Parsi involvement in Hong debts.

52. Morse, *Chronicles*, vol. 2, p. 111; Guo Deyan, op. cit., pp. 59-61.

53. Guo Deyan, op. cit., p. 60.

54. Ibid., pp. 49-50.

55. *Canton Register*, vol. 3, no. 7, 29/3/1830.

56. Morse, *Chronicles*, vol. 3, pp. 200-1.

57. *Canton Register*, vol. 7, no. 40, 7/10/1834.

58. Ibid., vol. 9, nos. 15 and 50, 12/4/1836 and 13/12/1836.

59. Ibid., 1/10/1839.

60. Letter from Jamsetjee Jejeebhoy to H.N. Lindsay in London, vol. 1/ 11/1842 - 23/12/1843, p. 5, 'Jamsetjee Jejeebhoy Papers' (hereafter referred to as JJP), deposited at the University of Mumbai Library.

61. N. Benjamin, 'Bombay's 'Country Trade' with China (1765-1865)', in *Indian Historical Review*, vol. 1, no. 2, Sept 1974, p. 301. The Indian firms that were subsequently compensated for their surrendered opium by the British government are listed in Vaid, *The Overseas Indian Community in Hong Kong*, op. cit., 1972, p.10.

62. Cited in Arthur Waley, *The Opium War Through Chinese Eyes*, Stanford, Calif.: Stanford University Press, 1958, p. 152. Yang Fang, the deputy of the Imperial Commissioner I Shan, sent a memorial to the Emperor on 3 April 1841, which mentioned a petition from some Indian merchants that they be considered as non-English and hence be allowed to continue trading.

63. The following account of Jamsetjee Jejeebhoy's career is based on information found in the Jamsetjee Jejeebhoy Papers, as well as in Asiya Siddiqi's 'The Business World', op. cit.

64. See Thomas N. Layton, *The Voyage of the 'Frolic': New England Merchants*

and the Opium Trade, Stanford, Calif.: Stanford University Press, 1997, p. 80.

65. Siddiqi, 'The Business World', p. 310.

66. Letter to Matheson, 8 December 1842, JJP, vol. 1/11/1842 - 23/12/1842, pp. 28-30.

67. Ibid., 28 January 1843, JJP, vol. 1/11/1842 - 23/12/1842, pp. 118-21.

68. Letter to Henry Pottinger, 18 March 1843, JJP, vol. 1/11/1842 - 23/12/1842, pp. 155-8.

69. Letter to Andrew Farquharson, 15 June 1843, JJP, vol. 1/11/1842 - 23/12/1842, pp. 241-2.

70. Letter to Donald Matheson, 1 April 1851, JJP, vol. 2/1/1851 - 29/12/1851, pp. 42-3.

71. See letter to David Jardine, Hong Kong, 16 August 1851, JJP, vol. 2/1/1851 - 29/12/1851, pp. 77-80. Also letter to Jardine, Matheson & Co., Shanghai, 11 September 1852, JJP, vol. 1/1/1851 - 30/12/1852, p. 278.

72. Siddiqi, 'The Business World', p. 315.

73. Ray (ed.), *Entrepreneurship and Industry*, p. 25.

74. This was the conclusion of Claude Markovits after studying the estates in China of six Parsis between 1882 and 1907. He analyses that real estate accounted for about 54 per cent of their total value, while shares, debentures and deposit receipts accounted for another 25 per cent. See Markovits, 'Indian Communities in China', p. 66.

75. F.R. Harris, *Jamsetji Nusserwanji Tata: A Chronicle of his Life*, 2nd edn., Bombay: Blackie & Son (India) Ltd., 1958, pp. 5-6.

76. Harris, *Jamsetji Nusserwanji Tata*, p. 13.

77. B.Sh. Saklatvala and K. Khosla, *Jamsetji Tata*, Builders of Modern India series, New Delhi: Publications Division, Ministry of Information and Broadcasting, Government of India, 1970, p. 63.

78. The most comprehensive account of this unusual family is provided in Stanley Jackson, *The Sassoons*, London: Heinemann, 1968. See also the earlier account by Cecil Roth, *The Sassoon Dynasty*, London: Robert Hale Ltd., 1941.

79. Chen Qilu, 'Xin Shasun Yanghang Pianduan' (a brief account of the New Sassoon Company), in *Jiu Shanghai de Waihang yu Maiban*, Shanghai: Shanghai Renmin Chubanshe, 1987, p. 179.

80. Chen Qilu, 'Xin Shasun', p. 183.

81. Zhang Zhongli and Chen Zengnian, *Shasun Jituan Zai Jiu Zhongguo* (The Sassoon Group in Old China), Beijing: Renmin Chubanshe, 1985, pp. 14-17.

82. Koh Sung-jae, *Stages of Industrial Development in Asia: A Comparative History of the Cotton Industry in Japan, India, China, and Korea*, Philadelphia: 1966, pp. 93-4.

83. Claude Markovits, 'Bombay as a Business Centre in the Colonial Period: a Comparison with Calcutta', in *Bombay: Metaphor for Modern India*, ed. Sujata Patel and Alice Thorner, Bombay: Oxford University Press, 1995, pp. 28-9.
84. Koh, *Stages of Industrial Development*, p. 142.
85. See Markovits, *The Global World*, pp. 139-44.
86. Markovits, *The Global World*, p. 143.
87. Asiya Siddiqi, 'Some Aspects of Indian Business under the East India Company', in *State and Business in India: A Historical Perspective*, ed. Dwijendra Tripathi, New Delhi: Manohar, 1987, p. 85. See also her introduction in Asiya Siddiqi, ed., *Trade and Finance in Colonial India*, New Delhi: Oxford University Press, 1995, pp. 25-6.
88. A. Westropp to Chief Secretary to Government Revenue Department, Bombay, 6 December 1909, Vol. 134, 1910, Comp. 842, Political Department, MSA, pp. 390-2.
89. Vol. 270, 1899, Comp. 1074, Revenue Department, MSA, pp. 165-6.
90. For example, a resolution of the Bombay Missionary Conference, dated 7 November 1910, urged the cessation of the trade, while pragmatically recognizing that this would lead to 'financial difficulties' in India which the British Government should be obligated to help overcome. Vol. 241, 1911, Comp. 1047, Revenue Department, MSA, pp. 97-104.
91. Vol. 242, 1911, Comp. 735, Revenue Department, MSA, pp. 103-10.
92. Vol. 163, 1912, Comp. 1335, Political Department, MSA, pp. 377-8.
93. Vol. 149, 1913, Political Department, MSA, pp. 25-41. According to one source, the Sassoons, sensing which way the wind was blowing, sent a memorial to the Government of India just before the end of the opium trade advocating its cessation! See Colin N. Crisswell, *The Taipans: Hong Kong's Merchant Princes*, Hong Kong: Oxford University Press, 1981, p. 141.
94. See Crisswell, *The Taipans*, pp. 15, 52-7.
95. Cited in Smith, *A Sense of History*, pp. 395-6.
96. White, *Turbans and Traders*, p. 34.
97. Vaid, *The Overseas Indian Community*, p. 57.
98. Ibid., pp. 59-61.
99. Interview with Jafferbhoy Ebrahim of Abdoolally Ebrahim & Co., Hong Kong, 17 June 2002.
100. One of the busiest and most prominent streets in downtown Hong Kong is named after Chater. Similarly, there is still a Mody Road in Kowloon and a Sassoon Road near the University of Hong Kong.
101. For a detailed account of Chater's many-sided business ventures, see Crisswell, *The Taipans*, pp. 186-97.
102. Crisswell, *The Taipans*, p. 140.

103. White, *Turbans and Traders*, p. 23.
104. Crisswell, *The Taipans*, p. 194.
105. *Report on the Census of the Indian Population of Hongkong Taken on twentieth May, 1911,* from the Sessional Papers, p. 103 (56) (available in the library of the University of Hong Kong).
106. Vaid, *The Overseas Indian Community*, p. 67.
107. Markovits, *The Global World*, p. 16.
108. Philip D. Curtin, *Cross-Cultural Trade in World History*, Cambridge: Cambridge University Press, 1984, p. 5.

CHAPTER 5

Indians in Western China

At a far remove from the Indian trading community on the China coast were the Indian traders and businessmen in the western-most region of China, Xinjiang. Here Indians constituted an altogether separate stream of travellers and migrants, whose fortunes were affected less by what was happening to their counterparts in eastern China than by the turbulent local politics of Xinjiang and by the great rivalry between British and Russian interests in this part of the world.

The origins of the overland trade between India and the oases south of the Taklamakan Desert in western China are obscure. Nevertheless, from the sixteenth to the eighteenth centuries AD in particular, there was a flourishing overland trade between India and the Asian land mass to the north and west, carried largely by Indian traders. Writing about the predominance of Indian traders in Central Asia in the early nineteenth century, a contemporary observer noted: 'Wherever there is a bazar, Hindoos are a necessary part of the establishment. These people are always found amongst the buyers in all the cities of Central Asia and constitute the bankers and money-changers in all commercial communities there. All financial affairs are entrusted to their management.'[1]

There were formidable natural limitations, however, to the overland trade between India and western China. The main trade routes were three, one through Afghanistan (Badakshan), another via Kashmir, Gilgit and the Pamirs, and the third via Ladakh and the Karakoram range. The one from Ladakh, which was much frequented by the traders, was a gruelling test of endurance and determination, with at least four mountain passes averaging heights of over 17,600 feet having to be crossed. The journey to Yarkand in Xinjiang took on an average thirty-eight days.[2] Francis Younghusband, one of the early British explorers of this terrain, described the stark landscape through which he passed as 'a pebbly waste, bounded by bare gravel hills, silent as the grave, without a single sign of life, but with every mark of death, for the valley is strewn with the bones of the poor baggage ponies employed by the enterprising traders, who risk the perils and difficulties of these mountains to carry their goods into the heart of Central Asia'.[3] His companion on his journey to Chinese Turkestan, George Macartney, who went on to become the first British consul at Kashgar, later noted that the difficulties owing to bad weather and poor supplies of feed for pack animals were so great that it was rare to have a season in which all the loads arrived at their destination.[4] Another source estimated that there was as much as a forty per cent loss of caravan animals en route.[5] The weather also limited the trading season, as the traders were obliged to cross the passes before they became snowbound and impassable in winter.

Due to these difficulties, the trade between India and western China tended to be of small volume although the commodities exchanged were of relatively high value. The first systematic account of this trade was given by Moorcroft in 1820-2. Moorcroft noted that at that time the balance of trade was heavily in India's favour, and that silver ingots called *yamboos* had to be imported into India from Yarkand to balance the trade. By the mid-nineteenth century, the principal exports from India were opium, cotton, piece-goods, spices, Indian tea, sugar, and indigo. From the Chinese side, the main goods were *charas* (hemp or cannabis), tea, silk, wool, felt, carpets, gold and silver, precious stones, and horses and mules.[6] Of these, *charas* was undoubtedly the most important, although when Moorcroft had made his visit, it was not yet significant enough to be noticed by him.[7] However by 1899, a British official report from Kashgar admitted that 'the Indian trade was dependent, to a large extent, on the export of *charas* to India, and that if the cultivation of this drug could be prohibited, the number of Hindustani traders would be considerably reduced, and the Indian trade with this country would become of a nominal value.'[8]

Various groups of Indian merchants participated in the trade. They were often referred to locally as *dawan-aashti* or 'men from over the mountains'.[9] The main Xinjiang centres where they traded were Yarkand, Yangi Hissar, Karghalik, Khotan, Maralbashi, Kucha, Kurla, and Usturfan. There were also Indians in Kashgar, the administrative centre of this part of Xinjiang, but not as many as in Yarkand and some of the other towns. Moorcroft noted the dominance of the Kashmiri merchants, who had ousted the Andijani traders from their earlier domination of the trade.[10] While some were seasonal traders, a number of them stayed on in Xinjiang for so long that they lost their ties with their homes in India and considered themselves as locals for all practical purposes.[11] Many of these people acquired land in Xinjiang and married Turki wives, and could no longer even speak in their original mother tongue. Besides the Kashmiris, traders from Punjab also visited Yarkand and other towns of Chinese Turkestan. Before the trade picked up in the late 1860s, many were small-time traders from the nomadic Gaddi tribe, whose routine circulation from lower to higher pastures took them sometimes to Ladakh and occasionally even to Yarkand.[12] Later, many of the Punjabi traders were Khatris from Hoshiarpur, Amritsar, Rawalpindi, and other towns, who operated either on their own account or else as agents of established firms in these places, such as Chelu Ram & Son of Amritsar, and Mella Mal Lachmun Dass of Hoshiarpur. They were in general treated well by the Chinese authorities, although they had to bear some discriminatory measures such as not being allowed to wear turbans or ride horses within the town.[13]

Another major group of Indian businessmen in Xinjiang were the Shikarpuris from Sindh. They were part of a larger network of Shikarpuri Sindhis that played an important role as financiers of the caravan trade between India and Central Asia.[14] The Shikarpuris followed what was known as the *shah-gumastha* system, in which the *shah* was the major partner who advanced the capital to junior partners called *gumasthas* who did most of the travelling. In southern Xinjiang, where they established a strong presence from the 1890s, they were predominantly moneylenders, and as such, earned a notorious reputation, charging on an average interest at the rate of 12 per cent per month, and using coercive methods to recover debts owed to them.[15] Their method of operation was to give out small loans at very high interest to a large number of people. Unlike their fellow Sindhis from Hyderabad in eastern China, the Shikarpuris in Xinjiang tended to be socially conservative, having their own *serais* or rest-houses and maintaining even their own panchayats which were linked with those in Shikarpur.[16] Although many remained in Xinjiang for a number of years, few settled there permanently. Some of them did form relationships with local women, often as a *quid pro quo* for unpaid debts owed by these women's families[17]—a practice that further fuelled local resentment against them.

Apart from the merchants and landowners, another group of Indians in Xinjiang in this period were slaves, mainly Kashmiris, Baltis, Gilgitis, and Nagaris, as well as a handful of Punjabis, numbering about 800 altogether.[18] Apparently, these hapless men and women had been captured by the Kanjutis from Hunza and taken to Xinjiang. Located mainly in the vicinity of Yarkand, Kashgar, Aksu, and Khotan, they were presumably engaged in agricultural labour or domestic service. In the 1890s, when the British representatives in Kashgar stumbled on the presence of these slaves, several of them had already been in bondage for more than thirty-five years, while others had even been born there. The British authorities insisted that the slaves be freed, but put responsibility for it on the Kashmir Darbar, which was obliged to 'ransom' them at the cost of Rs. 60-100 per head.

ANGLO-RUSSIAN RIVALRY AND THE INDO-XINJIANG TRADE

When the British traveller, Robert Shaw, visited Xinjiang in 1869, there were already 'hundreds' of Indians there.[19] Shaw's visit marked the beginning of a process that was to significantly change the complexion of the age-old relations of Indians with Xinjiang. From the middle of the nineteenth century, the innocuous trickle of trade over the mountains between India and Xinjiang developed into a key factor in the so-called 'Great Game', the strenuous efforts made by the British and Russian empires to assert their supremacy in this part of the world through a combination of diplomacy, intrigue, pressure tactics, and brinkmanship.[20] Among other things, this rivalry came to affect the routes and facilities used by the Indian traders, their status in

Xinjiang and the attitude of Chinese officials towards them, as well as the commercial competition they faced in the bazars of Xinjiang.

With the victory of the British in the last of the Sikh Wars in 1849, the frontiers of the British empire in India had expanded virtually up to India's natural frontier with China in the northwest. Meanwhile, the parallel process of Russian imperial expansion had brought it too up to the borders of Chinese Turkestan. Particularly after its bitter defeat in the Crimean War of 1854-6, tsarist Russia began to show interest in the lands to the east. In the 1860s, it managed to subjugate the Central Asian khanates of Tashkent, Bokhara, Samarkhand, Khiva, and Khokand. It secured a diplomatic coup in 1860 by becoming the only Western power to have consular representation at Kashgar. To the British, it seemed as if the Russian 'bear' was looming dangerously close to the border of India and that it had managed to strategically outmaneuvre them in the region just to the north.

Beginning with Robert Shaw's visit, a series of British travellers, both officials as well as private adventurers, explored Chinese Turkestan and the routes thereto. Many were quick to recognize the value of the trade between northwestern India and Xinjiang as an already existing bridgehead for British political and diplomatic penetration into a region in which British penetration would otherwise have little justification. The low volume trade suddenly became the object of considerable official concern, as well as of a series of measures designed to give it a boost. In 1862 a detailed report on the possibilities of the Indo-Xinjiang trade observed that Xinjiang was rich in silk, fruits, jade, sulphur, copper, lead, emeralds, gold, silver and wool, and that the main items from Punjab in demand there were cotton piece-goods and tea.[21] For various reasons, the trade across the Karakoram route had slumped in the mid-nineteenth century. Kashmiri and Ladakhi traders were particularly plagued by raids by Kanjuti traders from Hunza on their caravans. The exactions of the officials in Jammu and Kashmir also drove many of them away. The Maharaja of Jammu and Kashmir as well as the Governor of Ladakh were themselves the biggest traders, and fixed prices and the terms of trade in an arbitrary fashion to suit themselves and their own agents.[22] To correct this problem, in 1865 the Maharaja of Kashmir was prevailed upon to reduce his taxes on trans-frontier trade, and a uniform transit duty of 5 per cent was fixed. Road and bridge improvements were also carried out. In 1867, a British officer was for the first time stationed at Leh. In 1868, a scouting mission to Xinjiang was despatched, and in 1869, the first officially-sponsored trade fair for this trade was held at Palampur.

Another measure adopted somewhat later by British Indian officials to encourage trade with Xinjiang was the grant of exemption from duty or refund of duty with respect to certain commodities exported to Xinjiang, such as foreign goods and cotton goods. No doubt at least in part because of this, English piece-goods could be sold in Xinjiang at a profit of 60 per cent to 80 per cent.[23] However, availing of this refund facility proved to be a problem for many of the traders because the posts where the rebate or drawback certificates could be collected were not conveniently located. Travelling to the seaports to collect these certificates was simply not worth their while for the traders, who mostly purchased their goods for export on a retail basis in Amritsar, Delhi, and other inland bazars. Even after a customs post was established at Srinagar, a petition of 1908 from 'many influential Central Asian traders' asked for one to be set up at Hoshiarpur as well, the reason being that the existence of a post only at Srinagar meant that they were forced to use exclusively that route, which was inadequately serviced by mules for transport. Recommending their case, the British Resident in Kashmir blamed the prevailing system for collection of drawback certificates for the low value of the trade, which he claimed had declined to a value of only Rs. 2,842 in 1904-5. His view was endorsed by his successor, Sir Francis Younghusband, who claimed that 'the traders have immense physical difficulties to overcome on the journey between Leh and Yarkand, and in my opinion deserve all the assistance it is in our power to give.'[24]

The British interest in this trade had several aspects. In the first place, it was hoped that it would keep in check Russia's growing commercial penetration of this region. In addition Indian traders were a useful source of information to the British authorities in Srinagar, Leh, and Kashgar. The official diaries of the British outposts in these places meticulously record the arrival of individual traders and any information they chose to give. For instance, one trader returning from Yarkand in September 1890, reported on the Chinese construction of a fort at Suget, on the undefined border between India and Chinese Turkestan.[25] Another, referred to only as 'Bura, Hindu', reported on Russian military preparations, the extension of the Russian telegraph line to Irkishtam, and their transport arrangements for commercial purposes.[26] Indian traders also performed useful services to British officials and travellers in Xinjiang by virtue of their network of connections and local influence, including acting as provisioners and suppliers. They even functioned as unofficial bankers to the British by encashing their cheques.[27] At least one British visitor to Xinjiang believed that Indian traders helped to spread a good image of the British among the local populace. Writing in July 1890, after returning to India, Major C.S. Cumberland wrote, 'I consider that the friendly feeling and respect shown to Englishmen in Chinese Turkestan is entirely due to the reports of our traders. . . .'[28]

Despite such efforts, however, the Indians were at a great disadvantage with respect to the Russians. The commercial advantages enjoyed by the Russians were both physical and geographical, as well as political and diplomatic. The approaches to Xinjiang from the territory of the Russian Empire were incomparably easier than the approaches from India, added to which the Russians subsidized the export of various goods to Xinjiang, covering the cost of their transport from Russia proper to the border with Xinjiang.[29] The difficulties and losses en route were thus much less for the trade coming from Russia, and it was possible for Russians to undersell Indians in most cases. An Indian merchant observed bitterly: 'We have no chance against them. As soon as any cloth or foreign thing imported by us becomes popular in Yarkand or Turkistan, they send agents who take samples, and they quickly copy them in their own factories, and, of course, can undersell us by reason of distance.'[30]

Moreover, by virtue of having been recognized by treaty with China, Russian trade was on a much sounder footing than the Indian trade, and less vulnerable to what were considered arbitrary and excessive restrictions and exactions imposed by Chinese officials. According to the British Joint Commissioner at Ladakh in 1886, the Chinese dreaded any misunderstanding with the Russians in case that became a pretext to seize part of the territory.[31] Britain, of course, could not contemplate mounting any serious military expedition against Xinjiang over the mountains from India. The favoured treatment accorded to the Russians also seemed to have extended to peoples like the Andijanis who were a strong presence in this region. Commenting on the subject a British official wrote in a sour vein:

The Russians have a treaty which gives them free and unrestricted trade, exempt from duty with those regions, and the fulfillment of the treaty is watched by a Consular Agent. They are able therefore to sell what they please where they please. We have neither Treaty nor Consul and . . . our trade there is in fact contraband. Whether it can be carried on at all depends on the good-will of the local authorities. In this case they are the reverse of well-disposed. . . . In fact, Russian traders, backed by a treaty and supported by the local influence of a representative can drive us from any market they care to occupy in Chinese territory outside the Great Wall. The position is as injurious as it is humiliating.[32]

There was a brief period, however, from 1864 to 1877, when the British were in a relatively favoured position in Xinjiang. This was during the revolt of Atalik Ghazi, better known as Yakub Beg. Yakub Beg invaded Xinjiang from Khokand and declared the formation of an independent state there. In his search for allies against the Qing whose power he had overthrown, Yakub Beg favoured the British over the Russians, and sent out feelers for support from the government of Lord Mayo in India. The pre-existing Russian treaty rights were de-recognized initially, although later under pressure, they were restored. In any case, the British saw their chance to get ahead in the rivalry with Russia. Despite Britain's apparent support for the Qing in the rest of the Chinese empire during this period, in Xinjiang it had no compunction about supporting a rebel regime. The mission under Robert Shaw was despatched and cordially received. Accompanying Shaw was a Punjabi merchant, Tara Singh, who was similarly well-treated, encouraging many other traders from India to follow him to Xinjiang with high expectations. In 1874, a treaty was signed by the British envoy T. Douglas Forsyth and Yakub Beg. It was ratified by the Government of India in 1876. As far as the British were concerned, things were going very well.

Just a year later, however, Yakub Beg was overthrown and killed by the Qing forces under the command of the formidable General Zuo Zongtang. The Qing retaking of Xinjiang was accompanied not only by considerable bloodshed but, more alarming from the point of view of Britain's long-term interests, by the revival of Russian influence in the region. The Chinese were in no mood to forgive British support to Yakub Beg.[33] In 1881, a new treaty between Russia and the Qing was signed which settled the question of the restoration of some territory in Ili which the Russians had occupied during Yakub Beg's regime. It led to the upgradation of the status of the Russian representative in Kashgar to that of Consul General.

What followed was a period of, on the one hand, difficulties for Indian traders and, on the other hand, persistent efforts on the part of the British to regain some measure of their lost influence and prestige in southern Xinjiang. The complaints of Indian traders about discriminatory treatment and persecution at the hands of the local authorities reached a crescendo— whether because conditions became much worse than they had earlier been, or because they found a sympathetic ear among British officials, is not clear. Soon after the restoration of Chinese power in Xinjiang, Indian traders from Yarkand reported that the Chinese were trying to systematically reduce the number of Indians in the region. They claimed that only those who had settled there with their families for twenty or thirty years were being allowed to stay, while others were expelled or pressurized to leave, and had their goods confiscated.[34]

Throughout the 1880s, British officials posted at the frontier outposts in Ladakh and Kashmir dutifully recorded and passed on the complaints of Indian traders. Some kind of prohibition on the import of Indian tea had been imposed. In 1881, a trader from Yarkand, Sadr Bai, reported that while this had been temporarily lifted, 'the transit or intermediate duties throughout Chinese Turkestan are now so high that merchandise from India cannot reach beyond the town of Yarkand. . . . The trader is taxed at every town or military post upon the road.'[35] Apparently, the taxes were imposed even on Chinese traders, but the Russians, including Andijanis, were exempt. That was galling to the Indian traders and British officials.[36] A note of 1883, reported the Chinese prohibition of the production and export of *charas* to India—an act which the British Joint Commissioner of Ladakh warned could lead to crippling 'half the import trade' from Xinjiang.[37] The British strongly suspected Russian intrigue behind this measure. In 1887, came the news that 300 pony-loads of

Indian tea worth Rs. 48,750 which had been transported to Yarkand were not being allowed to be sold until a consignment of Chinese tea brought by a Chinese merchant there was sold. Again, no such prohibition was known to have been imposed on the Russian traders.[38] The report pointed out that the tea trade had, because of such restrictions and irritations, dwindled from Rs.100,000 the preceding year to just Rs.15,000.

THE QUESTION OF CHINESE AND BRITISH JURISDICTION OVER INDIANS IN XINJIANG

It was under these circumstances that George Macartney was despatched to Kashgar in 1890. His primary objective was to establish Britain's clout with the Chinese there and to aggressively protect the highly vulnerable Indian trade on the basis of which much of the British empire's designs in this part of the world rested. For eighteen years until 1908, when the Chinese finally agreed to his designation as British Consul at Kashgar, Macartney had no official status in their eyes and hence no real *locus standi* to deal with them on behalf of the Indians or anyone else. To compensate for this lack of status, the British Government in 1892, endowed Macartney with the unique title, 'Special Assistant to the Resident in Kashmir for Chinese Affairs'. But this turned out to be rather a hollow honour since it was not backed by anything more than a minimal official establishment at Kashgar, not even, as Macartney often complained, a proper official dress for ceremonial occasions!

Despite this, what Macartney managed to achieve was to carve out a sphere of 'British interests' in Xinjiang by claiming that whatever happened to anyone of Indian origin was of concern to Britain, and to insist on his right to intervene in any case involving an Indian. The 'Macartney era' saw an ongoing tussle in this respect between the British on the one hand and the Chinese authorities at the local and regional levels and at Beijing on the other hand.

A good part of Anglo-Russian rivalry in this period tended to be played out through this struggle between the British and the Chinese, with the Russians encouraging the Chinese authorities to take a firm stand against Macartney. However, Anglo-Russian rivalry in this region shortly afterwards began to diminish and became less of a preoccupation for the British. In 1895, the Pamir Boundary Commission established a strip of Afghan territory, the Wakhan tract, as a buffer between the Russian and the British Indian empires. British fears of Russia were further lessened by Russia's defeat in the Russo-Japanese War of 1904-5, and by 1907 the two former rival powers even found themselves bound together in an alliance under the Anglo-Russian Convention.

Because of their overall importance in Britain's strategic plans in this part of the world, the cases involving conflict between Indians in Xinjiang and the local authorities and people are richly, even minutely, documented in the files of the Government of India from that period. While these documents present only a one-sided picture of the tenor of relations between the Indians and Chinese, they nevertheless indicate some of the major points of friction between them.

In spite of their relatively small number, Indians were involved in a large number of cases. In 1898, Indians were involved in about 600 cases of dispute, totalling about Rs. 100,000 in value.[39] The causes of disputes included breach of faith by carriers who failed to deliver the goods entrusted to them for transport between India and Xinjiang, stolen goods, assault, and expulsion from the bazar.[40] However, by far the largest number of cases involving Indians revolved around the problems of moneylending and the difficulty of recovering debts.

Much of the problem of adjudicating these cases depended on the fine distinction between selling on credit, and money-lending. Since few of the local traders or shopkeepers in the bazars of Xinjiang possessed enough means to purchase outright the goods brought by Indian merchants, the common practice was to take them on credit. The Indians were paid when the goods were sold or when they left for home at the end of the trading season. Apparently, in a large number of cases, the repayment was never made, or was not made in full. Macartney described the situation in the following words:

A common feature of trade in Central Asia is the long credit system. Retail traders commanding little or no capital, it is difficult to get them to take goods on immediate payment, and so the importer is obliged to give credit extending from 6 to 18 months. In the interval between the delivery of the goods and the payment therefor, accidents frequently occur. The retail trader may become insolvent, or may abscond or die;

and in such eventualities in this country, where commercial faith is low and justice erratic, the importer runs great risks of losing his money.[41]

Several Indian traders complained that they had been forced to stay back in Xinjiang after the end of the trading season and thereby incur significant losses merely because of their inability to collect debts in time. A Punjabi named Husain Baksh came to Macartney with more than half a dozen bonds dating back eight years or more which he had been unable to redeem. He claimed to have been a once prosperous merchant who had sunk into poverty because of this, and sought Macartney's help in recouping some of his losses so that 'he might recover from poverty and be able to return to his native land in his old age'.[42]

Of course, there *was* a way of distinguishing between merely selling on credit and moneylending, and that was by seeing whether interest was involved. The Chinese argued, quite justifiably, that most of the Indian complainants were money-lenders who charged exorbitant rates of interest. Since money-lending was a prohibited practice, the Indians who indulged in it could expect no sympathy. Even otherwise, Chinese officials argued, they could not be expected to squeeze out money from a debtor who possessed nothing with which he could repay. It was up to the Indian traders to be more careful before they entered into deals. This was in fact the gist of the reply issued by the District Magistrate of Yarkand in 1899, to a complaint by Macartney on behalf of some Indian merchants. He noted: 'the Hindus lend money on interest, and their rates are such that a capital of 10 taels will become, together with interest, at the end of a year, 40 or 50 taels, the hardship suffered by the borrower being of the keenest description'. The District Magistrate also condemned the practice of penalizing a debtor by expropriating what little he had. 'It is the custom', he said, '... with the wealthier merchants to give an extension rather than harass a debtor by undue haste, and thus, by being enabled to carry on his trade, the debtor is offered the means of paying off his debts.'[43] Interestingly enough, this was the same viewpoint that had been expressed several decades earlier by 'the Beg of Khotan' in an incident narrated by Robert Shaw. Shaw had heard the story from an Indian merchant, Chinjoo, who had had an encounter with the Beg.

On the way to Khoten he met the Beg of Khoten and his retinue going to Kashgar . . . When they came up to him, the Beg pulled up and asked who he was; on being told that he was a Hindoo going to earn two 'rotees'. . . at Khoten, the Beg said, Well, go and prosper, but keep your eyes about you and don't trust anybody. Take your money before you give your goods. For if you are swindled, we shall, it is true, seize the delinquent and sell his house and property to pay you; but if he has none, whence can you get satisfaction?[44]

Despite this advice, Indian traders came to Macartney in droves begging for action on their complaints, when he made the rounds of the various oasis towns in which they were to be found. In the course of just one visit to Yarkand early in 1898, Macartney received as many as seventy-five petitions. Not all of these were against Chinese or local people, since there were a large number of disputes among Indians themselves.[45] Macartney's superior, Younghusband, had been particularly critical of the mutual squabbling among the Indians there. During a visit to Yarkand in 1891, he had even used the occasion of a dinner to publicly castigate them for it, asking them why the British Government should go to all the trouble of appointing a consular representative on their behalf. Younghusband's attitude to the Indian traders was summed up in his report of the visit, in which he wrote:

. . . the traders themselves are not so very deserving of our compassion: very few of them are real British subjects, the most part are Kashmiris, who on many occasions have shown themselves ready to intrigue against us: Afghan and Bajauris, who will not let an Englishman go a single yard into their own country; and Badakshis who as we have seen are half inclined to go off to the Russians. They are all keen enough, though on having an English consul up here to whom they can bring their grievances. . . .

Deputy Secretary Elias at Delhi, who read his report, concurred, saying that he would do well to stay away from their 'petty intriguing' and 'let the traders stew in their own juice'.[46] Macartney's own assistant Shuttleworth wrote: 'Shikarpuris will never meet the Chinese half-way, and the amount of trouble they are giving to the magistrate is considerable. . . there is no satisfying these vultures.'[47]

However, in Macartney, who took a more long-term view of British interests in the region, the traders found a more receptive audience, one who took their complaints at face value and followed up on all of them with great energy. He conducted his own investigations, forwarded the traders' petitions to the concerned Chinese officials, and prodded and goaded the latter relentlessly. What was worse, from the Chinese point of view, was that he pointed out shortcomings and delays in their system of justice, accused the lower functionaries of being corrupt, demanded their dismissal, and in short, appeared to be telling them how to do their jobs. All this was done when the principle of extraterritoriality was still not recognized in practice as applying to British and British Indian subjects in Xinjiang. To his superiors, Macartney repeatedly complained that he did not have adequate powers to deal with the problems facing him. But in practice, in his dealings with the Chinese, he did not let this limit him.

There already existed a well-established, if part informal, system on the part of the Chinese in Xinjiang to deal with the problems of Indian merchants. Where the problems concerned only British subjects the custom was for those involved to select a 'respectable person' who would act as arbitrator. Only if this failed to produce a settlement did the Chinese authorities intervene. The Chinese instituted a system of *aksakals*, or headmen, for the foreign traders. While the Russians were privileged to choose their own *aksakal*, the Chinese appointed an *aksakal* for the Indians. The *aksakal*, who was usually a local personality, was supposed to conduct on-the-spot investigations, and then advise the Chinese District Magistrate or *amban* on how to decide the cases. At times, minor officials called *shiang yo* and *begs* were asked to deal with offences on the part of the foreigners. More serious cases, however, were dealt with by the District Magistrate. The *taotai* (or *taoyin*), the Prefect at Kashgar, was supposed to exercise overall supervision over this system of justice and to deal with particularly complicated problems, especially after British representatives became involved.[48]

The complaints of the Indian traders with regard to this system pertained almost exclusively to the behaviour of their *aksakal*, a man called Ahmadyar. Their complaints portray him as corrupt, avaricious, manipulative, and vindictive to a high degree. They expressed few complaints about the higher Chinese officials, and insofar as they had complaints about the District Magistrate of Yarkand, it was that he relied too heavily on the judgement of

Ahmadyar. Even the Indians admitted that the District Magistrate, when not swayed by Ahmadyar, was capable of handing out justice quite even-handedly. In one case, for example, he summoned several Indian traders to answer charges put forward by twenty-five to thirty local *charas* dealers that the Indians were organizing to force down the sale price of *charas*. Munshi Bunyad Ali, Macartney's assistant, reported on the official's verdict:

The District Magistrate replied to the plaintiffs that the Hindus were at liberty to make or not to make a league for the purpose of purchasing charas, that the plaintiffs had nothing to do in the matter, the fall in the price of charas was their misfortune, and if they used to derive profit on charas before, they could suffer some losses this year, by selling at cheaper rates.[49]

Ahmadyar, like several of the other *aksakals*, was something of a versatile businessman himself, who had dealings in his own right with some of the Indians, and was not averse to using his clout to get the best deal for himself. It was natural that there would be considerable antagonism between him and the Indian traders. For instance, Ahmadyar was supposed to have purchased some brocades from one Basanta Mal on credit. When Basanta Mal demanded payment, Ahmadyar was reported to have challenged him to go and petition Macartney about it.[50] In another case, 18 Indian traders complained to Macartney that Ahmadyar was trying to scuttle an amicable settlement between an Indian Ludar Mal and a local person who was in his debt, Rahmatulla, because Ahmadyar wanted Rahmatulla to be formally penalized and his lands expropriated, since he himself had an interest in acquiring that land.[51] Ahmadyar had, in addition, an even more important position by which he could harass the Indian traders, since he was also the sole *charas* broker.[52] The list of complaints against Ahmadyar included his deliberately humiliating them in public while conducting investigations, taking bribes from all sides in disputes and being vindictive when he was thwarted. A trader named Kadir Arghun, who had appealed to Macartney against the *aksakal*'s behaviour when he had visited Yarkand, wrote to him about Ahmadyar's vengeance after Macartney had returned to Kashgar: 'It is difficult for me to pass life in this town . . . I write to inform you beforehand that if Ahmadyar gets a "razinama" from me, it will be by force.'[53]

It is possible that the Indian traders would have been satisfied with the dismissal of Ahmadyar and the appointment of another *aksakal* in his place. One indication of this was their reaction when the Yarkand District Magistrate, probably in response to repeated complaints about Ahmadyar, transferred two cases involving Indians to the Russian *aksakal,* one Mirza Jan. Macartney was highly indignant about this. But according to the report of Munshi Bunyad Ali, 'the Hindus were delighted, because the case would now be decided by a trustworthy and sensible man. Mirza Jan is a merchant, and will dispose of the case with discretion.'[54] Macartney, however, decided to use the discontent with Ahmadyar as the thin edge of the wedge to make changes in the system of justice as it applied to British subjects in Xinjiang. During the course of his visit to Yarkand in 1898, he suggested to the District Magistrate that since the current *aksakal* was not functioning properly, he should be dismissed and replaced, not by another official appointee, but by an *aksakal* chosen by the traders themselves. This made the Chinese official immediately cautious about British intentions. He replied that the Indian trade, unlike the Russian trade, was still not on an official footing. Hence, they could not have an *aksakal* of their own, but were nevertheless under the District Magistrate's protection.[55]

When it became clear that Macartney would not limit himself to forwarding complaints and making suggestions to the Chinese officials, but was assuming judicial powers himself in settling cases among Indians and other British subjects, the District Magistrate was angered. He warned Macartney not to receive any more petitions from the Indian traders. He also countermanded Macartney's settlement of various cases, and bluntly commanded the traders not to have anything to do with any Englishman or to show him any favours.[56] Chaudhri Ram Dass, whom Macartney referred to as 'Chief Hindu trader', reported that after Macartney had returned to Kashgar, the District Magistrate summoned them to demand an explanation as to why they had had dealings with the British representative. According to Ram Dass, the official railed against their ingratitude and threatened them with lashings.[57]

Macartney was not daunted, and on the contrary, escalated the struggle by formulating a five-point proposal or set of demands, which he presented to the Chinese authorities with the support of his superiors in Delhi and London. The demands stipulated: the dismissal of Ahmadyar; the right of British subjects to elect their own *aksakal*; no restrictions on traders dealing with Macartney; joint adjudication of civil suits between British and Chinese subjects by the District Magistrate and Macartney acting conjointly (excluding those involving Indians permanently domiciled in Chinese territory); and the right of British subjects to petition either the District Magistrate or Macartney.[58] With pressure being applied by the British Minister at Beijing on the *zongli yamen* (Foreign Office) as well, the authorities in Xinjiang were compelled to accept these demands. Nevertheless, implementation of the accord turned out to be a mixed affair. For instance, in July 1898, Ahmadyar was dismissed, deprived of his hat button and flogged. But his replacement, one Sadik Akhun, was not an elected choice of the Indians, and what was more, just a few weeks later, by September, Ahmadyar was back at his original post! More important from Macartney's point of view was the establishment of the Joint Court, which began functioning, although with some amount of friction. Overall, the British agency at Kashgar had reason to be pleased. Munshi Bunyad Ali wrote effusively on 22 September:

The Amban has once more turned his attention to the welfare of the Indian merchants, and his Begs too, have begun more or less to work fairly well. Akhoon Beg and Sadik Akhoon, Shiang-yo, now enquire into the cases with zeal from morning till evening in the Hindus' serai. Tahir Beg also pays occasional visits, and all of them exert their best to settle the Hindus' affairs.[59]

Eventually, even the principle of an *aksakal* being chosen from among the Indians themselves was recognized. By 1901, the *aksakal* was an Indian, Gauri Mal.[60]

The final twist to the story of the British struggle in Xinjiang over the question of jurisdiction over Indians, involved the question of who precisely constituted a British Indian subject. This question was a major preoccupation of British officials from 1903, when the Chinese agreed to allow trade benefits to British subjects in Xinjiang on the lines of those enjoyed by the Russians. This led to a sudden swelling of the numbers of those who claimed status as British Indians. Even Macartney admitted to being perplexed as to how to cope with the situation:

One of my duties here is to watch over the interests of British subjects in this country. But it is not always clear to me who those are that should be included under that denomination. Some persons, originally from British Indian territory, have settled in the Yarkand district for great many years, and now practically have no connection either with their country of origin or with the Indian trade. Others have executed bonds before the local authorities declaring themselves Chinese subjects, and have, in consequence, been admitted to privileges denied to ordinary foreigners, such as the owning of land, admisssion to administrative employ, etc. The whole situation is one of remarkable complexity. Yarkand appears to have always extended a special hospitality to all foreigners, and the result is that there are now amongst them several hundreds of Kashmiris, Baltis, Ladakhis, Gilgitis, and Indians, living in the country more as members of the native society than as sojourners. Such persons often apply, as British subjects, to me for protection, or assistance in litigation, whilst the local authorities, considering them as Chinese subjects, not unnaturally resent intervention. Again, the persons referred to have a tendency to proclaim themselves British, or Chinese subjects, according to the convenience of the moment. . . .[61]

On the whole, British officials seemed to agree that British protection should be extended only to Hindus, and not to Afghans and Bajauris, or to Indian or Kashmiri Muslims considered to have settled permanently in Xinjiang (defined as those who had not visited India for five years). This left only about 150 persons, according to Macartney's assessment made in 1900, who were entitled to British official protection.[62]

By 1913, however, circumstances had changed. With the overthrow of the Imperial Government in China, the British had an eye on the possibilities of furthering their interests in the western regions. This led to a vigorous drive to register second-generation Indians in Xinjiang as a basis for expanding the number of those considered as British subjects. Not doing so, in Macartney's opinion, 'in the event of our wishing to have a say as to the future of this part of the New Dominion, would scarcely give us a broad basis' for pushing forward British interests. The scruples about not registering Afghans and others as British Indian subjects were conveniently thrust aside, and Macartney managed to come up with the count of 209 British subjects at Yarkand, 50 at Karghalik, 40 at Goma and 70 at Khotan (most of whom were actually Afghans). According to one estimate, if those who had been second generation landowners had been disqualified, there would have been no more than a dozen Bajauri and Kashmiri farmers and twenty Punjabi merchants.[63]

PROBLEMS IN THE TWENTIETH CENTURY

In February 1907, a major riot broke out between the Indian Hindus and the Muslim population in Yarkand. According to Macartney, this was the first instance of large-scale conflict between the Hindus and Muslims in the region.[64] The immediate cause seems to have been the discovery of a local Muslim woman in the room of a Hindu cook, Ram Ditta, in the *serai* where he lived.[65] This led to an altercation between his supporters and members of the local population, which rapidly escalated into a riot. Angry crowds of more than 6,000 persons gathered and demanded punishment of the Hindus. Chinese officials who sought to defuse the situation were intimidated and their words went unheeded, and the situation threatened to rage out of control.

Eventually, a solution was found, for which Macartney claimed credit. The cook was fined Rs. 50, the Hindus who were found to have used insulting language against the Muslims and their mosque were admistered mild beatings, and further amends were made by the gift of carpets and a salaam in front of the mosque. On the other side, it was stipulated that no slaughter of cows or selling of beef in front of the Hindu serais were to be permitted. The *taotai* of Kashgar issued a proclamation berating the local Muslims for their unruliness and urging them to live in harmony with the Hindus. 'The Court of China', it ran, 'sets store on the keeping of good faith, and on the maintenance of friendly relations with foreigners; and when any of such comes to us for purposes of travel or trade, he should be treated with hospitality and be given protection. And how can little people like you, for the sake of your little opinions, be allowed to create an uproar!'[66] The *taotai* further said that anyone with a grievance against the Hindus should petition the authorities and not take the law into their own hands, and he particularly forbade 'headmen and intriguers' from collecting crowds and marching to the places of residence of the Hindus. Macartney declared himself satisfied with the effect of these words on the local people.

Nevertheless, it was not local flare-ups of this kind, but subsequent major political upheavals that were to decisively affect the Indian trade with Xinjiang and the situation of Indians there. The coming decades were to see momentous developments: the collapse of imperial rule in China and the control of Xinjiang by a series of warlords; the October Revolution in Russia; the Civil War and Allied Intervention in the Soviet Far East, and its spillover into Xinjiang and neighbouring regions; as well as the repeated insurrections in Xinjiang, particularly serious being the Tungan rebellion of 1933-4 and the revolt in Kashgar in 1937. These developments affected the condition of Indians in Xinjiang in different ways.

With the Revolution of 1911 in China, power in Xinjiang passed into the hands of Yang Zengxin, who ruled as Provincial Governor from 1912, until his assassination in 1928. One effect of the Revolution on Indian trade was that, because of the political instability, there was less movement of goods within the province, leading to the accumulation of stocks in Yarkand and Khotan.[67] The Revolution in China, however, seems to have had less effect on the fortunes of the Indians than the October Revolution in Russia. The immediate effect of the Russian Revolution was that the main competition for the Indians was suddenly eliminated. With the trade in Russian goods disrupted, the volume of Indian trade with Xinjiang soared to about Rs.10 million worth.[68] This could be considered the most prosperous time ever for the Indian trade in Xinjiang. However, within a decade, the trend began to reverse itself. After the Government of China recognized the USSR in 1924, Soviet consulates were reopened in Xinjiang and political hurdles to the resumption of trade with Russia were in the main removed. Soviet trade revived briskly and overtook the levels of the earlier trade with Russia. Soviet textiles, for instance, seemed to have displaced to a considerable degree the trade in Indian textiles.[69] In 1931, the Soviet Union constructed the Turksib Railway almost up to the border with Xinjiang, immensely facilitating the transport of commodities to Central Asia. By 1932, British officials privately admitted that 'Indian trade is at a hopeless disadvantage' with respect to Soviet Russia.[70]

Indians and their trade received the final crippling blows in the 1930s. In 1933, Tungan rebels under Ma Zhongying succeeded in overtaking much of Xinjiang. Yang Zengxin's successor, the warlord Jin Shuren, was forced out of office. A new warlord, Sheng Shicai, came to power, and began a offensive against the Tungans. The rebels retreated from Urumchi, falling back on the road to Kashgar and Yarkand, where they held out even as late as 1936, although their leader Ma Zhongying retreated into

Soviet territory in July 1934. In the meantime, the situation was further complicated by the setting up of a Turki 'Independent Muslim Republic of Eastern Turkestan' which lasted for just two months.[71] Needless to say, in those years, control over the main centres where Indians traded and resided changed hands several times, leading to considerable loss of life and property. Indians (Shikarpuris in particular) came in for special attack in mob violence, no doubt due to resentment over their moneylending activities. Apparently, during the 1933 uprising, one of the demands raised was for the cancellation of all debts. Rumours which inflamed local opinion at that time included the charge that the Indians refused to hand back local women with whom they had formed relationships.[72] Among the Indians who were killed in the course of all the turbulence were Rai Sahib Dipchand, Tarachand and Tulsidas Jethanand. The Government of India forwarded claims for compensation to the Government of China, but the Chinese Government only gave a certain sum which they termed a 'present', and would not otherwise accept liability for the losses suffered by Indians.[73]

By 1935, Indian trade with Xinjiang was estimated to have shrunk to about one-twentieth of its volume just after the Russian Revolution.[74] India's share of Xinjiang's external trade was estimated at just about 5 per cent, as opposed to the share of Soviet Russia, which stood at 82.5 per cent[75] The Tungan Rebellion which broke out in 1937, led to further losses for the Indians, through the loot and confiscation of goods in transit, and the occupation and plunder of their households. About 70 individuals and firms again submitted claims for compensation.[76] Public opinion in India began to show anxiety about the condition of Indians in Xinjiang, and questions about their welfare were raised in the legislative assemblies.

Sheng Shicai at around the same time launched a crackdown on the sale and export of *charas*, which at that time still accounted for about 42 per cent of all exports to India.[77] A major exodus began of Indians who found it too difficult to carry on with their trade and business under the circumstances. In addition, between 1940 and 1941, a total of 179 British subjects, most of them Indians, were deported from Xinjiang.[78] These included many who claimed to have no more ties with relatives or homes in India and whose families had been in Xinjiang for more than a half-century. Some of the deportees were charged with crimes like rape and selling opium. Some of them, however, were charged with 'sedition', probably with reference to their stand or activities during the Tungan rebellions. One of them included the Indian *aksakal* at Yangi Hissar, Rattan Singh, whose deportation was ordered in the winter and who died of exposure and frost-bite en route.

Trade between India and Xinjiang nevertheless continued in a desultory fashion in the 1940s. The main items imported into India were silk, silk yarn, carpets and *namdas*, woollen cloth and gems, while the main exports to Xinjiang were cotton piece-goods, muslin, dyes, spices, tea, and western medicines.[79] In 1942, the Provincial Government issued regulations requiring all sales and purchases by Indian traders to be made exclusively through the Native Products Co. Indian traders complained that the Native Products Co. quoted arbitrary rates and also would not supply them with goods equivalent to the value of what they had imported. They also accused the company manager of colluding with one of their number, a certain Munu Ram, in trying to undercut the trade of the others. Besides Munu Ram, there were only four other Indian traders at Kashgar by this time, of whom the most prominent was Pandit Bihari Lal, agent of the firm Messrs Shadilal Dwarkanath. Pandit Bihari Lal had had a long association with Xinjiang and had even collaborated with the British Consul-General M.C. Gillett in compiling an English-Uighur dictionary, and was one of the last three traders to leave Xinjiang for India, the other two being Pandit Bishambar Das and his son-in-law Arjun Singh.[80]

British officials complained that even after Britain became an ally of China during World War II, its subjects received no consideration from Sheng Shicai. In 1944, the Guomindang Government at Chongqing managed to remove Sheng Shicai from the governorship of Xinjiang by elevating him to the position of Minister of Agriculture and Forestry! He was replaced by a series of short-lived appointees of the Guomindang Government. Hopes of an improvement in Indo-Xinjiang trade were quickly belied, however. Writing in November 1944, Gillett noted:

I am not very optimistic . . . about the future of Indo-Sinkiang trade. The negotiations just completed make it abundantly clear that the

Sinkiang authorities are not interested in giving our traders fair play, but only respond to practical sanctions applied where they will feel it most. . . . In the question of international trade, as in every other matter, the new Government has failed to live up to its early promise of being an improvement on the Sheng regime.[81]

The final blow to the fortunes of Indians in Xinjiang, particularly those who had settled down there and acquired some property, came when increased rates of taxation and rigid collection procedures led to many of them being dispossessed of their lands. The taxes were not applied only to the Indians, since the Chinese were required to pay at the same rates. However, the Agent-General for India at Chongqing, K.P.S. Menon, who travelled through Xinjiang in 1944, wrote in December: '. . . the main complaint of British subjects in all the oases which we visited, other than Yarkand, was that they had been dispossessed of their lands'. He claimed that these landowners, of whom at least 50 sought to meet him in this connection, stood in great danger of becoming paupers as a consequence. An Indian of Yarkand called Mohammad Usman wrote that 'there are all kinds of taxes, yearly, half-yearly, monthly and daily. If one tax collector comes then another and so on that the whole day is spent in doing nothing but weighing corn and counting money.' One year's income from the land, he claimed, was not enough to pay one month's tax. He also reported on the fate of his friend: 'Abid Hajee was charged 12,000 coys but he was unable to pay it and was consequently imprisoned. I stood security for him and he was released. As a result of this he has sold his land and paid the amount. 'Now of course,' he added, 'he has no land to cultivate.'[82]

Of the various segments that made up the Indian population of China in the modern era, the merchants in Xinjiang constituted the oldest. Over the course of several centuries, they had survived both the rigors of passage as well as the numerous political changes in this region of the world. Yet they could not survive the explosive combination of political turbulence and targeted violence against them in the Xinjiang of the 1930s and 1940s. It is possible to conjecture that the dispersal of Indians from Xinjiang in that period could have been just an interlude, a temporary disruption, following which Indians would once again cross over the mountains with their goods for sale, as they had done in the past. After all, the 1949 revolution in China did not altogether put an end to border trade of this kind between India and China. However, the deterioration in the relationship between India and China in the post-colonial era precisely over the issue of the demarcation of the border, and the strategic importance of this region where India, Pakistan, and China meet, made such an eventuality virtually impossible. Furthermore, today trade routes that are not amenable to either rail or road traffic have also become something of an anomaly. As Janet Rizvi has pointed out,

Among the paradoxes of the modern world is the way in which change, development and technological progress have rendered the mountain barriers between different regions not less but more formidable than they were before. Ancient routes, crossing savage ranges by high and often glaciated passes, could be negotiated by the feet of traders and pilgrims and their pack animals; but it is only those whose gradient is gentle enough for the road and rail systems on which modern overland communications depend that remain in use today. On many another the ibex and the marmot now roam undisturbed.[83]

NOTES

1. General Josiah Harlan, cited in Kiran Datar, 'The traders of Punjab and Asian trade (seventeenth to early nineteenth centuries)', *Punjab Past and Present*, vol. 20, Oct. 1986, p. 83.
2. Janet Rizvi, *Trans-Himalayan Caravans: Merchants, Princes and Peasant Traders in Ladakh*, New Delhi: Oxford University Press, 1999, p. 34.
3. Francis E. Younghusband, *Report of a Mission to the Northern Frontier of Kashmir in 1889*, Calcutta: 1890, p. 8. See also Bir Good Gill, 'Trade of the Punjab with Eastern Turkistan: its ramifications - 1865-1879', *Proceedings of the Punjab History Conference, Nineteenth Session*, 22-24 March 1985, Publication Bureau, Punjabi University, Patiala, pp. 303-4.
4. Foreign/Frontier-A/Oct. 1907, National Archives of India (hereafter referred to as NAI), pp. 153-6.
5. Owen Lattimore, *Pivot of Asia: Sinkiang and the Inner Asian Frontiers of China and Russia*, Boston: Little, Brown & Co., 1950, p. 173.
6. Gill, 'Trade of the Punjab', pp. 303-4. See also C.P. Skrine and Pamela Nightingale, *Macartney at Kashgar: New Light on British, Chinese and Russian Activities in Sinkiang, 1890-1918*, London: Methuen, 1973, p. 10.
7. Rizvi, *Trans-Himalayan Caravans*, p. 37.
8. Foreign/Sec.F/Jan. 1899, NAI, pp. 28-33. Until as late as the 1930s, when the import of *charas* was finally banned, there was even a Charas Office at Leh under the Government of Punjab.

9. C.P. Skrine, *Chinese Central Asia: an Account of Travels in Northern Kashmir and Chinese Turkestan,* Hong Kong: Oxford University Press, 1986 edn., p. 108.

10. Rizvi, *Trans-Himalayan Caravans,* pp. 32-3. See also Marc Gaborieau, 'Kashmiri Muslim Merchants in Tibet, Nepal and Northern India', in *Asian Merchants and Businessmen in the Indian Ocean and the China Sea,* ed. D. Lombard and J. Aubin, New Delhi: Oxford University Press, 2000, pp. 193-6.

11. British files record the plight of several second and third-generation Indians in Xinjiang when the regime of the provincial governor Sheng Shicai deported them in 1940-1. They had lost all their property and claimed not to know anyone in their places of origin back in India. Ext. Affairs/External/ 1941/ 678-X (Sec.), NAI.

12. Rizvi, *Trans-Himalayan Caravans,* pp. 46-7.

13. Ibid., pp. 48-9.

14. For the most detailed account of the Shikarpuris of Sind, in Xinjiang as well as other parts of Central Asia, see Claude Markovits, *The Global World of Indian Merchants, 1750-1947: Traders of Sind from Bukhara to Panama,* Cambridge: Cambridge University Press, 2000.

15. Markovits, *The Global World,* pp. 190-1.

16. Ibid., pp. 256-7.

17. Ibid., p. 267.

18. References to these slaves of Indian origin can be found in the following files in the National Archives of India: Foreign/Secret F/Feb. 1893, pp. 389-416; Foreign/Secret F/May 1893, pp. 380-90.

19. Robert Shaw, *Visits to High Tartary, Yarkand and Kashgar,* London: John Murray, 1871, pp. 285, 289.

20. See Gill, 'Trade of the Punjab', for a discussion of this aspect of India's trade with Xinjiang.

21. Gill, 'Trade of the Punjab', p. 302.

22. Rizvi, *Trans-Himalayan Caravans,* pp. 38-9, 40-1.

23. Ibid., pp. 48-9.

24. Political Department, vol. 58, 1908, Comp.1554, Maharashtra State Archives (hereafter referred to as MSA), pp. 191-206; see also Revenue Dept, vol. 75, 1900, Comp. 1182, pp. 1-10.

25. Foreign/Secret-F/Oct. 1890, NAI, pp. 141-70.

26. Foreign/Secret-F/Aug. 1894, NAI, pp. 300-5.

27. Foreign/Frontier A/Dec. 1893, NAI, pp. 1-12.

28. Foreign/Secret-F/Oct. 1890, NAI, pp. 141-70.

29. Rizvi, *Trans-Himalayan Caravans,* p. 56.

30. Foreign/Frontier-A/Jan. 1904, NAI, pp. 137-44.

31. Foreign/Secret-F/Dec. 1886, NAI, pp. 1-17.

32. Foreign/Frontier-A/Dec. 1888, NAI, pp. 106-33.

33. Skrine and Nightingale, *Macartney at Kashgar,* p. 11.

34. Foreign/Secret/Nov. 1878, NAI, p. 151.
35. Foreign/Pol.-A/Jan. 1882, NAI, pp. 242-60.
36. Foreign/Sec.-F/Dec. 1886, NAI, pp. 1-17.
37. Foreign/A-Pol-E/Sept. 1883, NAI, pp. 231-4.
38. Foreign/Frontier-A/Dec. 1888, NAI, pp. 106-33.
39. Skrine and Nightingale, *Macartney at Kashgar*, pp. 104-5.
40. Foreign/Sec.-F/Jan. 1900, NAI, pp. 91-3.
41. Foreign/Frontier-A/Oct. 1907, NAI, pp. 153-6.
42. Foreign/Sec.-F/Jan. 1899, NAI, pp. 28-33.
43. Foreign/Sec.-F/May 1899, NAI, pp. 319-33.
44. Shaw, *High Tartary*, pp. 385-6.
45. Foreign/Sec.-F/July 1898, NAI, pp. 251-72.
46. Foreign/Sec.-F/Sept. 1891, NAI, pp. 176-7.
47. Cited in Markovits, *The Global World*, p. 95.
48. Foreign/Sec.-F/July 1898, NAI, pp. 251-72.
49. Foreign/Sec.-F/Sept. 1898, NAI, pp. 332-63.
50. Foreign/Sec.-F/July 1898, NAI, pp. 251-72.
51. Foreign/Sec.-F/Sept. 1898, NAI, pp. 332-63.
52. Foreign/Sec.-F/Sept. 1898, NAI, pp. 332-63.
53. Foreign/Sec.-F/July 1898, NAI, pp. 251-72.
54. Foreign/Sec.-F/Sept. 1898, NAI, pp. 332-63.
55. Foreign/Sec.-F/June 1898, NAI, pp. 501-4.
56. Ibid., pp. 501-4.
57. Foreign/Sec.-F/July 1898, NAI, pp. 251-72.
58. Foreign/Sec.-F/Sept. 1898, NAI, pp. 332-63.
59. Foreign/Sec.-F/ Mar. 1899, NAI, pp. 257-73.
60. Foreign/Sec.-F/Apr. 1903, NAI, pp. 28-37.
61. Ibid., NAI, pp. 28-37.
62. Skrine and Nightingale, *Macartney at Kashgar*, pp. 116, 133.
63. Ibid., pp. 232-3.
64. Foreign/Secret-F/June 1907, NAI, pp. 632-43. See also Foreign/Secret-F/ Sept. 1906, pp. 69-72 for an account of this incident.
65. There were Hindu and Muslim *serais* established for the use of Indian and other merchants in some of the towns of southern Xinjiang. There were at least four Hindu *serais* in Yarkand. One of the *serais* was constructed by a long-time trader from Hoshiarpur, Jawala Bhagat, at his own expense. Even after circumstances led to his losing most of his wealth, he sought to keep up the *serai*. See Foreign/Frontier A/Dec. 1893, NAI, pp. 1-12, for a description of this trader.
66. Macartney's translation of the proclamation of 30 May 1907. Foreign/Secret F/Sept. 1907, NAI, pp. 69-72.
67. Rizvi, *Trans-Himalayan Caravans*, p. 61.
68. Peter Fleming, *News from Tartary: a Journey from Peking to Kashmir*, London: Macdonald & Co., 1936, rpt. 1980, p. 260.

69. Owen Lattimore, *Pivot of Asia: Sinkiang and the Inner Asian Frontiers of China and Russia*, Boston: Little, Brown & Co., 1950, p. 176.
70. Foreign & Political/External Branch/1932/F.No. 365-X(Secret), NAI.
71. Fleming, *News from Tartary*, pp. 256-7.
72. Markovits, *The Global World*, p. 268.
73. Foreign & Political/1938/F.No. 234-X/38(Secret), NAI.
74. Fleming, *News from Tartary*, p. 260.
75. Lattimore, *Pivot of Asia*, p. 174.
76. External Affairs Dept/External Branch/1941/678-X(Secret), NAI.
77. Lattimore, *Pivot of Asia*, p. 173. Silk, nevertheless, had overtaken *charas* as the main export from Xinjiang to India in the early 1900s. See Rizvi, *Trans-Himalayan Caravans*, pp. 58-9.
78. External Affairs Dept/External Branch/1941/678-X(Secret), NAI.
79. Rizvi, *Trans-Himalayan Caravans*, p. 64.
80. I am deeply grateful to the former Foreign Secretary, R.D. Sathe, who had been posted as the Consul General for India at Kashgar from December 1948 to September 1950, for sharing with me this and other information regarding the Indians in Xinjiang during this period.
81. External Affairs Dept/1945/335-C.A.(Secret), NAI.
82. Ibid.
83. Rizvi, *Trans-Himalayan Caravans*, p. 27.

CHAPTER 6

Indian Soldiers, Policemen and Watchmen in China

As soon as the rickshaw puller straightened up to go, the outstretched hand of an Indian policeman holding a gun blocked the way. The appearance of the man frightened the child. He hid his face in terror. 'There's nothing to be afraid of', Mr. Pan told the child. 'He is just an Indian policeman. Look at his red turban. Because back home we don't have policemen like him, we have to come here. With his gun he will protect us. Look at his beard, it's amusing. It looks like that of the arhats in the temples.'

The child was too frightened to look even at a beard like that of an arhat.[1]

Soldiers, policemen, and watchmen formed a large and highly visible segment of the Indian population in China between the 1840s and the 1940s. This was a unique feature of Indian migration to China, standing in contrast to the situation in other countries in this period, to which the emigration of labour to work the fields, mines, and railroads was the major trend. (In China, unlike in many of those other countries, the British and other western powers found a plentiful supply of suitable cheap labour for their enterprises.)

Soldiering and guard duties were a field in which the demand for Indians was great among the colonial powers in China.[2] Britain, singly or in alliance with other powers, fought three 'China Wars' in this period, not to mention her involvement in the suppression of the Taiping Rebellion. The colony of Hong Kong required continuous garrisoning, in addition to a regular police force which, for various reasons, the British were unwilling to raise entirely from the local population. Moreover, because of the turbulent conditions in China during much of this period, as well as the strong undercurrents of hostility to the foreign presence that periodically surfaced into open clashes, the British required the presence of reliable and experienced troops. Given the limited number of British-born military and police personnel available for Britain's global interests, it was not surprising that the British authorities turned to Indian soldiers for their needs in China.

Although their duties were not exactly identical, soldiers, policemen, and watchmen formed a single socio-economic category among the Indians in China. Generally speaking, ex-soldiers or those from soldiers' families were the ones who found employment as policemen in Hong Kong and the treaty ports of China. In the same way, those retired or discharged from police or army service were the most sought after as private watchmen by Chinese and European employers. Hence, the background and experience of these persons, the factors motivating them to come to China, and their reactions to the conditions around them, tended to be broadly comparable. Besides, with their high visibility and striking and colourful appearance (with uniform, turban, and beard), this particular category of Indians tended to dominate the popular Chinese perception of Indians as a whole.

THE ARMIES OF BRITISH INDIA
AND OVERSEAS SERVICE

The First Bengal Native Regiment was raised by Robert Clive in 1757. This force included not just Bengalis, but also Pathans, Rajputs, Jats, Rohillas and men from other communities who were to be found in this region because of the Muslim conquest of Bengal and the politically unsettled conditions generally prevailing in northern India in this period.[3] In the initial stages, the three Presidencies under the East India Company, which were in a more or less constant state of hostilities with the forces of neighbouring Indian principalities and of other European powers like the French, recruited and organized forces of Indian soldiers on an ad hoc basis to meet their military requirements. The Madras Regiment was founded in 1758, when the forces of the French were threatening to besiege Madras. Of the Madras Army, less than 12 per cent were actually Tamils, with nearly three-quarters of the force consisting of men from Telengana as well as other communities.[4] By 1798, there were about 24,000 Indians in the Bengal Army, about the same number in the Madras Army, and about 9,000 in the army of the Bombay Presidency.[5]

It was Marquis Wellesley who, as Governor-General from 1798 to 1805, for the first time introduced the practice of sending Indian troops overseas. Overseas service for Indian regiments was a voluntary affair under the East India Company. Initially, it was not popular with many soldiers, particularly Brahmins, of whom there were a particularly large number in the Bengal Army. To induce Indian soldiers to volunteer to serve abroad, special benefits were offered, including enhanced pay, rations and pensions, extended leave with pay on completion of the tour of duty, and the choice of which regiment they wanted to rejoin in India once their service overseas was completed.[6] The reluctance of the Bengal Army soldiers permitted only a small force of Bengal volunteers to be sent to China when hostilities first broke out there in 1840. However, in the case of the soldiers of the Madras Army, the willingness to serve overseas appeared to be greater. The entire regiment of the 14th Madras Native Infantry (MNI), for instance, volunteered for service in China in 1840. These batallions of the MNI also came to be known as 'the Golden Galley' for their repeated tours of service overseas.[7] According to a contemporary source, more than 20,000 Indian sepoys and camp followers had volunteered for overseas duty between 1824 and 1844.[8]

In 1801, a force of Indian soldiers was sent by Wellesley to Egypt to help check Napoleon's advance. Their services, however, were not required by the time they arrived, as the French general there had surrendered the day before.[9] The Napoleonic Wars also saw the first occasion for the despatch of Indian troops to China. 600 Bengal sepoys under the command of Rear Admiral Drury arrived in September 1808 in Macao, the island leased to the Portuguese by the Qing Empire for commercial purposes. The purpose of their visit was allegedly to prevent Macao from falling into the hands of the French. The Portuguese did not welcome this intrusion, but were powerless to prevent it. Having already landed with his troops, the British admiral then made a formal request for permission to land which was conveyed to the Jiaqing Emperor at Beijing. The Emperor was incensed, and refused permission for the fleet to stay:

Nine warships have come one after another, all loaded with cannon, ammunition and gunpowder. They dared to anchor at the Chi-Ching Ocean of the Hsiang-shan hsien. 300 barbarian soldiers boldly landed at Macao and lived in the churches of San-pa-ssu and Lung-sung-miao. They were divided into groups and ordered to guard both the eastern and western fortresses. . . . When the foreign barbarians dare to occupy the strategic spots of our frontier, we must not show the least sign of weakness or cowardice![10]

Unwilling to enter into a confrontation with the Qing Empire at this stage, the British forces withdrew from Macao on 23 December of the same year.

THE FIRST OPIUM WAR, 1840-1842

More than three decades were to pass before Indian soldiers of the British Indian Army engaged in actual combat with the Chinese for the first time, during the First Opium War. It is an interesting fact that the Sanyuanli episode, famous in Chinese patriotic folklore as the occasion when thousands of Chinese villagers got together to drive off a detachment of British troops in May 1841, involved mainly a company of Indian soldiers from the 37th Madras Native Infantry. For more than a century from the time of the First Opium War, a very large number of Indian regiments did a tour of duty in China and Hong Kong and acquired battle experience there.[11] These soldiers did a major share of the fighting in Britain's wars with China, and were also extensively involved in patrolling and guard duties. They were not confined to border areas. On the contrary, the scene of their operations was the most densely populated region of China— the bustling cities and towns of the eastern seaboard and the Yangzi river region, like Canton, Shanghai, Tianjin, Beijing, Hankou and the surrounding areas, as well as the fast developing colony of Hong Kong. Hence the impact of the presence of these soldiers on the Chinese perception of India and Indians is something worth considering.

The First Opium War involved not a single, continuous

engagement of forces, but a series of armed encounters between the forces of the British and the Chinese, punctuated by negotiations and fairly lengthy periods of waiting for the arrival of reinforcements and for replies to communications sent to Beijing and London by the leading military officers and officials on the spot. The first real armed encounter took place, not near Canton which had been the locus of Sino-British confrontation till that point, but much further northward along the coast, at the town of Dinghai on Zhoushan Island in Hangzhou Bay. This town was attacked and occupied in July 1840, by a British force which included a batallion of Bengal Volunteers, the Madras Sappers and Miners, the Madras Artillery, and the 18th, 26th, 49th and 41st regiments of the Madras Native Infantry. Some of these troops were left in occupation of Dinghai for several months. Two companies of the Bengal Volunteers also took part in the same year in an armed action near Macao in the south, which was the only other such clash in the year 1840.

With the arrival of seven companies of the 37th MNI in December 1840, the force available to the British in China was greatly augmented.[12] In January, they resumed active hostilities, this time choosing to force their way through to Canton by attacking the numerous forts en route. On 7 January action commenced with an attack on Chuanbi fort, which was taken rapidly. As a condition for a truce, the British demanded among other things the cession of the island of Hong Kong, which they lost no time in taking possession of (on 26 January 1841), despite the Imperial Court refusing to ratify the terms of the truce. The next two months saw the fall of the various defences on the approach to Canton, until an armistice was signed on 20 March. Following this, the occupation of Zhoushan was lifted, and some of the earliest arrivals from India, including from the Bengal volunteers, were sent home.

The British carried out patrolling and reconnaissance activities in the countryside around Canton, resulting in depredations by their troops against local inhabitants.[13] They also sought to put pressure on the town of Canton by occupying the heights to the north of the city towards the end of May 1841. All this led to the raising of tensions to a fever pitch in the area and to a groundswell of hostility to the British on the part of the local population. This was the setting for the Sanyuanli incident. On 29 May, thousands of Chinese from the villages north of Canton began gathering in response to a general call to arms, following a clash between a British army patrol and some villagers in the hamlet of Donghua. On the 30th, the British sent troops from the 37th MNI and 49th MNI, as well as from the Bengal Volunteers and Cameronian Regiment, to disperse the Chinese. Initially troubled by the intense heat that caused several men to collapse from sunstroke, the troops ran into even greater trouble in a sudden, ferocious thunderstorm. In the confusion of the blinding rain and consequent flooding of paddy fields and ditches, a detachment of about fifty to sixty Indian soldiers from the 37th MNI got separated from the main force. As the Chinese closed in on them, the rain also rendered the muskets of the soldiers useless. Eventually they were rescued from possible annihilation by the timely arrival of a detachment of marines, and the armed villagers were quickly ordered to disperse by the prefect of Canton. Nevertheless, this particular incident greatly contributed to the confidence of the militia groups that sprouted in this period.

The second northbound expedition of the British in this war, which set sail in August 1841, included among others, men from the 36th and 49th regiments of the Madras Native Infantry, as well as the Madras Sappers and Miners. After taking the fortified island of Gulangsu just opposite the port of Amoy, the expedition proceeded to recapture Dinghai. It then occupied Zhenhai on the point opposite the island on the coast and proceeded up the river to the town of Ningbo. Ningbo was taken and was occupied throughout the following winter by troops of the 36th MNI among others. During this period, the battered 37th MNI, two companies of Bengal Volunteers, and troops from the 18th and 49th regiments as well as the Madras Artillery and Sappers and Miners remained on garrison duty on Hong Kong.

In April-May and in June 1842, fresh reinforcements that arrived from India included troops of Bengal Volunteers (Rajputs) and the 2nd, 41st and 14th Regiments of the Madras Native Infantry. They arrived in time to take part in the third major phase of British operations, which was an offensive against the towns along the Yangzi river. While Ningbo was evacuated on 7 May, the troops headed for Zhapu, capturing it on 18 May. In June, Shanghai was briefly occupied. A bloody engagement

which led to the taking and virtual destruction of the town of
Zhenjiang in July was the prelude to the final major assault,
that on the Yangzi river port of Nanjing. It was there that
the treaty that finally ended the First Opium War was concluded,
on 29 August. The troops left Nanjing only after the Emperor's
assent to the Treaty was received on 15 September. In November,
the bulk of the British forces reassembled at Hong Kong. Apart
from the garrison left there, the rest of the troops left China on
20 December 1842.

The climate and disease took a heavy toll of the early
detachments of soldiers in China. Not just the European soldiers,
but the Indian ones in even greater numbers succumbed to the
heat and dampness, particularly during the summer months. In
1842, 25 per cent of the garrison on Hong Kong died of disease,
while in 1843, casualties mounted to 39 per cent. Of the troops
from the 41st MNI sent to Hong Kong after participating in the
campaigns at Zhenjiang and Nanjing, 150 died of illness and 87
had to be sent back to Madras to convalesce, leaving only about
100 on the island.[14] The British Commander, General D'Aguilar
remarked that at that rate, the retention by the British of Hong
Kong would require the loss of an entire regiment every three
years![15] The problem was compounded by the lack of suitable
accommodation. In the main theatre of war in south China, dry
firm ground on which to pitch tents was rarely to be found, and
tents often had to be set up in the midst of wet paddy fields.
Even on Hong Kong, it took some years before the troops were
suitably accommodated in barracks.Before that, while the
European soldiers were permitted to stay on board the relatively
healthier environs of their transport ships, the Indian soldiers
were compelled to stay on shore in the 'wretched mat-sheds' made
of bamboo leaves, which exposed them to the rigours of both
the hot sun and the torrential rains in equal measure. Of the
troops at Amoy too, half had to be hospitalized, while many of
the rest were also unfit for duty.[16]

The situation was serious enough to warrant the institution of
a 'Special Committee to enquire into the causes of the mortality
amongst the troops at Chusan' (Zhoushan). Among other things,
the Committee appears to have discovered food poisoning to be
a factor in the high incidence of disease among the soldiers: 'a

very great proportion of the Calcutta provision served out was of exceedingly bad quality, and this too at a time when good and wholesome provisions were procurable, at a reasonable price from two merchant vessels lying in Chusan Harbour which the Committee are surprized [sic] were not purchased by the Commissariat'.[17] Among the other regiments that suffered the most during the China campaign were the 37th MNI and the Rajput detachment of the Bengal Volunteers, which set out from Calcutta in 1842 900 strong, but returned the following year with only 400 men.

Shipwrecks, mainly on account of fierce typhoons encountered in the China Sea, also took their toll. The danger was not merely of capsizing and drowning in the stormy waters, as in the case of the *Golconda* in 1840, but of falling into the hands of the local people and authorities. H.B. Morse, in his *Chronicles*, claimed that usually crews of wrecked ships were treated with 'great consideration' by the Chinese authorities.[18] But during wartime, they were obviously treated as enemies and received harsh treatment. This is what appears to have happened to the *Nerbudda*, which was shipwrecked in the Straits of Formosa in September 1841. Its 274 passengers were almost all Indians—mainly ship's lascars and camp followers rather than soldiers. When the ship foundered,[19] all twenty-nine Europeans on board, together with just two crew members from Manila and three Indians, escaped on lifeboats, making sure that the others could not follow suit by burning the last boat and pushing back the desperate men with bayonets. Of the 240 Indians left, many were killed by the Chinese while trying to reach the shore. The rest—133 Indians altogether, according to the Chinese authorities—were immediately captured and sent to jail. A Swede who happened to be in the same jail where these Indians were lodged and who later escaped, described how they had suffered from the cold and from frequent thrashings. However, they were permitted to purchase rice and vegetables once a day from Chinese vendors who were allowed inside the jail. Life in the jail went on until a day in August 1842, when they were carried off in chairs without knowing the fate that was in store for them. At a public execution-ground, they were executed in groups of three or four—an act believed to be in retaliation for the slaughter of the Manchu defenders of Zhapu.

Only two out of the 240 Indians left on board the ship survived, and were eventually handed over to the British authorities after the conclusion of the Treaty of Nanking.

The account of the capture of these Indians contained in the memorial of the military commander on Taiwan purported to be based on the confessions of the 'chief' (*tou mu*) of the prisoners, a certain 'Mu-li-kong', and others. In an effort to elicit information about the moves and the intentions of the British, as well as to gauge their strength, prisoners were systematically interrogated, through the medium of interpreters known as 'linguists'. In some cases, these interpreters were captured Chinese 'traitors' (*han jian*) who had worked for the foreigners. Between the dubious linguistic skills of these interpreters on the one hand, and the obvious ignorance and naivete of many of the captured Indians, the Chinese authorities were hard put to ascertain anything of real value to their military preparations. The American William C. Hunter witnessed one such farcical 'interrogation' of two captured lascars, in which neither the linguist nor his assistant could understand a word of what the lascars were saying, but nevertheless continued to gravely 'translate' for the officials' benefit.[20] The military commander Da Hong A lamented that the Indians (*hei yi*) were illiterate and a 'disorderly mob' of 'dolts', who were 'not able to clarify secret and important matters concerning the foreigners' affairs when asked'.[21] In a later memorial, the Imperial Commissioner Qi Ying commented on the Indians encountered in the service of the British in a more sympathetic vein. While remarking that they were savage by nature, he also referred to them as 'simpletons' who 'don't know how to avoid when the foreign chiefs press them into servitude and use them like brutes. After all, they have to listen to their directives and submit to their commands without trying to understand them.'[22]

The confessions of the Indian prisoners,[23] while revealing little knowledge of British military plans, nevertheless throw some light on the circumstances under which they came to be in China (allowing for some distortion in the process of rendering their testimony into Chinese). Whether because they wanted to avoid harsher punishment at the hands of their captors or not, most of those interrogated claimed that they were only hired hands on board ship and denied being soldiers or having had anything to do with the fighting. They mentioned doing jobs like cutting grass (for fodder), washing clothes, and so on. The confession of one 'Ma-mo' makes poignant reading:[24]

I don't know my age or my parents' names. I have a wife and two younger sisters. I come from Fan-lian in Bengal. . . . The Englishmen came to our country and told our headmen to sell them black men as labourers at the price of three or four *yuan*. If someone was not willing to go, the headman beat him up. I was sold to an English ship to wash clothes, sweep and do other odd jobs some months ago. . . . The Englishmen call soldiers *shu-zhi*. I am no use as a *shu-zhi*. I beg your lordships to give me food to eat and I would be very willing to serve here.

Ma-mo's confession in addition included his description of some of the social and religious conditions in his country, which the Chinese authorities duly recorded as follows:

There are three classes of people in Bengal: the upper are white, the middle are (also) white, and the lower ones are black. They are all believers in the religion of the Lord of Heaven (*tian zhu jiao*). Those of the lowest class are black and can barely earn their living. . . . It is a long-standing custom that there is a king who looks after the country's affairs. Besides, there are several kings who only look after religious matters. Believers ascend to Heaven after death, while non-believers go to Hell. After eating food, I press my palms together and chant hymns to God.

Elaborating further on Ma-mo's account, the official forwarding his confession added that, of the different classes of society in Bengal, 'the whites are shrewd, while the blacks are simple-minded'. He further mentioned that while the English were all white, there were also some 'whites' among those from Bengal which hence made them hard to distinguish. 'It's easiest to distinguish the black ones', he added.[25]

Except for the large group of Indians captured from the shipwreck, it appears that many of the others were captured when they strayed away from their camps in search of fodder, or to wash clothes, cut firewood, purchase provisions, etc. In one case, a surveying party consisting of one Englishman and five or six Indians was surprised by a Chinese patrol.[26] The British generally referred to this as 'kidnapping'. One of them who was present during the campaign in China described how, during the occupation of Ningbo in particular, soldiers wandering the town in search of entertainment were often plied with drink by their

Chinese hosts. Then, when they had become senseless with alcohol, they were tied up in a sack and bundled out of town disguised as a sack of goods.[27]

In those towns that fell under British occupation, the local Chinese had many encounters with the foreign troops. On most occasions, the towns were given over to systematic looting. A resident of Jinjiang which was occupied in July 1842, recorded in his diary how some Indian soldiers (*hei gui*) planted themselves at a river crossing and demanded foreign money from all those wanting to cross, getting incensed at those who could not pay.[28] The extortion and plunder was so systematic that looters even issued some kind of security certificates to the victims as a guarantee that they would not be harassed again. A perhaps more friendly form of interchange between the foreign soldiers and the Chinese was in the market. An English eyewitness described how troops who had occupied a pawnbroker's shop in Shanghai held a 'fair' to auction to local Chinese traders the goods they had looted from the shop! The exchanges and bargaining were carried on in a mixture of Chinese, English, and Hindustani.[29]

A resident of Shanghai during the British occupation of the city, a certain Cao Sheng, left a colourful account of an encounter with a wayward Indian soldier who turned up at his house.[30]

In the afternoon a *hei gui*, all drunk, tried to push his way in. When I anxiously pointed out the security certificate to him, he shook his head without any trace of fear . . . and incessantly demanded foreign money using sign language. . . . When he indicated that he wanted 50 foreign dollars, I shook my head and didn't reply. He gradually reduced it to 10, but I still didn't reply. Then, mimicking me, he left.

The door hadn't shut, when the devil, holding an umbrella, suddenly summoned me. Seeing his intoxicated state, I went out . . . I hadn't crossed the threshold when he started to rain blows on me. I initially put up with it, thinking to escape and run. Then I remembered that there were people inside; if he became recklessly cruel, what was to be done? Moreover, if I struggled with him and his cohorts arrived, then too what would happen?

Then a passerby said: 'Quickly go call out in the direction of the warehouse. The white devils will come and catch him. Every day this happens. Why not go quickly?' The foreign devil seemed to understand his words and looked at him angrily. Seeing his reaction, I called out loudly: 'I am going rightaway to the warehouse to ask the white devils to come', and hurriedly made as if to leave, though I didn't actually go.

I hid a little while and then went back. The fellow had already vanished. There were only some broken teacups and winecups and things lying around. When I asked my son about this, he said: 'When you left, Father, he came inside and stumbled and fell down flat twice. When he came to the middle room, he threw around the household goods and went out.' I told my son, 'This security certificate is no use. Barely two days have gone by and they are being so wild and unruly like this. What kind of havoc will they wreak in the days to come?'

THE SECOND OPIUM WAR AND THE TAIPING REBELLION

About the Indian troops under the East India Company, it has been said that 'While they were conquerors in other lands they were defeated and enslaved at home.'[31] Perhaps at no other time was this anomalous position of the Indian soldiers more obvious than during the Second Opium War. As early as 1856, the British had determined to attack and occupy Canton, because they continued to be prohibited from entering that city even after the Treaty of Nanking. For this purpose they marshalled a sizeable force under Lord Elgin. However, the Rebellion of 1857 broke out in India, involving a major proportion of the soldiers of the East India Company. Elgin's force, intended for China, was in fact diverted to India for some time to help in the suppression of the uprising. In vain did the military authorities in Hong Kong complain that the troops on the island were 'in a most debilitated state'on account of sickness, and were 'unfit to take the field'.[32] In reply, Governor-General Canning in India declared that 'it would be madness' to remove the European troops that were already overstretched in combatting the Rebellion in different provinces.[33] However, it was felt that it would be a good idea to send off any detachment of sepoys that volunteered to go to China, as this would in a way 'save' them from the infection of the rebellious spirit. By June 1858, some Indian troops were sent to China. These included soldiers from the 47th, 65th and 70th Bengal Native Infantry, as well as the 38th Madras Native Infantry.

These took part mainly in operations in and around Canton, which included the burning and destruction of several villages which were perceived as strongholds of resistance to the British even after a peace treaty had been signed at Tianjin in June 1858.

After a second northward military expedition to the mouth of the Beihe river near Tianjin in June-July 1859 was beaten back by the defenders at the Dagu forts, the British and French jointly marshalled forces for another, more powerful, offensive. By this time, the Rebellion in India had been suppressed, and the British could mobilize many more troops from India. The Indian troops included the 8th, 11th, 15th and 19th Punjab Infantry and the Ludhiana Sikh Regiment, as well as the 1st Sikh Irregular Cavalry (Probyn's Horse) and the 2nd Sikh Cavalry (Fane's Horse). Apart from these, there also were the A and K companies of the Madras Sappers & Miners and the 2nd and 12th Madras Native Infantry, and the 1st Light Infantry. Altogether nearly 4,000 Indian soldiers were despatched. Out of a total of 419 officers on the 1860 expedition to Beijing, 70 were Indian. Since the terrain in north China was relatively dry and flat, this was the first of Britain's China campaigns in which the cavalry was deployed. The preparations for and provisioning of this expedition were also much more elaborate than the earlier ones, with hay and forage for the horses being sent from Bombay, and even the despatch of Indian mules and bullocks accompanied by bullock-drivers from Madras and Bombay for the purposes of transport.[34]

Between August and October 1860, the combined forces of the British and French armies pushed their way from the coast to Beijing, entering the capital city for the first time on 13 October via the Anding gate in the north. Beijing was given over to loot and destruction, with the Summer Palace, *yuanmingyuan*, left in ruins and many of its priceless treasures carted off.[35]

Following the conclusion of the second peace treaty on 24 October, which was deliberately accompanied by a display at Beijing of the military strength of the Western powers, most of the troops apart from the garrison at Hong Kong sailed home. The exceptions were the detachment left at Tianjin and Dagu to enforce the payment of indemnity and that part of the expeditionary force that had been sent to the region around Shanghai to counter the advance of the Taiping army. The latter included the Ludhiana Regiment, the 11th and 19th Punjab

Infantry, the 5th Bombay Light Infantry and a part of the Madras Artillery. These troops occupied the approaches to Shanghai, as well as the north gate, a building on Suzhou creek and the Ningbo guild-house.[36] A.F. Linley, an Englishman who sided with the Taipings and appears to have had the confidence of the Taiping King Li Xiucheng, mentions in his account that soldiers from a detachment from Agra also took part in fighting against the Taipings.[37]

It was in the course of the campaign against the Taipings that many Indian soldiers deserted and went over to the side of the Chinese.[38] Zeng Guofan, the general in command of the Qing forces, wrote: 'I have heard that in laying siege to Yushan county town [in Jiangxi province] the rebel Loyal Prince Li Xiucheng had a number of dark-skinned foreigners among his ranks.'[39] Obviously, such Indians who deserted to the Taiping ranks were not a few in number. Reporting on another battle in Shaoxing in Zhejiang province, the general Li Hongzhang also referred to '50 or 60 dark-skinned foreigners' who stood atop the wall of the city they were defending for the Taipings and shot dead the French officer Tardif de Moidrey.

In some cases, these Indians appeared to have been among those who were captured during battle and made prisoner by the Taipings and were thereafter converted to the rebel cause. The fact that the Taiping operations around Shanghai were under the direction of Li Xiucheng, by all accounts one of the most enlightened and committed of the Taiping leaders, may have had something to do with their change of heart. On the other hand, some Indians seemed to have decided to go over to the Taipings even without being captured by them. Linley's account mentions an incident in which his co-passengers in a sampan travelling upriver from Shanghai included a European and a 'bearded, swarthy East Indian' who were obviously running away to Taiping territory and taking pains to hide at the sight of any European vessel on the way. On another occasion, he describes how he recruited for the Taipings the services of a Sardinian adventurer. This Sardinian, who apparently knew Hindi well, was then left behind in Shanghai to assist in the recruitment of several Indian officers whom he knew in the 22nd Regiment[40] and in the 'Baluchi' regiment who were eager to join the Taipings.[41]

It must be remembered that Indians were not the only

foreigners who went over to the side of the Taiping movement. A few westerners also served under the Taiping command, such as Linley. Nevertheless, the desertion by Indians in the service of the British during this period, however limited in scope, presaged a similar phenomenon half a century later when Indian soldiers and policemen in China, motivated by discontent with their conditions of service and by the call of the struggle against colonialism and imperialism, once again turned their arms against the British.

THE GARRISON AT HONG KONG

With the 'unequal treaties' and a relatively weakened and pliant Qing dynasty in place after the conclusion of the Opium Wars and the Taiping Rebellion, it was nearly forty years before Britain needed to again import soldiers into China to fight a war. Nevertheless, throughout these years, Britain maintained a ready force, which at all times included some detachments of Indian soldiers, at Hong Kong.[42]

About 2700 Indian soldiers were present at Britain's takeover of Hong Kong on 26 January 1841.[43] These soldiers were accompanied by camp-followers, including provisioners of Indian food items and other such goods. Indian troops were mostly accommodated at Sai Yung Pun, the Western military camp at West Point, Central, Chek Pai Wan (Aberdeen), Chek Chu (Stanley) and Sai Wan. As the colony of Hong Kong took shape, the temporary mat-shed accommodation for troops was gradually replaced by barracks. This took care of some of the problems of the troops, but not all. As late as 1850, one-quarter of the troops in one particular regiment died of fever. In September 1864 soldiers from one of the Indian regiments rioted for two days, along with some of the policemen and Malay seamen.[44]

Certain specialized corps of Indian military and semi-military personnel were formed on Hong Kong. One of these was the company of 'Gun Lascars', established to assist the main artillery units by doing some of the heavy pulling and other work associated with artillery. It initially consisted of 1 Jemadar, 2 Havildars, 4 Naiks and 81 Lascars. In 1892, it became the Asiatic Artillery Company, and was later reorganized with the more exalted titles of Hong Kong and Singapore Batallion Royal

Artillery and Hong Kong and Singapore Batallion, Royal Garrison Artillery, in 1898 and 1899 respectively.[45] The military establishment also included a 'Mule Corps' composed mostly of Indian mule-drivers brought over from India specially for the purpose of facilitating transport on the island. In 1921, it had 580 men. This corps was even armed during World War II.[46]

In 1890, it was decided to raise a special regiment in India for service in Hong Kong.[47] A prolonged discussion took place in the various concerned departments of the British empire about what kind of men would prove most suitable for this purpose. When at last it was decided to recruit from among the Muslims of Jhelum in West Punjab, the Governor of Hong Kong gave his approval somewhat grudgingly: '. . . the people of Hong Kong [sic!] wanted to have Sikhs not Madrassee troops if they could not get Europeans. These Mohammedans of Upper India, if not actually Sikhs, will at any rate presumably be more warlike than the Southerners from Madras. . . .'[48] A force of 1,012 men—all Indians except for eight British officers—arrived in Hong Kong in May 1892, and moved into the Whitfield Barracks at Kowloon constructed specially for the purpose. Within the first few days, the soldiers of this regiment got into a clash with local Chinese workers, which ended only with the arrival of the police who drove the soldiers back to their barracks.

A more serious clash took place when the British attempted in April 1899 to take over the New Territories of which they had obtained the lease from the Qing Government. The British military camp, consisting of soldiers of the Hong Kong Regiment at Tai Po, was bombarded with guns and artillery fire from several thousand Chinese who had gathered on the ridge of the hills surrounding it to drive the British forces away. Reinforcements were brought up, and the Chinese were eventually defeated. Nevertheless, tension was rife for some time afterwards, and the Indian soldiers on duty had to keep within the bounds of the camp.

The Hong Kong Regiment was disbanded in 1902, but soldiers from the Indian Army continued to garrison the island. Another flash-point which brought these troops into action in Hong Kong again was during the Revolution of 1911 which brought down the imperial government in China, and which had repercussions on the British-governed island as well. The British were alarmed and dispatched post-haste the 25th Punjabi Regiment from Multan, the 26th Punjabis from Samana and the 24th Hazara Mountain Battery from Maymyo to pre-empt any attempt by Chinese to push back into the New Territories. During the agitations in Hong Kong that accompanied the Revolution in 1911, it was found necessary to have the Indian troops stage a flag-march.

The Indian detachments on Hong Kong during World War II, which included the 7th Rajputs and the 2nd Batallion of the 14th Punjabis, suffered heavy losses in the fighting that took place. The casualty rate was as high as 30 per cent. The forces surrendered to the Japanese on 25 December 1941. The end of the War, accompanied as it was by preparations to transfer power in India, saw the beginning of the end of the nearly century-long deployment of Indian troops in Hong Kong. From November 1946, the phased withdrawal from Hong Kong of the Indian troops (minus the Gorkha regiments) began with the departure of the Jaipur Guards.[49]

THE BOXER REBELLION

Sentiment against the intrusive foreign presence in China steadily picked up in north China in the 1880s and 1890s, leading to a series of clashes and culminating in a popular movement to drive out the foreigners, known as the Yi He Tuan Movement, or, in the west, as the Boxer Rebellion. With the Qing Court giving backing to the Movement after some initial hestitation, the Western powers, including Britain, France, Russia, and America, together with Japan, mounted a sizeable military force to march to Beijing, cow down the Qing rulers, lift the siege of the foreign legations in the capital, and suppress the Boxers' fighting forces. 18,000 Indian troops formed a major portion of the Allied forces.[50]

The first set of Indian troops to be despatched was the 7th Bengal Infantry, which arrived at Dagu in mid-July 1900.[51] It was joined by the remainder of the force from India, barring those in the 2nd Brigade, consisting of about 3,000 men, which was left to garrison Shanghai throughout the operations in the North.[52] The Hong Kong Regiment too was sent to join active operations in north China.

This was the first of Britain's military operations in China which saw the despatch of troops from various princely states of India. Apparently, the rulers of these states vied with each other to offer men, money and equipment to be placed at the disposal of the Allied Expedition in China. 'I need not remind you,' wrote the Inspector-General of the Imperial Service Troops, Major J.G. Turner, 'of the enthusiasm with which certain Chiefs offered their Imperial Service regiments.' In the end, only four detachments of the Imperial Service Troops were carefully selected and sent to China. These were one cavalry regiment from Jodhpur, one infantry regiment from Alwar, the Camel Corps from Bikaner and one company of the Malerkotla Sappers.[53] The Maharajas of Bikaner and Gwalior personally went with the troops to China, and were granted honours for this show of support. Except for a brief skirmish between a section of the Jodhpur Lancers and Chinese fighters near the Great Wall in January 1901, the rest of the Imperial Service Troops were not involved in actual fighting. They were instead engaged in garrison and escort duty and patrolling lines of communication, while the Malerkotla Sappers were employed in building stables and temporary bridges, and laying roads.

Aided by abnormally dry climatic conditions, which assisted in the movement of men and equipment, the Allied Forces advanced towards Beijing, with major engagements with the Chinese at Beicang and Yangzun, and an encounter between the First Bengal Lancers and Chinese cavalry near Hexiwu. Dongzhou was occupied on 12 August. Entry into Beijing was forced through the numerous gates of the city on 13 and 14 August in the face of heavy resistance. The 1st Bengal Lancers, the 24th Punjab Infantry, the 7th Bengal Infantry and the 1st Sikhs were among the contingents that took part in the seizure of Beijing. The siege of the legations was said to have been lifted with the arrival of the 7th Rajputs.[54]

For the second time in less than half a century, the capital suffered looting by the rampaging foreign troops. While the Allied command was consolidating their occupation of the city, more detachments of Indian troops continued to arrive right through September 1900, including the 16th Bengal Lancers, the 3rd Bombay Cavalry, the 34th Pioneers, the Bengal Sappers and the 20th Punjab Infantry. These took part in the various reconnaissance and 'mopping up' operations against the Boxers, which included the burning down and complete destruction of several villages and towns in the regions, as well as the punitive expedition against the town of Baoding in October.

Besides the usual booty, Indian soldiers during these operations also acquired all kinds of arms and ammunition—something that was a cause for some anxiety on the part of the authorities. The Bikaner detachment acquired 30,900 rounds of Lee Metford ammunition as a gift ('a very inconvenient gift', according to the Foreign Department) from the provincial authorities in China. However, in other cases, the arms and ammunition were acquired through loot and through a brisk trade in arms that appears to have been conducted amongst the soldiers of the Allied Forces during the campaign. The British authorities decided to temporarily waive the regulations forbidding the private import of arms and allowed the soldiers to bring the arms they had acquired back to India with them. Nevertheless, they kept a careful record of each soldier and the arms in his possession.

The China Expeditionary Force despatched by the British began to be gradually reduced from April 1901 and was deemed to have been formally disbanded by mid-July, but the troops were not fully withdrawn even after that. In fact, at the end of July, the British Government ordered the temporary re-occupation of the Summer Palace at Beijing by its troops, including two companies of the 7th Bengal Infantry, to bring pressure to bear on the Qing Government.[55] For a number of years afterwards, Indian troops under British command continued to be stationed in both north and south China as a reminder of the power of the Western states and Japan to enforce their dictate.[56]

A unique and sensitive first-hand account of the Boxer operations by an Indian who was part of the Allied Expedition has come down to us. Gadadhar Singh was a Rajput soldier with the 7th Rajputs of the Bengal Army, one of the first Indian contingents to arrive in north China as part of the Expeditionary Force. He recorded his impressions from the battlefield, and these were later published in India in Hindi . His is not just the only extant Indian record of the Expedition, but one of the few surviving eyewitness accounts in any language. His record of what he saw and thought throws light on the feelings that may have agitated some Indian soldiers who were gradually awakening to a sense of the injustice that was being perpetrated on the Chinese by the foreign powers, and were filled with despair at the role being played by Indians in it.[57]

Even before he arrived in China, Gadadhar Singh appears to have been filled with misgivings about his mission. 'A fear gripped my heart. God! Are you going to mete out the same fate to China too?.... Is the beautiful moon of China about to set? The dazzling sun of the land of the Aryans has already set.' Further on in his record he again expressed his empathy with the Chinese after actually witnessing some of the destruction that had been wrought by the foreign troops on their soil:

There was no occasion for our hearts to melt because after all we had come to fight against these very Chinese. But . . . seeing their colour which was similar to ours—a sort of feeling arose in our hearts. The Chinese are Buddhists, India's co-religionists. Being inhabitants of the Asian continent they are our neighbours too. There is not much difference between their colour and ours, their customs and manners and ours. Why did God inflict such a calamity on them? Should we not have come to their aid instead?[58]

Drawing a parallel with the way soldiers had traditionally been used as mercenaries in the numerous battles fought in India in the past, he questioned: 'What sort of persons were our ancestors who used to go to war against Lahore on behalf of Delhi and who used to fight against Jaipur on behalf of Chittor! What sort of men were they who were ready to fight the Rathors for Akbar and Ranjit for the British. Had their hearts and minds really gone into decay?'[59]

Gadadhar Singh graphically described the horrors of the war and the atrocities inflicted on the Chinese in particular. By the time his regiment had reached Tianjin on 17 July, that city had already been laid waste by the foreign armies. 'Tientsin is a very big and prosperous city of north China,' he wrote. 'Or rather, I should say it was. For today it was a city without citizens, a house without the householders, a body without life!' 'The sky was still covered with smoke' when they arrived. 'The river Peiho's water had become a cocktail of blood, flesh, bones and fat. Even to touch this water was to invite danger.' He described the systematic killings, arson and rape to which the populations of Tianjin, Beijing, and the numerous villages en route were subjected. Some of the incidents he mentioned showed that the atrocities were purely wanton, in which hapless persons were tortured for the fun of it. And 'all these sportsmen', he noted in disgust, 'belonged to what were called the civilized nations!'[60]

Gadadhar Singh particularly castigated the French and Russian troops for their cruelty, but at the same time he did not spare his own countrymen. 'When the British Indian Troops reached Tientsin, the city was already under foreign occupation and all the inhabitants of the city had fled away. Only the sick, the wounded and the lame were left behind and seizing their possessions at the point of gun was the glorious pastime of our soldiers.' Describing how the soldiers did not hesitate to kill those from whom they looted, the diary acerbically commented:

In India, the Municipalities used to engage Doms to kill dogs by paying them at the rate of two to four annas per dog and thus every six months or a year organized a campaign to give salvation to the souls of poor dogs. Same thing was being done here to human beings. Whoever had a few goods, got the gift of salvation. The only difference was that the dog-killers in India used to be Doms, the man-killers here included also the civilized gentle Hindus.[61]

However, there were also other Indians, like an Indian Army doctor called Pandit Ram Datt, whom Gadadhar Singh noted tried their best in the face of all the odds to save the lives of some Chinese.

For another fifty years after the Boxer operations, Indian soldiers were sent to the shores of China to defend the interests of the British. Yet the type of soldier represented by Gadadhar Singh was an altogether different sort from that represented by the 'Mamo' of the First Opium War, one torn between his duties as a paid soldier and the promptings of a nascent anti-imperialist consciousness. The beginning of the twentieth century saw the growth of militant nationalism in India which was bound to have, and did have, its effect on the soldiers, particularly on those whose horizons had been broadened through service outside India.

EARLY GROWTH OF THE
HONG KONG POLICE FORCE

The archetypal image of the Indian in the eyes of many Chinese from the mid-nineteenth to the mid-twentieth century—an image that has persisted even afterwards—was that of the turbaned, bearded Indian policeman. The Indian policeman first made his appearance in China in Hong Kong shortly after its takeover by the British. William Caine, the first Chief Magistrate of Hong Kong, recruited a few ex-sepoys as policemen. In 1844, Assistant Superintendant of Police J. Bruce organized about twenty-five Indians discharged from the army as a night guard that patrolled the area along Queen's Road. Under Charles May, the Captain Superintendent of Police from 1845 (and Police Magistrate from 1862), the police force consisted initially of almost equal numbers of Indians, Europeans, and Chinese. Sir Hercules Robinson, Governor of Hong Kong from 1859 to 1865, also recruited soldiers from the Bombay Native Infantry detachments which were stationed in Hong Kong after the Second Opium War. In addition, he brought over about 150 recruits to the police force from Bombay. By 1867, there were 377 Indians in the police force (mainly ex-sepoys from the Bombay Army), along with 132 Chinese and 89 Europeans.[62]

The demand for Indian policemen in Hong Kong came from the British conviction that the local Chinese were entirely unsuited to carrying out what was perceived as the main task of the police on the island at this stage, which was 'to overawe the Chinese *lumpenproletariat*, composed in European eyes of the sweepings of Kwangtung Province'.[63] Hong Kong in its early days as a British colony was a hotbed of crime, and a base for the operations of smugglers, pirates, gamblers, pimps and others of their kind. Governor Davis, writing in 1844, declared categorically that he was 'convinced that a Chinese Police can never be trusted in this Colony. If not actually collusive with their countrymen, they have not the resolution to do their duty in case of Emergency, and it therefore follows that either a European or a Sepoy Police, or a mixture of both, will always be necessary.'[64] As it turned out, the European and Indian policemen and officers were themselves not in the least immune to the temptations of crime and corruption. Nevertheless, it took nearly half a century before a conscious policy of reducing the foreign element and 'sinicizing' the Hong Kong police force was taken up in earnest.

The search for a suitable type of candidate to police the local Chinese population eventually led to the preponderance of men from Punjab, and particularly Sikhs, in the force. Both in Hong Kong and in the Malay States in this period, the British experimented with recruits from the local people, from Europeans and from different parts of India. European policemen were considered hard to satisfy and to control, while south Indians and others apparently failed to strike sufficient terror into the Chinese. On the other hand, Sikhs were considered suitable on account of their physique and fighting qualities, coupled with their reliability and willingness to work for low pay.[65] Initially, fifty Sikhs were brought in to supplement the policemen from Bombay. With the appointment to the Hong Kong police force of Giles Creagh, who had earlier served with the Punjab Police, the recruitment of Sikhs began in a systematic fashion. Creagh was a strong advocate of the desirability of recruiting from this particular community, and in 1867 he went personally on a mission to Punjab with the aim of bringing back a contingent of Sikhs for the police force. The first batch that he recruited consisted of 108 men. The following year, he brought back another 100 or so in a second recruiting mission, which led to the formation of the first mounted police unit on the island. Creagh preferred to pick those who had had little exposure to the world outside their villages and who could be moulded into the kind of policemen he wanted. They came mainly from Amritsar, Jalandhar, Ludhiana, and Ferozepur districts. As a kind of balance to the presence of these Sikhs, Punjabi Muslims from Jhelum, Multan, and Kamalpur districts were also brought into the force. By 1871, there were 182 Sikhs and 126 Muslims in the Hong Kong police.[66]

It was Governor Kennedy (1872-7) who began to reverse this policy. He pushed for the development of a predominantly Anglo-Chinese force, and took the initiative to shift most of the Sikhs in the force to jail duties. After him, in 1879, the police and jail staff were formally differentiated. Nevertheless, it was only from the 1890s that large scale recruitment of Chinese into the police force began to be conducted. Even thereafter, there was a rough parity between the numbers of Indians and those of Chinese in the force.[67]

INDIAN POLICE IN SHANGHAI

Indians were also employed in the police service in Shanghai and other cities of China which had foreign concessions, such as Hankou and Tianjin. In Shanghai, the origins of the police of what came to be known as the International Settlement (*gonggong zujie xunbu* or *gongbuju xunbu*) lay in the joint efforts of the British, French, and Americans in 1854, to establish a force to guard their interests when faced with the Taiping Rebellion and the uprising of the Small Knife (*Xiaodao*) society. However, although Indian soldiers were used to confront the Taiping forces, it was not until a number of years had passed that Indians began to be employed in the police force. In 1880, only four Indians were listed as being present in Shanghai, but by 1885, this number had increased to 58 mainly on account of the Indian policemen recruited in the preceding year.[68] Indians were employed in the area police stations as well as in the military reserve corps. A contemporary Chinese source noted: 'In the 12th year of Guangxu (1886), there was established on the road south of the Song Lan Ge tea-house in the Hu Jia locality of Si Ma Road, a post exclusively manned by new police brought from India. With their faces as black as lacquer and their heads wrapped in red cloth, the Chinese call them "red-headed flies" (*hongtou cangying*)!'[69]

Pay and service conditions were obviously attractive enough to ensure a steady supply of Indians at most times to the police and jail services. For instance, in 1908, the pay of a sepoy in the Indian Army was Rs. 9 per month, whereas an Indian policeman in China could earn the equivalent of Rs. 26 to 30 per month.[70] The work was also considered to be less arduous than that of a soldier. Shanghai policemen were expected to do eight hours of duty every day in addition to attending at fires and being present in Court when required.[71] Policemen were hired on contract for a limited term, usually five years. During the period of their contract, they were not given leave (except for medical or other emergencies), but they were given an extended furlough at the end of their term. On the average, less than 5 per cent of the rank-and-file policemen could bring their families out to China with them. Most were supposed to have led very isolated lives, with almost no intermingling with either the local Chinese or the Europeans in the force.

The pay and promotion prospects of Indian policemen were considerably inferior to those of their European counterparts. This was a source of dissatisfaction among them, particularly from the end of the nineteenth and beginning of the twentieth century.[72] Indian policemen, although they shouldered much of the heaviest burden of policing, could not usually aspire to rise above the rank of sergeant. In 1930, out of a total of 691 Indian policemen in Shanghai's International Settlement, 594 were constables and 88 were sergeants. Out of 255 police personnel above the rank of sergeant, only six were Indians (four sub-inspectors and two inspectors.)[73] Jail staff considered themselves at a further disadvantage with respect to policemen. Nominally, the pay of the jail guards was higher than those of the police constables. However, the policemen had benefits in the matter of leave and pension as well as the terms of remittance of pay, which effectively gave them a better deal when compared to the jail staff.[74]

Overall, Indians, and particularly those from the Sikh community, made themselves indispensable in the British police forces in China. Writing to the British Minister in Beijing in 1906, a judge of the Supreme Court of the International Settlement at Shanghai noted: 'The opinion is held here that Sikhs make cheap and efficient police for the rougher work of keeping order among the Chinese in the streets, and that they have done very well in cases of riot.'[75] However, the image of the Indian police and the colonial police force in general took a battering over a number of corruption and moneylending scandals. The most notorious of these was the one in Hong Kong in 1897-8, in which it was alleged that a large number of policemen were on the payroll of various illegal gambling houses.

A raid on some gambling houses had led to the discovery of account books which recorded identification numbers purported to be those of policemen who were on the take. On interrogation, the gambling house owners and watchmen testified that various Indian policemen stationed in the area used to visit them in plain clothes when off duty and demand money on a regular basis to leave them alone. The investigation, conducted in a summary fashion by the Captain Superintendant of Police May, led to the sweeping dismissal of a number of policemen, including nineteen Indians, of whom at least five had over ten years' service to their credit. One of them, Utter Singh, had attained the highest rank of an Indian policeman, that of Sergeant-Major. The whole case turned out to be highly controversial.[76] The police authorities themselves were of the opinion that the charges and testimony against the policemen would not hold up in a court of law, and chose to opt for dismissal rather than prosecution. The case against Utter Singh was particularly controversial, because the evidence against him in the gambling scandal was so weak that it was not mentioned as a reason for his dismissal. Instead, he was dismissed for having been a go-between in a case of moneylending for the rather trifling sum of fifty dollars three years earlier. Utter Singh challenged his dismissal and succeeded in taking the matter all the way to London, while in Hong Kong itself, he secured the support of a large number of Indian traders and businessmen. Forty-five of them in fact sent a petition to the Governor in which they charged that the case against Utter Singh had been 'pre-judged and prejudiced'. They testified that the Sikh policemen, while not being free of certain failings, were by and large 'dignified, sober and orderly men, obedient to discipline and devotedly attached to their officers.' While the Governor and the Hong Kong authorities tended to uphold the action of the police chief, the authorities in London were more sympathetic to Utter Singh, particularly on the admission of the Governor that for reasons extraneous to the case at hand, it had been decided to make an example out of Utter Singh in order to root out the phenomenon of moneylending in the police force. Using his discretion, the Secretary of State for the Colonies, Joseph Chamberlain, reduced Utter Singh's punishment while not reversing his dismissal from the Hong Kong police force.

WATCHMEN

The number of Indian policemen in Hong Kong, Shanghai, Hankou, and other Chinese cities was roughly matched by the number of Indians privately employed as watchmen. Right from the founding of Hong Kong as a British colony, Indian watchmen played a major role in guarding various establishments from the robberies and burglaries that were rife at that time. Jardine and Matheson employed a number of Indians as guards, drawn from the ranks of ex-sepoys and lascars. According to the report in the 1911 Census of the Indian Population of Hong Kong, Indian watchmen were to be found in the service of nearly all the foreign commercial companies, shops and hotels. A large number were also employed by Chinese.[77] The Secretary of the Shanghai

Municipal Council, J.O.P. Bland, in 1903 noted approvingly: 'there is no doubt that as watchmen in the local mills and other places, these men perform very useful functions.' Indians who could not get employment as policemen in the bigger cities often managed to find jobs as watchmen in the smaller towns and treaty ports where the foreign concessions were small and which did not have their own police services. 'In case of local disturbances,' Bland added, 'their presence in many places added to the available defence forces.'[78]

However, the watchmen also appeared to have been a cause for concern on the part of the British authorities. Unlike the policemen, they spread out more widely, often landing up in small towns where there were few other Indians to fall back upon when they met with hard times. British consuls in these places not infrequently had to deal with cases of destitute ex-watchmen who had no money even to proceed to Shanghai or one of the bigger cities when they ran out of employment. Moreover, several watchmen were men who had been dismissed from the British police forces for some reason or other and were generally considered by them to be 'bad characters'. The British authorities would have liked to see these men return home to India, but as long as they could get private employment in China, it was difficult to get them to do so. Since moneylending seems to have been an important secondary source of income for many Indian watchmen, this also led to their involvement from time to time in disputes with local people.[79] The authorities in Hong Kong at one point even considered the idea of registering all private watchmen and of enrolling them either in the police rolls or, since most were ex-soldiers, as a special section of the Indian Army reserve under the command of regimental officers of the garrison stationed at Hong Kong.[80]

MIGRATION TO AND FROM CHINA

Strictly speaking, the emigration of unskilled labour outside India without the prior permission of the Government was prohibited under the Defence of India Rules.[81] However, for a long time the Government of India was well aware of the emigration on independent intitiative, of Indians, particularly Sikhs, to China in search of jobs, and in fact could have been said to have encouraged it.

The situation seems to have changed somewhat in the beginning of the twentieth century. The authorities in India, Hong Kong, and London, as well as the British consular representatives in China, all repeatedly expressed apprehension over any unchecked emigration of Indians to the Far East. Various reasons were given. One was related to the growing problem of destitution. As a British Consul expressed it: 'It is seldom that a week passes in a port such as Chefoo without the arrival of some "Civis Britannicus" who has come to the end of his resources and can neither support himself nor get away again.'[82] The Secretary of State for India commented that the Government of India 'consider it undesirable to encourage the emigration of Indians generally and of Sikhs particularly by undertaking liability on their account when abroad.'

A more serious cause for concern was the discovery that Indians from the police and armed forces were drifting into the employ of other foreign powers in the Far East. The decade or more preceding the outbreak of World War I saw increasing militarization on the part of the big powers, new alignments amongst them, and the intensification of big power rivalry in the Far East. As early as 1902, there were reports that Sikhs had been employed by the Germans at Kiaochou, while some had been selected for service by the French in north China.[79] The British were even more worried by the news that Indians were proceeding to Manchuria to seek employment under the Russians, with whom they had a particularly intense rivalry. The Acting Consul-General in Shanghai reported that since January 1902, 114 Indians had applied for passports to 'Asiatic Russia'.[84] The fear was expressed that, even though these men were to be employed mainly as watchmen, they would be used by Russia against Britain in the event of war. Most of those wanting to go to Vladivostock were refused passports, except for 'substantial Indian merchants'.[85] It was felt that the recruitment of Sikhs by foreign powers was particularly undesirable at a time when it was getting difficult to find enough suitable men from 'the fighting races' to man the Indian Army regiments, and when the British police forces in Hong Kong and China were plagued by constant resignations by men in search of better pay and service conditions in other places. The fears of the British authorities were only to some extent relieved after the conclusion of the Russo-Japanese War of 1905, which resulted in Russia's defeat and her evacuation from Manchuria.

From the last years of the nineteenth century, China and Hong Kong also increasingly came to be transit points for Indians seeking employment in the Americas. Canada and the United States were favoured destinations for these men who sought employment in the railway and lumber companies of Canada and the farms of California. The wages they could get in those places was usually far more than they could aspire for in China. Men who were getting paid 16 to 22 *yuan* a month as salary in Shanghai heard reports about how their compatriots in America and Russia were earning as much as the equivalent of 60, 80 or even 100 *yuan*. The word spread quickly, and triggered off a spate of resignations from the police and jail services in the treaty ports and Hong Kong. In 1907 the policemen of the Shanghai International Settlement went on strike for the first time over their pay and service conditions. Ultimatums were given to the authorities by the police and jail staff there and in Hong Kong to either increase their remuneration or else face mass resignations. Regarding the petition of the jail staff of Hong Kong in 1910, the Secretary of State for the Colonies, the Earl of Crewe, remarked with some concern that 'something will have to be done if the present terms don't keep men in the service or attract newcomers'. Both in the case of the jail staff of Hong Kong as well in the case of the Shanghai policemen, the situation was deemed serious enough to warrant pay increases.[86]

Yet Canada and the United States soon imposed regulations drastically curtailing the immigration from Asian countries. This did not deter aspiring job-seekers using the China route to emigration. On the contrary, it led to hundreds of Indians seeking to leave China for other countries that were ill-prepared to receive them. In July 1907, the British Consul at Lima, Peru, reported on the arrival of an 'invasion' of some 200 Indians from Hong Kong, most of whom he declared were destitute and in ill-health and unfit for work of any kind. That did not stop him from literally passing on the problem by directing them on to Jamaica where they were told they could find jobs. The Government of Peru, the laws of which apparently did not prohibit the landing of immigrants, for its part tried to deter the Indians from coming by raising the consular fees at Hong Kong from $5.40 to $63 at one go![87] In 1908, there was an equally sudden arrival of Indians from Hong Kong in German New Guinea. According to the Governor of German New Guinea, the Indians here were not satisfied with the terms of work offered, and most of them ended up by going back to Hong Kong.[88] Apparently, both in the case of the rush to Peru and the exodus to German New Guinea, competition between rival steamship companies seems to have had something to do with it. For instance, two rival steamship lines on the Yokohama-Callao route were believed to have offered through their agents a premium of one pound sterling per head for passengers, and this had led to local agents within the Indian community promising an 'El Dorado' in Peru to waiting emigrants.

Some Indian emigration agents seemed to have used ingenious methods to try and get their clients from China to the Americas. From mid-1911, about 150 Indians per year left Hong Kong for Manila in the Philippines, where an Indian watchman named Barkat Ali would get them registered and arrange for their stay in Manila for six months. After that, they would sail for America on the Great Northern Railway Company steamer 'Minnesota', which plied the Hong Kong-Manila-Seattle route. The reason for this was that the Commission for Immigration in Seattle had apparently ruled in the preceding year that, since the same immigration laws applied to the Philippines as to the United States, any Indian who had established a minimum of 6 months residence in the Philippines had an automatic right to land in the US![89]

To control the phenomenon of Indians leaving their police and jail jobs in China and Hong Kong and seeking more lucrative employment elsewhere, and to ensure the repatriation of Indians from China, the British authorities came up with various schemes and regulations. One of these was the scheme to end the practice of recruiting Indians for the services locally in favour of recruitment directly from the Indian armed forces in India, which took shape in 1906-7. In September 1906, a call was issued for volunteers from Indian Army cavalry and infantry regiments from among Jat Sikhs, Dogras, Punjabi Muslims and Pathans only, for three years' service with the Shanghai Municipal Police. On 31 October, a notice was issued by the British Consul-General at Shanghai ending local recruitment of Indians by colonial and municipal administrations in their own settlements as of 1 January 1907. In addition, the 'British Concessions in China Municipal Police Regulation, 1907', together with 'The Police Discipline Regulations, 1907', prohibited and made provisions for the punishment of those who (a) while serving with the Municipal Police of British concessions in China, deserted or tried to desert; (b) incited a serving policeman to desert.

The authorities were optimistic initially about the effectiveness of these measures. A note from the Military Department of the Government of India dated 26 January 1908 claimed:

Sikhs now go out to Hong Kong and Shanghai at their own expense in order to get service in the police, because that is at present the only way in which such employment is obtainable. As soon as they find that men on the spot are rejected in favour of those recruited through the recruiting staff in India, free emigration, if not actually stopped, will at any rate be effectively checked, which is what is wanted by the Government of India.[90]

However, by mid-1908, there is evidence that they had begun to doubt the success of these schemes, and by the end of 1909, the Secretary of State for India decided to altogether abandon the scheme of trying to recruit candidates for the police forces in China through the recruiting staff in India.[91]

Within a couple of years, the British authorities had the opposite problem on their hands: Indians had begun to *return* to China from America, frustrated by lack of employment opportunities. The 1911 Census of the Indian Population of Hong Kong mentioned that emigration to America was 'practically at a standstill'. In 1914, the Governor of Hong Kong reported to the Secretary of State for India about the passage of 415 Indians through Hong Kong on their way back to India from Canada and the United States.[92] The effects of the legal restrictions on immigration into the United States and Canada, as well as economic factors such as a slump in the lumber trade, had begun to make themselves felt. The return of Indians from those countries contributed to a situation of growing unemployment among the Indians in China. A resolution of the Government of India, Commerce and Industry Department (Emigration) of 26 June

1913 warned that there was 'little probability of natives of India finding employment in Shanghai and Hankou as watchmen or in similar capacities. The Governor-General-in-Council accordingly requests all Local Governments and Administration to make the above intimation as widely known as possible, particularly in places from which emigration to China is believed to be most common.'[93]

The forward movement of Indians continuing to try and proceed to America, combined with the wave of returning Indians, led to a congregation of Indian males in Hong Kong and Shanghai in particular, who had no jobs and an uncertain future. The situation coincided with the spread of militant Indian nationalism, including the growth of movements that found a strong base among Indian workers and students outside India, especially in the United States and Canada. The British authorities in Hong Kong and China knew that they had a tinderbox on their hands, and orders were issued to keep a close watch on the movements of Indians with a view to nipping in the bud any signs of 'sedition'. Their greatest fear—one that turned out to be justified—was that the contagion of disaffection would spread from these Indians to those in the garrison and police forces. From being the ones who did the policing for the British in China, Indians there began to become the *object* of policing. The Shanghai Municipal Police, for instance, created a special 'Indian section' whose objective was to gather information on Indians, infiltrate their organizations, and gather evidence for their conviction and deportation in case they were engaged in activities construed as seditionist.[94] Initially, it had four Sikh staff members and infiltrators in it under the command of D.I. Sullivan. Later it was expanded, and by 1936, it had collected detailed biographies of 250 activists and 280 sympathizers of Indian nationalist groups, and less detailed ones of 3500 others![95] The British sought cooperation with the Public Security Bureau of the Guomindang in their drive against Indian 'seditionists', but the Guomindang was reluctant to act against them unless they were suspected of having communist leanings as well.

During the Japanese occupation of China during World War II, the Indians in the police and prison services found themselves in a problematic situation. On the one hand, they were a part of the British forces but the attitude of a sizeable number of them was 'sullen and uncooperative' towards the British.[96] On the other hand, the Japanese made a point of distinguishing between them and the British, and asked the Indians to keep on working in the force. Those who refused to do so were executed.[97] Most continued to serve under the Japanese.

Having been brought to China specifically for the purpose of safeguarding British interests, it followed that the presence of Indian soldiers and policemen in China would not be required (a) if there were no longer such interests to serve, (b) if they were found to be unfit for this kind of work, or (c) if there was some other group found to be more suitable. It was a combination of all these factors that marked the end of the community of Indian soldiers and policemen in China. The 1930s was a period of growing nationalism among the Chinese and of a campaign to recover the elements of sovereignty lost through the 'unequal treaties' of the nineteenth century. However, this in itself did not significantly affect the demand for Indian soldiers and policemen, because the foreign concessions in the treaty ports were not wound up. In fact, this was a period of further growth in numbers of this group, which included an increasing proportion of family members.[98] However, the Japanese occupation of eastern China prior to and during World War II, and later the 1949 Revolution that put an end to the foreign presence altogether, combined to ensure that there was no place for Indian soldiers and policemen in China by 1950.

Yet unlike in the case of Indian businessmen, many of whom shifted their base of operations to Hong Kong, there was no room for the Indian soldiers and policemen even on this island which continued to be a British colony for nearly another half century, except for a small number of private watchmen. Those Indian members of the police force who remained in Hong Kong at the end of the War were hopelessly compromised by their association with the Japanese and the militant Indian National Army. The British policy since the beginning of the twentieth century, of slowly sinicizing the Hong Kong police force, was now implemented with greater zeal, aided by the huge influx of Chinese from the mainland from the late 1940s. In addition, the approach of Indian independence, coupled with the desire of the British to reduce the number of Indians who could claim

British nationality, were undoubtedly factors which made the British take measures to eliminate Indians from the police force in Hong Kong as rapidly as possible. By 1952, there were only three Indian policemen left in Hong Kong. The longest continuous presence of Indian security forces in a foreign land had come to an end.

NOTES

1. From Ye Shaojun, 'Pan Xiansheng zai Nanzhong', in *Zhonghua Xiandai Wenxue*, Shanghai: Shanghai Jiaoyu Chubanshe, p. 102. I am grateful to Sharmishta Gupta Basant for drawing my attention to this passage and for translating it for me.

2. Needless to say, Indians served as soldiers and policemen in China only for the British. Nevertheless, at times other European powers also did seek to enlist the services of Indians in their police and armed forces in China and the Far East. A letter from the Portuguese Consul-General in Bombay to the Secretary of the Government of Bombay Political Department in 1921 sought permission to raise a 'military police force consisting of Indian Mussulmans' on behalf of the Government of Macao. General Dept/Comp. 478/1921, Maharashtra State Archives (hereafter referred to as MSA), pp. 1-16.

3. Lt. F.G. Cardew, *A Sketch of the Services of the Bengal Native Army to the Year 1895*, New Delhi: Today and Tomorrow's Printers and Publishers, 1971, p. 5.

4. H. Dodwell, *Sepoy Recruitment in the Old Madras Army*, Calcutta: Government Printer, 1922, pp. 45-6. See also E.G. Pythian-Adams, *The Madras Regiment*, Wellington: The Defence Services Staff College Press, 1958, pp. 2-3.

5. Brig. Rajendra Singh, *History of the Indian Army*, New Delhi: Sardar Attar Singh, Army Educational Stores, 1983, pp. 76-7.

6. Cardew, *Bengal Native Army*, p. 193. See also Correspondence regarding relief of the 2nd Madras Regiment at Chusan, between the Government of India Military Department, the Government at Fort St. George Military Department, and the Major General commanding the British forces at Hong Kong between August and November 1844. Foreign/8 Feb.1845/4-6/S.C., National Archives of India (hereafter referred to as NAI). In 1824, the 24th Bengal Native Infantry mutinied over the issue of going 'overseas' to fight in Burma. See Hugh Tinker, *A New System of Slavery: the Export of Indian Labour Overseas, 1830-1920*, Oxford: Oxford University Press, 1974, p. 46.

7. Geoffrey Betham and H.V.R. Geary, *The Gold: en Galley: The Story of the Second Punjab Regiment, 1761-1947*, New Delhi: Oxford University Press, 1956, pp. 21-4.

8. *The Friend of China and Hong Kong Gazette*, 13 and 17 July 1844.
9. Brig. Rajendra Singh, *History of the Indian Army*, pp. 77-8.
10. Cited in Fu Lo-shu, *A Documentary Chronicle of Sino-Western Relations (1644-1820)*, Tucson: University of Arizona Press, 1966, p. 371. Admiral Drury's troops apparently landed in Macao in two lots of about 300 each. That is why this version mentions just 300 soldiers, whereas the actual number of sepoys was 600. See *Frontier and Overseas Expeditions from India*, Simla: Intelligence Branch, Army Headquarters, 1907-1913, vol. 6, p. 356, and Morse, *Chronicles*, vol. 3, pp. 87-8.
11. See Appendix B.
12. In fact, the forces of the 37th MNI were to some extent diminished en route from India, when the transport ship *Golconda* sank with heavy losses on encountering a fierce typhoon in the South China Sea.
13. John Ouchterlony, a contemporary witness accompanying the British expedition, admitted to 'some excesses perpetrated by stragglers from the British outposts' around Canton in May 1841. See his *Chinese War: an Account of all the Operations of the British Forces, from the Commencement, to the Treaty of Nanking*, rpt. New York: Praeger Publishers, 1970, p. 150. See also the reference in Frederick Wakeman, *Strangers at the Gate: Social Disorder in South China, 1839-1861*, Berkeley and Los Angeles: University of California Press, 1966, pp. 16-17, 55-6.
14. *Friend of China*, 6 April, 1844.
15. Alan Harfield, *British and Indian Armies on the China Coast, 1785-1985*, Farnham, Surrey: A.&J. Partnership, 1990, pp. 43, 47.
16. *Friend of China*, 14 August, 1844.
17. India despatch to Secret Committee, No. 60 of 1841, NAI.
18. Morse, *Chronicles*, vol. 3, p. 96.
19. This incident is described by Ouchterlony, *Chinese War*, pp. 203-7 and 500-9, and the newspaper *Friend of* China, 6 December 1842, as well as in Chinese official documents. See the memorial of Da Honga, the military commander on Taiwan, in the *Qingdai chouban yiwu shimo* (hereafter referred to as *YWSM*), Beijing: Palace Museum comp., 1930, Dao Guang, juan 47, pp. 14-20. The Chinese version stresses that the ship foundered after being hit by guns fired by Chinese shore defenses as it tried to enter Jilong harbour, and that Chinese patrol boats gave vigorous chase to the escaping boats.
20. The scene is described in William C. Hunter, *Bits of Old China*, Shanghai: Kelly and Walsh Ltd., 1911, pp. 21-31.
21. *YWSM*, Dao Guang, juan 59, p. 49.
22. Ibid., p. 49.
23. The *YWSM* collection of documents record the transliterated names of several Indian prisoners captured on different occasions, including Ma-mo, Jia-hai, Jin-hai, Ma-la-nan, Hu-lin, Wen-gan, Ma-la-hua-li, Tu-

xia (Dao Guang/juan 15, p. 22); Mu-li-kong (Dao Guang/juan 47, p. 15); Shuang-guo and An-ma-na (Dao Guang/juan 11, 1964 edn., p. 314); Zhan Ke and Chi Cha (Dao Guang/juan 18, 1964 ed, p. 607); and Chou-man, Ha-wu-li-er, Wu-bing-you, Sha Mu (Dao Guang/juan 62, 1964 ed., pp. 2425-6).

24. *Yapian zhanzheng ziliao congkan* (hereafter referred to as *YPZZ*), Shanghai: 1954, vol. 1, pp. 245-7. An excerpt from Ma-mo's confession is also translated in Arthur Waley, *The Opium War Through Chinese Eyes*, Stanford, Calif.: Stanford University Press, 1958, pp. 243-4.

25. *YPZZ*, pp. 246-7.

26. *YWSM*, 1930 edn., Dao Guang/juan 15, p. 22.

27. Ouchterlony, *Chinese War*, pp. 226-7.

28. *YPZZ*, 1957 edn., vol. 3, p. 83.

29. Ouchterlony, *Chinese War*, pp. 312-20.

30. *YPZZ*, vol. 3, pp. 132-5. See also Waley, p. 191.

31. Brig. Rajendra Singh, *History of the Indian Army*, p. 92.

32. Foreign & Political/27 Nov. 1857/60-65/S.C., NAI.

33. Foreign & Political/27 Mar. 1857/65/S.C., NAI. •

34. *Frontier and Overseas Expeditions*, vol. 6, pp. 420-1.

35. Members of Probyn's Horse and Fane's Horse are said to have acquired 'fortunes' through loot in this campaign. See Byron Farwell, *Armies of the Raj: From the Mutiny to Independence, 1858-1947*, London: Viking Press, 1990, p. 32.

36. *Frontier and Overseas Expeditions*, vol. 6, p. 422.

37. See A.F. Linley, *Taiping tianguo geming qinliji*, Shanghai: Guji Chubanshe, 1985, vol. 1, pp. 214-19.

38. Various references to this phenomenon, in contemporary Chinese and Western documents, are listed in Yu Sheng-wu and Chang Chen-kun, 'China and India in the Mid-Nineteenth Century', in *Rebellion 1857: A Symposium*, ed. P.C. Joshi, Calcutta: K.P. Bagchi & Co., 1986, pp. 346-52. See also Lin Chengjie, *Zhongyin renmin youhao guanxi shi, 1851-1949*, Beijing: Beijing Daxue Chubanshe, 1993, pp. 48-51.

39. Cited in Yu Sheng-wu and Chang Chen-kun, 'China and India', pp. 346-7.

40. Same as the 11th Punjab Infantry.

41. Linley, *Taiping tianguo*, vol. 2, pp. 526-8, 540-1.

42. See Appendix B for a list of Indian regiments which garrisoned Hong Kong at different times.

43. K.N. Vaid, *The Overseas Indian Community in Hong Kong*, Hong Kong: Centre of Asian Studies, University of Hong Kong, 1972, p. 15.

44. Barbara-Sue White, *Turbans and Traders: Hong Kong's Indian Communities*, New York: Oxford University Press, 1994, pp. 4, 18-19.

45. Harfield, *British and Indian Armies*, pp. 52, 211.

46. White, *Turbans and Traders*, pp. 31-2.

47. See Harfield, *British and Indian Armies*, Chapter 10, pp. 185-203, for a detailed description of this regiment.
48. Cited in Harfield, *British and Indian Armies*, p. 186.
49. Ibid., pp. 437-45, 459-60.
50. Ibid., p. 250.The name *Yi He Tuan means* 'righteous and harmonious fists'. The members of this movement practiced a form of boxing as well as other rituals which, they believed, made them invulnerable. Hence the name 'Boxers' given to them by Westerners. See Appendix B for the list of Indian regiments who participated in this expedition.
51. The former Bengal Army had been bifurcated in 1895 into the Bengal and Punjab commands. Cardew, *Bengal Native Army*, pp. 429-31.
52. *Frontier and Overseas Expeditions*, vol. 6, pp. 455-6.
53. Foreign/Internal-A/July 1900, NAI, pp. 223-49, and Foreign/Internal-A/August 1902, NAI, pp. 137-42.
54. Harfield, *British and Indian Armies*, p. 229.
55. *Frontier and Overseas Expeditions*, vol. 6, p. 514.
56. Harfield, *British and Indian Armies*, pp. 309, 316, 318, 323. See Appendix B of this work. Some Indian soldiers seemed to have remained behind in China of their own volition when the rest of the troops were withdrawn, and to have sought employment in the treaty ports and points further north, in Manchuria and Siberia. See the case of Sohan Singh, Foreign/External-B/June 1906, NAI, p. 214.
57. See excerpts from this account in the article by O.P. Sangal, 'An Indian Soldier Indicts War', in *New Age* (January 1953), pp. 53-9. The excerpts are taken from the original account written in the form of a diary from the battlefield in Hindi, and which was later published in India. The title of the original work has been translated by Sangal as *Thirteen Months Spent in China* by Gadadhar Singh.
58. Cited in Sangal, 'An Indian Soldier', p. 55.
59. Ibid., pp. 55-6.
60. Ibid., pp. 57.
61. Ibid., pp. 57.
62. Colin Crisswell and Mike Watson, *The Royal Hong Kong Police (1841-1945)*, Hong Kong: Macmillan, 1982, pp. 13, 15, 25, 41. See also, Henry Lethbridge, *Hong Kong: Stability and Change*, Hong Kong: Oxford University Press, 1978, p. 122.
63. Lethbridge, *Hong Kong*, p. 106.
64. *Colonial Office 129* records series, University of Hong Kong microfilm (hereafter referred to as *CO 129*), 6:26 (21 June 1844), p. 282.
65. Kernial Singh Sandhu, 'Sikh Immigration into Malaya during the Period of British Rule', in *Studies in the Social History of China and South East Asia*, ed. Jerome Ch'en and Nicholas Tarling, Cambridge: Cambridge University Press, 1970, pp. 338-40.
66. Vaid, *The Overseas Indian Community*, pp. 37-8.

67. Ibid., p. 38.

68. *Shanghai yanjiu ziliao*, Shanghai: 1984, pp. 99-100.

69. Cited in *Shanghai yanjiu ziliao*, p. 100.

70. Secretary of State for India Morley's letter to the Governor-General of India, 19/6/08. Foreign/External-B/March 1909, NAI, pp. 40-1.

71. Foreign/External-B/September 1906, NAI, p. 185.

72. See petition from Indian jail guards in Hong Kong of 25 January 1892. *CO* 129/254, no. 28, p. 151.

73. 'Shanghai gonggong zujie shigao', in *Shanghaishi ziliao congkan*, Shanghai: Shanghai renmin chubanshe, 1980, p. 122.

74. See petitions from jail staff of 1892, 1900, 1910, *CO 129/254*, no. 28, p. 151; *CO 129/300*, no. 368, pp. 354-61; *CO 129/*365, no. 101, pp. 564-72.

75. Foreign/External-B/March 1909, NAI, pp. 40-1.

76. The details of this scandal, and the case of Utter Singh in particular, are to be found in the following *CO 129* files: 277/200, p. 138; 277/206, pp. 293-300; 277/217, pp. 347-90; 278/254, p. 249; 293/149, p. 192; 296, pp. 238-68.

77. *Report on the Census of the Indian Population of Hong Kong Taken on twentieth May, 1911* (from the Hong Kong Sessional Papers), p. 103 (56).

78. Foreign/Secret E/March 1907, NAI, pp. 96-8.

79. For references to such problems involving Indian watchmen, see for instance Foreign/External-B/June 1906, NAI, p. 214 and Foreign/External-B/March 1909, NAI, pp. 40-1.

80. *CO 129/*346, 11 Feb. 1908, pp. 215-22; *CO 129/*415, 1 Dec. 1914, pp. 19-23.

81. Rule 16-B of the Rules read: 'No native of India shall depart by sea out of British India for the purpose of, or with the intention of, labouring for hire in any country beyond the limits of India: 'Provided that the prohibition imposed by this rule shall not extend to any person of class of persons permitted so to depart by general or special licence granted by such authority as the Governor-General may appoint in this behalf.' General Dept/Comp. 478/1921, MSA, pp. 1-16.

82. Foreign/External-B/June 1906, NAI, p. 214.

83. *CO 129/*312, 25 July, 1902, p. 86.

84. Foreign/Secret E/March 1907, NAI, 96-8.

85. Ibid., pp. 96-8; *CO 129/*353, p. 455, 11 Dec. 1908.

86. *CO 129/*365, no. 101, pp. 564-72. See also *Shanghai yanjiu ziliao*, p. 100.

87. *CO 129/*344, pp. 512-15; *CO 129/*341, no. 249, p. 444.

88. *CO 129/*395/ pp. 355-62.

89. Similar factors made many Indians also sail for Mexico, since US regulations permitted aliens with two years' residence in Mexico to enter the US bypassing quota restrictions. Foreign & Political/1923/1306-G, NAI.

90. Foreign/External-B/September 1906, NAI, p. 185; Foreign/External–B/ March 1909, NAI, pp. 40-1; Foreign/Secret E/June 1908, NAI, pp. 386-90.

91. *CO 129/*354, pp. 5-12, 15 June 1908; Political Department/186(1910)/ 141, MSA, pp. 29-34.

92. *Report of the Census of the Indian Population of Hong Kong Taken on Twentieth May, 1911* (Table XLI), 103 (56); *CO 129/*414, 29 October 1914, pp. 69-72.

93. General Department/51/1913/979, MSA, pp. 1-4.

94. Frederick Wakeman, Jr., *Policing Shanghai, 1927-37,* Berkeley: University of California Press, 1995, pp. 142-5.

95. Wakeman, *Policing Shanghai,* p. 370, fn. 72.

96. Crisswell and Watson, *The Royal Hong Kong Police,* p. 180.

97. Vaid, *The Overseas Indian Community,* pp. 41-5. In the first two months of the occupation, eight Indian policemen were executed by the Japanese.

98. Markovits, 'Indian Communities in China', pp. 59-60. See also Appendix A of this volume.

CHAPTER 7

The Politicization of Indians in China

... they go out to the East primarily to make money, and something very substantial in the way of a pecuniary inducement would be necessary to persuade them to take an active part in a movement which is aimed at destroying the commercial interests which provide them with a living.

> Extract from a CID report on political activity
> among Indians in China, 1925[1]

Oh Brother, do not fight in a war against the Chinese. Beware of the enemy. He should not deceptively instigate you to fight your Chinese brothers. The enemy splits brothers and makes them kill each other. The people of Hind, China and Turkey are real brothers. The enemy should not be allowed to besmirch their brotherhood.

> Poem in *Ghadar ki Gunj*, a publication widely
> circulated among Indian soliders
> and policemen in China
> around World War I[2]

The major impetus behind the different streams of Indian emigration to China in the nineteenth and early twentieth centuries was undoubtedly economic—the pursuit of trade or the search for a better livelihood. Moreover, the interests of the emigrants were closely bound up with the defence and expansion of Britain's economic and political interests in the Far East and with Britain's privileged position and enclaves in China. Consequently, before the twentieth century, there is little evidence of Indians engaging in political activity in China, and particularly not against the British connection. Least of all did they seem to be troubled by the anomaly of their position in China, at the fact of their being used as 'pawns' by the British and being 'regarded by other Asiatic powers as a menace to their freedom', as Rabindranath Tagore was to describe them in anguish.[3] Cases like those of the Indian soldiers who defected to the side of the Taiping rebels, or of the soldier whose conscience troubled him so deeply during the suppression of the Boxer uprising, were exceptions.

This chapter now explores the steady transformation of this outlook among the Indians in China in the twentieth century, and their growing political mobilization in the struggle against British rule in India and in the worldwide struggle against imperialism for the resurgence of Asia. The extent and duration of this mobilization distinguished Indians in China from virtually all the other Indian diasporas in East and Southeast Asia, except perhaps from the Indian residents in Japan, who in any case were considerably fewer than those in China.[4]

Three factors were primarily responsible for the politicization of the Indians in China in the twentieth-century. These were: the personal experience of racial discrimination and humiliation at the hands of colonial government; the growth and spread of the national movement in India; and the upsurge in revolutionary nationalism in China and the anti-imperialist struggle there and in other countries. All these factors combined to produce a situation of ferment among Indians in China persistent enough to cause anxiety for the British and their allies. In this process, three phases can be distinguished: the first lasting from the early years of the twentieth century through to the end of World War I; the second encompassing the period between the two World Wars, and peaking in the late 1920s; and the third covering the years of the Japanese invasion of China and World War II.

THE BEGINNINGS

The beginnings of political activity among Indians in China in the years immediately preceding World War I can be understood only by appreciating the close identity between this group of Indians and their counterparts in North America. In fact, it was developments in Canada and the United States between 1907 and 1914 that first triggered off restlessness among Indians in China and contributed to their early politicization. Emigration to North America among Indians, particularly from Punjab, was in many cases via Hong Kong and Shanghai. In some cases, Indians already employed as watchmen, soldiers, or policemen in China, moved on to Canada and the United States, attracted by higher wages and also the possibility of acquiring land there. In other cases, Indians passing through Chinese ports to and from North America, waiting for considerable lengths of time for the desired onward passage, also had to seek some kind of interim employment, making them virtually indistinguishable from the resident Indian population in China.

The restrictions imposed on the immigration of Chinese into North America at the beginning of the twentieth century seems to have spurred the demand for Indian labour there. Only 45 Indians entered Canada in 1905, but in 1906 the number rose to 387, while in the following year it jumped to 2,124. In 1908 2,623 Indians emigrated to Canada.[5] Yet, just as the doors appeared to be opening for Indian labour in Canada, they were closed: in 1908, the Canadian Government passed two Orders-in-Council specifically designed to drastically curtail Indian immigration. One raised the money requirement for prospective immigrants from $25 to $200 per head, while the other stipulated that only those Indians would be allowed to land who had arrived in Canada by 'continuous journey' from India—a virtual impossibility for Indians because of the steamship routes prevailing at the time. The United States also, in the same year, began to curtail Indian immigration, not by enacting any new laws but by the so-called 'strained application' of the existing laws. This resulted in the rejection of as much as 50 per cent of the Indian applications in the years 1909, 1911, and 1913.[6] Moreover, the Alien Land Law instituted in the United States in 1913 dashed the hopes of those Indians who had hoped to acquire some land. Administrative measures against Indians were accompanied by active campaigns against them in the media in both countries and by the hostile activities of societies such as the Asiatic Exclusion League.

The reaction of many Indians in North America, a large number of whom were ex-soldiers of the British empire and had been proud of the connection, rapidly turned from bewilderment to resentment and then, under the influence of various societies and journals founded by militant Indian nationalists in North America, to grim hostility towards the British rule. As in England and France, so too in Canada and the United States, various political exiles and intellectuals from India had begun to actively espouse the cause of India's freedom.[7] Foremost among these was an organization founded in May 1913 in Portland in the US by Lala Hardayal and Parmanand, which came to be known as the Ghadar Party after its famous paper of the same name. The Ghadar Party soon shifted its headquarters to San Francisco. Because it reached out to, and consolidated itself among, the Indian workers and agricultural labourers in the region, this movement was qualitatively different from that of practically all the other Indian nationalist struggles abroad which had a much narrower base. 'The movement is entirely one of the people,' wrote Hardayal, 'The members of the party are peasants and working men. There are only about half a dozen educated men to edit the paper, carry on correspondence, deliver lectures and think out plans.' Talking about the circulation of *Ghadar*, Hardayal said it

reaches the masses, men poor in wealth but rich in courage; it does not appeal merely to the so-called educated men and aristocrats, whose heart is in their bank accounts while their lips prate of liberty and sacrifice. When the common people understand something they want to risk life in order to realise the ideal. They have no property to make them cowards.[8]

The Ghadar Party believed in the necessity of the armed overthrow of British rule in India. They systematically began to collect money, men, arms and material for this purpose. A key aspect of their work was propaganda to undermine the loyalty of the Indian armed forces, a substantial proportion of which by now were drawn from Punjab, to the British crown. Various channels were used to send copies of *Ghadar* to different regiments. Much of the literature destined for India was routed via China, and the Hankou post office was an important point of transit.[9] Other channels were also used. A consignment of subversive literature found in Lahore, for instance, contained the name of one M. Kohli, a station master of the Shanghai-Nanking Railway line.[10] The *Ghadar Directory* compiled by the

Punjab Government in 1916 listed a number of individuals in Hankou, Shanghai, and Hong Kong who were known to have forwarded copies of *Ghadar* to various regiments and persons in India.[11]

Ghadar was not the only militantly nationalist paper in circulation among Indians in China. The *Jehan-i-Islam*, a proscribed paper published in Constantinople, was discovered to be circulating from hand to hand among Indian Muslim members of the police force of Hong Kong, calling on them to join in a Holy War against the British, and warning them to be vigilant against British schemes to 'create disturbances between the Hindoos and the Mussulmans'.[12] The Indian troops stationed in China and Hong Kong, along with their compatriots in the police, were themselves the target of propaganda, as well as the means of reaching out to other regiments in India.

A large number of the young Indian men, most of them Sikhs, who had to bide their time in Hong Kong and Shanghai on their way to and from North America, sought shelter in the gurudwaras such as the one on Baoxing road in Shanghai and those at Central and Wanchai in Hong Kong. Commenting on their plight, the Indian businessman from Singapore Gurdit Singh, better known as the man who later chartered the famous ship *Komagata Maru*, said:

When I came to Hong Kong for some private business in January 1914, I could not bear the grief and hardship of the Vancouver emigrants who had been waiting in the Sikh temple in Hong Kong. It was a matter of injustice and darkness, I thought, because our brethren were passing their days in a miserable state for the hope of arriving at Vancouver while staying here for one year and spending money for their eating from their own pockets.[13]

As their frustration over inordinate delays and obstructions and humiliation mounted, the gurudwaras became cauldrons of insubordination in British eyes. The gurudwaras were regularly visited by men of the regiments stationed in Hong Kong as well as members of the police force, and the British were most alarmed at the impact of all the fiery talk on these men. In 1914, they tried to prohibit Indian soldiers and policemen from visiting the gurudwara in Hong Kong, but this was violently resented. An unsigned letter from 'A True Friend of the British and Indian People' to the colonial authorities threatened:

Is our humiliation before the Civilized World by you people not complete yet? Religion is the only thing left to us but that too seems to be in danger now. . . . Remember it is only the Sikh who saved your entire annihilation and extinction in India in 1857. . . . Don't you know that you are your own enemy for you are undermining the foundations of your Government yourselves by your own silly and cowardly rash acts like the present one. The consequences will be far reaching. . . . [14]

Deciding that it would be wiser to reopen the gurudwara to the men of the armed forces while keeping a discreet watch over them, Governor May rescinded the closure. The Governor was at the same time under pressure from the military authorities, particularly Major-General Kelly of the China Command, who charged that the colonial authorities were lax in their supervision of the gurudwaras as well as in checking the credentials of Indians passing through from North America to India. While claiming that the description of the gurudwara as a 'hotbed of sedition' was 'exaggerated', Governor May admitted that 'it is certain that a good deal of loose talk and no doubt some sedition has taken place there especially. . . among the very large number of Indians', who passed through from the USA and other countries, 'where they had imbibed an unwholesome freedom of both manners and thought'. He claimed that he was personally keeping a close watch on the affairs of the gurudwara with the assistance of its main office-bearers who, he claimed, were fully cooperative. [15]

Not all the functionaries of the gurudwara were cooperative in this sense, however. Several of the granthis were known to be sympathizers of the Ghadarites, or even more. The best known among these men was Bhagwan Singh, the fiery granthi at Central Gurudwara from 1910 to 1913. The Colonial Office files are full of the doings of this individual and the measures taken to keep track of him as he moved from city to city across the Far East and North America. Coming from village Viring, Tarn Taran, Amritsar district, Bhagwan Singh left India in 1909-10. He made his way to the Federated Malay States, where he was granthi at a gurudwara at Perak. The management of the gurudwara committee fired him for preaching 'sedition', following which he came to Hong Kong. After three years there in 1913 he was dismissed as granthi for his fulminations against the British, and had to leave for Japan. From there he arrived in Vancouver where his stay, although of very short duration, was supposed to have been a turning point in the radicalization of the movement. He seems to have formally become a member and an office-bearer of the Ghadar Party. He was externed from Canada in November 1913 and made his way back to Japan. There he came into contact with other Indian revolutionaries like Rash Behari Bose, as well as with Sun Yat-sen. Bhagwan Singh remained active for a number of years in the movement of Indians in North America and the Far East against British rule. Years later, another famous Indian nationalist in the Far East, Raja Mahendra Pratap, recalled meeting him at a gurudwara in San Francisco, and described him as 'a poet, an orator of distinction, firebrand by nature and constitution'.[16]

Two events occurred in 1914 which had far-reaching consequences for the politicization of Indians in China. The first was the ill-fated voyage of the *Komagata Maru*. The second was the outbreak of World War I. Both contributed to the further radicalization of the movement among the Indians, as well as to the stepping up of the tempo of their activities against the British.

The *Komagata Maru* was a Japanese ship chartered by the Indian businessman Gurdit Singh in Hong Kong to carry aspiring Indian emigrants to Vancouver. After several delays, during which the passengers, the majority of them ex-armymen, started to get restive, the ship was finally permitted to set sail in April 1914. It was only a few days afterwards that a communication from the Canadian Government refusing the ship permission to come to Vancouver reached the authorities in Hong Kong. Of the 337 passengers of the *Komagata Maru*, 165 boarded at Hong Kong, while 73 boarded at Shanghai (the rest embarking at Moji and Yokohama in Japan). Governor May of Hong Kong noted that most of those who boarded had 'come here during the last two years with the object of going to the United States of America. They failed in accomplishing that object and have been maintaining themselves here as watchmen and in other civil employment. They are said to be illiterates and of the agricultural classes.'[17]

The Canadian authorities refused the passengers permission to land at Vancouver, citing the 'continuous journey' clause. Since the passengers refused to sail back, a stalemate ensued, in which the passengers were confined to the ship for several weeks and denied essential supplies. The issue became a highly emotive one for all Indians in Canada, encapsulating as it were all the humiliation and harshness which they had been facing as aliens. The Indians in Vancouver actively organized themselves in support of their beleaguered countrymen on board. Eventually, the Canadian authorities forced the ship to turn back in July. Whatever the political inclinations or extent of political commitment of the majority of the passengers on the *Komagata Maru* before it had set sail from Hong Kong, there is no doubt that by the time their ship reached India, they were virulently anti-British, almost to a man. The reception that they received from the police on arrival at Calcutta, when an attempt on their part to march in procession was brutally suppressed, and a large number were either killed or arrested and jailed, further inflamed public opinion in India and abroad.[18]

Anger over the *Komagata Maru* episode directly contributed to the mutiny of the Indian regiment posted in Singapore in 1915, the first such mutiny by a regiment of the British Indian army since 1857.[19] In the gurudwaras of Hong Kong and Shanghai feelings were at a high pitch, and men were exhorted to return home to avenge the humiliation inflicted on the *Komagata Maru* passengers. The Ghadar Party had already started sending activists home from North America, in preparation for a planned uprising in India. The first *jatha* of Ghadar activists from Shanghai reached Calcutta in 1914 just after the *Komagata Maru*.[20]

The involvement of Britain in the first World War, and the hostilities between Britain and Germany, seemed to the Ghadar Party organizers to provide a favourable opportunity to further the cause of armed uprising. China, where the political situation was still in a flux following the 1911 Revolution and where the Germans retained their concessions in Tianjin, Hankou and other places, assumed great importance in their plans. According to Don Dignan,

the conditions in neutral and semi-colonial China made it second in importance only to the United States as a source of recruitment for revolutionary activities. Not only was revolutionary nationalism in China a source of encouragement to the Indian revolutionaries there, but Chinese politicians and officials increasingly resisted pressure from the British to cooperate in combating the Indo-German conspiracies. During the war years, Sun Yat-sen and some other Chinese nationalist leaders became directly involved in Indian revolutionary schemes.[21]

After two attempts to ship arms to India directly from California and from the Philippines had proved abortive, Indian revolutionaries preferred to use the Shanghai—Amoy / Swatow-Bangkok route. A letter of 1916 from one of the leaders of the Ghadar Party in San Francisco, Chakravarty, testified to the willingness of influential Chinese to assist in the process of arms shipments to India. One of the conditions for such assistance was that the Chinese would retain one-tenth of the arms and ammunition. Chakravarty's letter referred to various Chinese sympathizers who were rendering valuable help to the Indian movement in China, including one King Su Chan, a former student at Columbia University in New York, Wu Ting-fang, Foreign Minister of the Chinese Republic, and a W.T. Wang who was a confidante of the then President of China, Li Yuan Hung, and who was acquainted with Chakravarty in the United States. Wang, according to Chakravarty, 'says Li Yuan Hung is in sympathy with the Indian revolution and would like English power weakened. Some of the prominent people are quite eager to help India directly, and Germany indirectly, without exposing herself to any great risk. . . .'[22]

The International Settlement in Shanghai not being under their sole control, the British were not as free to keep a rein on the activities of Indian revolutionaries there as they wished. Several Indians were directly in the employ of the Germans, such as those working in the German Club, the German Bank, and other German concerns in Shanghai, while in Hankou twenty-six Indians were employed as policemen in the German Concession.[23] The British Foreign Secretary, Sir Edward Grey complained in a memorandum to the Japanese of 12 November 1915: 'Not only have the Germans been attempting to fit out armed expeditions to India and in the Shanghai settlement have accumulated large stocks of arms and ammunition, but they have been tampering with the Sikh police and watchmen and also intriguing with the Chinese.'[24] The Japanese were formally allies of the British in the War. Nevertheless, British measures to contain Indian revolutionary activities in the Far East at all costs, including the detention of Japanese ships carrying Indians, were factors contributing to the increasing strain in the relationship.

Some idea of the kind of help given by the Germans to the Indian militant nationalists in China during World War I can be gauged from the following testimony of Nawab Khan, a one-time Ghadar Party activist who turned police informant after his arrest in India in December 1914. Nawab Khan had passed through Hong Kong in September of 1914 as part of one of the several detachments of men sent back to India in preparation for the uprising. He was important enough to be elected as one of the eight members of a Central Managing Committee set up by the returning Ghadar activists in Hong Kong to coordinate their plans. Describing his visit to the German consul at Canton in the company of three other comrades, Nawab Khan said in his testimony:

We . . . took the train and arrived the following morning at Canton. Rur Singh, being acquainted with English, was sent on to ask the German Consul whether he would permit our deputation to wait on him. The German Consul expressed great willingness to see us. He, however, advised caution as, he said, he was being carefully watched. He asked us to limit the number of our deputation to two or three members. And so Rur Singh and I alone attended on him. We found him in his office and explained to him at some length of our intention of going to India and stirring up a revolution. We further asked him to make arrangements with some Norway-Swedish Shipping Company for our conveyance to India. He replied that, at that moment, there was no ship of the company in question in port and that the necessary arrangements could be made within the next eight or ten days. We then asked the Consul whether he could procure us passports from the Chinese Government and thus enable us to buy arms in China and journey unhindered by land to India. In reply he pointed out that the Chinese Government was neutral and that the passports required were not likely to be granted. He further added that we should take the Japanese boat of which we made mention. This would, he said, be our best course of action as Japan was merely allied to England because of the financial advantages which such an alliance gave the former. In reality, Japan was no friend of England. In fact nothing would be more gratifying to the Japanese than to see us go to India and raise the standard of rebellion. We then asked the German Consul whether, in the event of our success in stirring up a revolution in India, whether we could count upon assistance from the German Navy. If such help were given us, we promised to allow Germany free trade with India. The German Consul said that he was not in a position to make us any promises in these matters. He explained that the news, received by him from Berlin, was extremely scanty and spasmodic. His correspondence had to travel practically round the world before he received it.

The German Consul then showed us photos of various German cruisers and warships such as the *Emden*, etc. He urged us to proceed to India and guaranteed us safety from the attacks of German cruisers. 'You must,' he said, 'make every effordirect or indirectt to raise a rebellion in India.'

We then left him. On our way out of the Consul's room we happened to glance into an adjoining room where we saw a Sikh seated. Rur Singh told me that this man belonged to Hong Kong and that he was a member of our party. His name, according to Rur Singh, was Sappah Singh.[25]

In the years 1914 and 1915, the gurudwaras in China were overflowing not only with disgruntled migrants waiting to go out to North America, but with groups of committed activists and organizers of the Ghadar Party sent to India from North America, who succeeded to a great extent in enlisting the sympathies of the local Indians for their cause. The British authorities in China became decidedly jumpy. Indians began to deported for the slightest signs of 'seditious' activities, and where the evidence against them appeared to be too flimsy to stand legal scrutiny, they were harassed and charged on various other grounds.[26] The heavy-handed methods of suppression employed by the British threatened to backfire. One particular round of arrests and deportations in Hong Kong in September 1915 engendered so much disquiet, that rumours of an impending revolt among the local Indian military and police personnel began to circulate in the Guangdong and Hong Kong Chinese papers. The colonial authorities even took the precaution of asking a US warship to stand by, though eventually nothing came out of it.[27] Nawab Khan described the charged atmosphere prevailing in the gurudwara in Hong Kong:

We had previously decided that, on arrival at Hong Kong, we would not betray our mission with wild and reckless talk against the British Government. But on entering the Gurdwara, we found the Sikhs from Canada in an exceedingly restive state. They were vociferous in their denunciations of Government. They further informed us that they had got the Sikh Sepoys of the 26th Punjabis whose barracks were in close proximity to the Gurdwara. The sepoys, they said, had become disaffected.

On hearing this, we decided to throw off our disguise and thenceforth we showed equal, if not greater, enthusiasm in inculcating revolutionary ideas into the minds of the Sikh sepoys who visited the Gurdwara under the pretence of worship.

Throughout our stay in Hong Kong meetings were held daily at 8 p.m. in the Gurdwara. The Sepoys of the 26th Punjabis also attended these meetings. . . .

The Sepoys of the 26th Punjabis and the Sikhs of other regiments stationed at Hong Kong had assured us of their willingness to join in any subversive movement which might be contemplated. They, however, warned us against the native officers who, they declared, were strongly pro-British and discountenanced Ghadr tendencies. After mature consideration I thought it inadvisable to foment any trouble in Hong Kong especially as we could never hope to hold any possible conquests owing to the fact that we possessed no naval force.[28]

The plans to mount an armed uprising in India from abroad, in which the Indians in China had played a notable part, suffered a serious blow with their betrayal just before the scheduled date by some informers. About 291 Ghadar activists were rounded up and brought before special tribunals in a series of trials collectively known as the Lahore Conspiracy Cases. The judgement, delivered in September 1915, resulted in 46 men being hanged and 64 being transported for life as exemplary punishment. By 1917, the tide of the War had begun to turn against Germany and its allies, leading to the further weakening of the revolutionary scheme. A permanent fall-out of this phase of nationalist agitation in China was the recognition by the British of the need for better, more coordinated and centralized intelligence. It was felt, for instance, that the Shanghai Municipal Police, being a multinational concern, was not sufficiently geared to safeguarding specifically British interests. During the earlier stages of the War, the British Ambassador in China had requested the deputation of an officer of the Indian CID to keep a watch on the Indian community in China, following which David Petrie was sent to China in this capacity. In 1916, it was agreed that a special Bureau would be set up in Shanghai under Petrie which would coordinate the activity of the Foreign Office, the War Office, the Admiralty, and all agencies concerned with the issue.[29]

By the end of World War I, the first upsurge in political activity among Indians in China had more or less come to an end. In

1925, an officer of the Indian Police sent to China to investigate the political activity among Indians there assessed complacently: 'The circumstances which gave birth to the Ghadar movement were unusual, and are not likely to be repeated. Certainly no parallel exists today. . . .'[30]

THE SECOND PHASE

Despite this assessment, the year 1925 turned out to be a significant point in the revitalization of the movement among Indians in China, in more ways than one. 1925 saw an upsurge in the movement against imperialism in China, particularly against British imperialism, following the shooting down of striking Chinese workers in Shanghai by British (and Indian) police on May 30. This triggered off a great sense of revulsion among Indians at being used by the British in the suppression of the Chinese. 1925 also was the year when a particularly dedicated group of Ghadar activists from North America, headed by Daswandha Singh, arrived in China in the company of the exiled nationalist leader, the colourful Raja Mahendra Pratap. The summer of 1925 was in addition the occasion of a conference of the International Union of the Oppressed Peoples of the East at Canton, the first of a series of international conferences with a radical tone held in China in this period, which gave a fillip to the revolutionary movement in China as well as to the solidarity between the national liberation struggles of different Asian peoples.

This second phase in the political activization of Indians in China was different from the first in certain significant ways. It was much more closely linked with the revolutionary nationalist movement of the Chinese people, which was approaching a new high tide in the mid-1920s. The ties went much beyond the earlier pattern of a few meetings between a handful of Indian nationalists in exile and Guomindang leaders like Sun Yat-sen. Secondly, with the success of the Russian Revolution and the establishment of the Comintern, the nationalist movements and organizations in both China and India came under the powerful new influence of the Communist movement. The Ghadar Party itself not only underwent some ideological change under this influence, but also developed organizational links with the Comintern. In India too, a new, internationalist, phase of the struggle against imperialism could be discerned in (among other things) the strong opposition voiced by different sections of political opinion to the despatch of Indian troops to China, and by the participation of Jawaharlal Nehru in the Brussels Conference of the League against Imperialism in 1927.

The shooting down of striking Chinese workers at Canton in the summer of 1925, in which Indians were used, was vehemently denounced by nationalists in India and abroad.[31] A mass meeting of Indians at Marysville, California condemned the massacre, as did another meeting of the Hindustan Club of Detroit, which also called on the Indian National Congress to put pressure on the British to withdraw Indian troops from China. The *United States of India*, July 1925, wrote: 'Our head goes down in shame to know that our brethren in China have sunk so low as to kill innocent Chinese, with whom we have no quarrel whatsoever. . . All that India can do now is to ask her sons to refrain from fighting against the Chinese and offer an apology to the Chinese nation for the misdeeds of Indian soldiers.' Rash Behari Bose in Japan reacted with the words: 'As an Indian I hang down my head in shame for the unpardonable sin of my Sikh countrymen. They have committed a great crime against humanity. Their action has tarnished the name of Mother India.'

Very soon, news began to filter out of China that Indian troops in China had started refusing to obey orders to fire on the Chinese, and that entire regiments had to be transferred and replaced as a consequence. The British sought to deny the truth of these reports.[32] Where they could not altogether deny instances of Indians fraternizing with the Chinese, they tried to dismiss them:

The Sikhs and Mahomedans who allied themselves to the strikers were either out of employment or mostly in the employ of Chinamen. Their position in Canton was rendered difficult by the extreme anti-British feeling prevailing there, and it is not unnatural that they should have allowed themselves to be drawn into the general agitation. While the leaders joined the movement because they were actively disloyal, many of those who subscribed their names must have done so because it was the easiest course to follow, and the only alternative to intimidation and possible loss of employment.[33]

The *United States of India* in September reported an instance of seventy Indian members of the Hong Kong police resigning, in sympathy with the Chinese and in protest against the repression unleashed by the British. These men were said to have then presented themselves en masse before the Governor of Guangdong, offering their services to him. The Governor initially hesitated to take them up on their offer, whereupon the men are reported to have told him: 'We have burnt our boats. There is no going back. You can utilize us for China's cause or kill us—as you please.' The Governor was then said to have given employment to these Indians.[34]

All efforts to condemn the atrocities on the Chinese and to offer Indian sympathy were apparently much appreciated by Chinese. Raja Mahendra Pratap contrasted the atmosphere he found in China in the course of his second visit in June 1925 with the friendly, but less enthusiastic reception he had received during his earlier visit in 1923:

It was very lucky that just then China was in one of her most revolutionary moods. Perhaps you remember that in spring 1925 British troops clashed with the Chinese masses at Shanghai. I openly condemned British police for killing Chinese! Chinese leaders at Peking welcomed me. Dinners were given, meetings were held and I lectured here and then there. One great mass meeting before the palace was exceptionally fiery. Here Madame Sun Yat-sen and myself spoke from the same platform. People wildly cheered us.[35]

The rapidly increasing tempo of the nationalist struggle in China further galvanized the process of the political radicalization of Indians in China. By 1927 the Guomindang-Chinese Communist Party alliance had launched the Northern Expedition to reunify the country, threatening the privileged enclaves and concessions of the foreign powers as well. The rapid pace of the expedition and its apparent power to sweep all before it seems to have had an electrifying effect on the local Indians. The experienced intelligence officer, David Petrie, commented:

. . . the Special Officer who visited China early in 1926 described the reactions till then discernible among the local Indian communities as unimportant, judged either by their extent or by the class and character of the individuals affected. This opinion was no doubt true as regards the early, and possibly the middle, months of 1926. But, by the beginning of 1927, the abandonment of the Hankow Concession had pointed its own moral as to the power of anti-British propaganda backed by mob violence; and from that time the position has rapidly deteriorated until, at the moment of writing, the anti-British agitation among Indians in China is of an extent and intensity that cannot be regarded without some anxiety.[36]

British efforts to rush troops from India at this time were again widely condemned by Indian nationalist forces.[37] The Shiromani Akali Dal in Amritsar called it a 'national humiliation'. Motilal Nehru, on behalf of the Swaraj Party, declared: 'Any use of Indian resources against the Chinese nationalists in the threatened war will be strongly deprecated by the Swaraj Party and deeply resented by the people of India', while Jawaharal Nehru, attending the Brussels Conference, said: 'It has been a matter of shame and sorrow to us that the British Government should venture to send Indian troops to China in an attempt to coerce the Chinese,' and that 'in spite of her weakness India is not so weak today as to permit herself to be employed as a pawn in the imperialist game.' The secretary of the Hindustani Ghadar Party, Munsha Singh, informed the Guomindang in a blunter vein: 'The Hindustani Ghadar Party declared any Hindu who fired upon the Chinese a traitor.'

The sentiments expressed by Indian nationalist opinion were accompanied with concrete measures to prevent the newly arrived Indian troops in China in 1927 from obeying the orders of their British superiors. According to a report in the *China Weekly Review* of 6 August 1927, Indian troops on their way to China had been told that the Chinese had vandalized Indian religious places and molested Indian women, and so on. 'But they were met, almost at the dock, by certain men of their own nationality, who were working for the cause of Indian freedom among the large groups of Indian police and watchmen already in Shanghai. . . . The reaction of the troops when they discovered the untruth of the stories which had been circulated among them was great', and the men had to be hastily shifted out to Hong Kong. Reports in various papers also claimed that the Indian police in the Hankou Concession had defected to the Chinese side, and that the entire Indian force in the Shanghai police were similarly preparing to go over. The revolutionary Hankou Government is said to have actually offered to give military training to one thousand Indians and to pay them not less than what they had been receiving from the Shanghai Municipal Corporation. The rank-and-file men were being offered $40 per month and more senior men $50, while a drill instructor was offered $100 per month as salary.[38]

Further evidence of the widespread sympathy among Chinese at this time is seen in Raja Mahendra Pratap's account of his efforts to visit Tibet and to enlist Chinese help during his second visit to China.[39] A party of ten Indians made up his team, including among them several Ghadar Party activists. About the object of his mission to Tibet, Mahendra Pratap wrote plainly: 'To tell the truth, I had a plan to surround India with anti-British empires and pro-India states and to establish on the frontier our outposts. In Afghanistan under King Amanullah we had our best friend. I said, why we not try to have the like friends in Tibet and Nepal!'[40] Despite the sensitivity of the Chinese on the question of Tibet, Mahendra Pratap received the friendly assistance of various Chinese officials and strongmen along the way, even though nothing concrete resulted from his mission. The warlord Feng Yuxiang not only gave him considerable aid, but arranged for several mass meetings to be addressed by Mahendra Pratap in which he too, like the others, sat cross-legged on the floor and diligently took notes![41] At Ningxia, the local Chinese general 'proposed that I took his 25,000 troops and attack the British in India and thus liberate my native land'. Even Mahendra Pratap regarded this as an 'astounding' proposal. The warlord Wu Peifu, who had driven out Feng Yuxiang and replaced him by the time the Indian mission returned from Tibet, and who was inclined to regard him with suspicion at first, later appears to have changed his attitude and also received Mahendra Pratap cordially.[42]

In his autobiography Mahendra Pratap wrote of an episode which occurred in 1927, which throws an interesting light on the relations at that time between nationalist Indians in China and their Chinese patrons, as well as on the relations among the Indians themselves.[43] Mahendra Pratap made his way to Kaifeng to see his old friend Feng Yuxiang who was now ensconced in this city. There he found Feng in the company of about twenty Indians, including two who had accompanied him to Tibet, Charan Singh and Bishan Singh, whose attitude Mahendra Pratap now found to be quite hostile towards himself. 'We were shocked to hear that Marshall Feng had received a wire from Shanghai advising him not to see us. He was told that the two Sikhs accompanying me would try to murder him! Such are we, I said to myself, Indians intriguing against Indians.' According to Mahendra Pratap, Feng went on to expel those Indians from his entourage, leading to further illwill against himself, although he claimed that the misunderstanding was later cleared up.[44]

In China solid organizational work of mobilization for the cause of freedom appears to have been largely the work of the nucleus of Ghadar activists who came to China along with Mahendra Pratap in 1925. After the end of the Tibetan mission, four of them—Daswandha Singh, Inder Singh, Dulla Singh and Gainda Singh—went to Beijing. In Beijing at that time, there was a Gurudwara Ghadar Party, with one Narain Singh as its Secretary, as well as a Ghadar Ashram.[45] There they carried on their organizational work, writing articles and delivering speeches in different gatherings on the need for Indians and Chinese to unite against British imperialism.

Daswandha Singh and Charan Singh shifted their base of operations to the more congenial climate of revolutionary Hankou in January 1927, to be followed by Inder Singh in March. Along with some Chinese, Koreans, Filipinos and Japanese, they played a leading role in the formation of the Eastern Oppressed People's Association, which had its headquarters at No. 39 Ko Min Li, just behind the former British Concession at Hankou. On 26 January, declared as India's 'Independence Day', the organization distributed 10,000 leaflets, the text of which was supposed to have been written by Mahendra Pratap.[46] They also set up the necessary arrangements to bring out the *Hindustan Ghadar Dhandora* as a fortnightly journal in Gurmukhi, for circulation among the Indian soldiers and policemen in Shanghai. Mahendra Pratap was acting editor of this paper for a while. Others associated with the paper included one Jiwan Singh, said to have been a passenger aboard the *Komagata Maru*, as well as a very active ex-watchman of Hankou called Ganda Singh. This Indian group in Hankou worked closely with the Guomindang forces there, and actively sought support from among the Indians in Hankou and Shanghai for the revolutionary movement in China. One of the issues of the *Hindustan Ghadar Dhandora* contained an appeal on 'The Duties of the Indian Army in China' which said: 'The dutiful sons of China are fighting for the freedom of their country. The freedom of India and the freedom of China have a close connection with each other. By the freedom of China the day of the freedom of India will draw near. It is the duty of Indians to help the Nationalist Party of China so that they may have the pleasure of seeing India free.'[47]

Another event of some significance that took place in Hankou in 1927 was the Pan-Pacific Labour Conference. It was originally intended to be held in Canton in May, and in fact, many of the foreign delegates to the Conference arrived in Canton weeks in advance, including M.N. Roy as the delegate of the Comintern. However, the coup carried out by Chiang Kai-shek compelled the Conference to shift to Hankou, still under the control of the left wing of the Guomindang. British intelligence sources reported that M.N. Roy came with 'instructions' as well as money for Daswandha Singh and his comrades, and that he had been specifically charged by the Comintern with the task of spreading 'sedition and disaffection among the Indian troops in China', though it is not clear what actual role, if any, Roy played in the work among the Indian community in China.[48]

While Daswandha Singh and his comrades carried on their work in Hankou, the Shanghai end of the work was carried out with great zeal by Gajjan Singh. He was joined in March 1927 by Gainda Singh from Beijing, one of the other Ghadar activists who had been part of Mahendra Pratap's party, and the two of them carried on their activity together, with their headquarters in the office of the General Labour Union, Chapei. The Shanghai group made considerable headway in organizing a network of infiltrators and distributors of the *Hindustan Ghadar Dhandora* among the local Indian police and troops. The modus operandi of the local activists can be seen from the following description of the charges against some of them who were later arrested by the British authorities:

. . . Gulzara Singh, . . . an ex-watchman with a bad record, spoke to a Mahomedan Lance Naik and three men of the 3/14th Punjab Regiment, and asked them why they come from the Punjab to fight against their Chinese brethren. Gulzara Singh went on to speak in a disloyal strain of the dishonesty of the British Government in paying Indian soldiers less than British, and ended by attempting to persuade these men to desert with their arms and equipment to the Chinese Nationalists. . . .

One Sangat Singh, . . . an ex-watchman and ex-dalladar of the 39th Central India Horse, approached a Naik and three men of the 4/1st Punjab Regiment and engaged them in coversation of a disloyal nature. . . .

One Asa Singh, . . . Police Constable No. 83 of the Shanghai Municipal Police, attempted to hand a copy of the *Ghadar* paper to a Hindu Naik of the 3/14th Punjab Regiment. . . .

Two Sikh watchmen, named Amar Singh and Dalip Singh, were arrested for hanging about the camp of the 3/14th Punjab Regiment in a suspicious manner and attempting to get into conversation with some of the men. . . .[49]

The Shanghai group was strengthened by the arrival of Daswandha Singh, who shifted his operations from Hankou, in mid-April. Others associated with them were a certain Lal Chand and Abdul Rashid Savul. Lal Chand and his 'group of seditious Sindhis' had a club at No.19, North Szechuan Road. Savul had a business also located on Szechuan Road, exporting tea and silks and importing skins.[50] The tempo of meetings and other activities escalated. The British authorities closed down the gurudwara in Chapei claiming that it had become a centre of 'seditious' activities. Eventually, in mid-May, using the excuse of the murder in early April of the seniormost Indian member of the Shanghai Municipal Police, Budha Singh by another Indian, the British in Shanghai swooped down on twelve Indian activists, including Daswandha Singh, Gainda Singh and Gajjan Singh. After an in-camera trial, they were sentenced to a year's rigorous imprisonment followed by deportation and imprisonment in India. Lal Chand and Savul were also forced to leave Shanghai because of the pressure of the police.

Although the arrest and departure of these leaders was a setback for the Indian revolutionaries in China, their associates continued to be 'as active as ever' according to Petrie's own admission. The centre of activity, however, once again shifted back to Hankou. There, Charan Singh and Inder Singh, two of the original Ghadarites, were joined by two more veterans who arrived from Moscow, Bishen Singh and Pritam Singh, and by another revolutionary, Rattan Singh, from India. In Shanghai, the granthi of the Szechuan Road Gurudwara, Jagat Singh, became the leader of the local activists.

In November 1927 in Shanghai, a Pan-Asiatic Conference was held. Mahendra Pratap managed to attend this Conference, eluding attempts by the British police to waylay him before he could reach the venue and to take him to the International

Settlement. Both in Shanghai and later in Nanjing, he stayed as a guest of Chinese Guomindang officials. He made two more trips to China, in 1928 and 1930, in the course of which he kept up his contacts with high-placed Chinese officials and members of the Guomindang, like Wang Jingwei, Chen Lifu and Sun Fo, the son of Sun Yat-sen. About Sun Fo, he wrote: 'His knowledge about the Indian affairs is very extensive, and he takes personal interest in the Indian problems . . . in thought and spirit he is very near to India and the Indians. He can count several Indians as his personal friends.'[51] However, Mahendra Pratap's efforts to use their influence to make a second trip to Tibet met with a rebuff. He got the clear feeling that his views on the Tibetan question were not liked by many in China. Undaunted, he carried on with his plans on other fronts, and actually established the headquarters of his World Federation in Beijing from 1931 to 1933 until a serious shortage of funds forced him to close it down.

In the meantime, the British continued their relentless pressure on the 'seditionists' and their sympathizers. The *Hindustan Ghadar Dhandora* of 1 August 1928 complained that Indians who read the paper were being harassed by the police and employers.[52] The arrests and deportations continued relentlessly from 1928 to 1931. The persecution was also directed against members of another Indian organization that seems to have come up around this time, called the Indian Youth League, which had its headquarters in Chapei. According to an OSS report, the Indian Youth League had 'some kind of agreement with the Kuomintang and the Bureau of Public Safety, which enabled it to hold meetings and carry on political activity. The leaders were young working men who were literate and intelligent.'[53] They seem to have worked in association with the Eastern Oppressed People's Association. In June 1930, their headquarters were raided by the British. Various leaders and activists of theirs, such as Zapuran Singh, Chanan Singh, Kartar Singh and Surjan Singh, were arrested, tried and deported.

Apart from direct British persecution, the Indian nationalist organizations were also subject to other troubles. One problem seems to have been factions and infighting within the community. One such quarrel led to the resignation of the editor of the *Ghadar Dhandora*, Tek Singh, and to the suspension of publication after 15 December 1931. Another problem was waning Chinese official support. According to a British intelligence report of 1932, the Eastern Oppressed People's Association in Nanjing had been deprived of its monthly subsidy from the Guomindang which gave financial difficulties as the reason. A bare living allowance for the main office-bearers was all that was given thereafter. These problems effectively stifled the activity of the organizations. According to the same intelligence report, the British authorities were choosing not to pursue too vigorously their campaign of arrests and deportation of Indians because 'the sedition movement at the present time has little vitality and it has seemed best not to provide it with any more martyrs'.[54]

THE THIRD PHASE

From 1931, the Japanese expansion onto the Asian mainland, beginning with its occupation of Manchuria, began to cast its long shadow on pan-Asian solidarity and the freedom movement among Indians in China. Until this time, Indian revolutionaries and nationalists in the Far East had sought and received sympathy and support from among both Chinese and Japanese, and there was no apparent contradiction in this. However, with the growth of Sino-Japanese hostility, any closeness to one of these countries on the part of Indian nationalists was viewed with suspicion by the other. Indian nationalists had to make a choice: either side with the Chinese in their struggle against Japanese aggression, or with the Japanese who seemed to be the only power in the East with the capacity to challenge the British empire in Asia. The choice was a difficult one, and led to divisions in the ranks of the nationalist Indians in China.

The rift in the Guomindang, which led to the ascendancy of the anti-communist faction around Chiang Kai-shek, and the subsequent toning down of the united, national revolutionary movement in China in the early 1930s, also affected the movement among the Indians and the support they had been receiving from prominent Chinese in the preceding period. The activities of the Comintern in China came to an abrupt end, even as the Chinese communists and other leftists were either killed, driven underground in the cities, or forced to flee to remote areas. Raja Mahendra Pratap expressed his anxiety about the domestic situation in China in a letter to the Chinese papers from Beijing in June 1932: 'It pains me to see that the forces of disruption are again active in this country. I cannot understand how is it possible that on one hand they can come to terms with the invading force but they cannot make peace with internal groups, they can think of re-establishing diplomatic relations with Russia but they cannot have friendly relations with the communists of China.' He ended with a suggestion which can only be considered amazing in the context of the times: 'I propose that we should try to found a Kuomintang-Communist-Congress (Indian) Party. This group will be able to bring all that internal and external peace that China needs.'[55]

It was the Japanese connection that eventually undid much of the goodwill that Mahendra Pratap had earlier built up in China. Mahendra Pratap was by no means as consistent a friend of Japan as, for instance, Rash Behari Bose. Nor did he decisively throw in his lot with the fortunes of the Japanese as Subhas Chandra Bose and his Indian Independence League did in the later stages of World War II. Nevertheless, the primacy he gave to 'Asiatic unity' as a step towards realizing his cherished dream of a 'World Federation' made him blind to the changing connotations of the concept of pan-Asianism, which was becoming the ideological bridgehead of Japanese expansionism in the 1930s and early 1940s. In the China of the 1930s, any variant of pan-Asianism left a bitter taste in the mouth, as the Chinese saw the Japanese armies cutting a vast swathe through the most flourishing eastern regions of their country. From the earlier charges he had had to face of being a 'Bolshevik agent', Mahendra Pratap began to be distrusted, if not outright reviled, as a Japanese 'puppet'.

In 1934, Mahendra Pratap, in conjunction with some Japanese of known militarist views, began a drive to collect volunteers for an 'Asiatic Army'. After attending the Japanese-sponsored Second Pan-Asiatic Conference at Dairen, he began his tour of China for the purposes of recruitment. The authorities of Canton arrested him on arrival. To Mahendra Pratap's great indignation, he was kept under armed guard for four days in a hospital ('though I was not ill'), after which he was unceremoniously placed on a cargo boat bound for Shanghai. In Shanghai, he was again arrested, but was released the following day due to the efforts of some friends. Mahendra Pratap chose to view this episode as a sign of the capitulation of the Guangdong authorities to British pressure from neighbouring Hong Kong, as well as a manifestation of a 'North-South struggle' (i.e. between the Nanjing and Guandong authorities). In a letter to the *Japan Times* of April 30, after he had returned to Japan, he admitted to being 'a little angry' over the reception he had received in China, but 'inclined to pity their foolishness' at not being able to 'see the salvation which our programme brings to all humanity'. A much less charitable attitude towards his activities, however, was taken by his critics in China. An article by Hollington K. Tong in the *China Press* of 18 March, Shanghai, roundly denounced 'this hodge-podge of ideas, these delusions of grandeur, this Pratapism, this unreal Asiatic army that is supposed to be under formation as a new weapon for the support of made-in-Japan Pan-Asianism.' The writer sarcastically claimed that

A zealous search is now being made in South China for a Chinese of some reputation to become a director of the Golden Corps of the Asiatic Army, another newly created instrument of Japanese aggression. Mahendra Pratap (Raja), a self-styled 'servant of mankind', has been commissioned by his Japanese colleagues to find three prominent Chinese to serve as army leaders. . . . His efforts have failed to produce a director for North or Central China, but undismayed, the 'Raja' is now trying his luck at Canton. . . . Pratap is . . . a puppet, not a prime mover and creator of the new idea that threatens to engulf modern civilization.[56]

Raja Mahendra Pratap was not daunted, and continued his visits to China in 1935 and 1936, and also tried to renew his contacts with 'old friends' like Sun Fo and Feng Yuxiang.[57] He also continued to try and explain why he believed that hostility to Japan was not in Chinese interests, for whoever was willing to listen: 'If any conflict occurs between Japan and China,' he said, 'a third country will probably come in to usurp whatever China has today. It would be suicidal for China and even for all Asia. The greatest problem which faces Oriental peoples today is to promote understanding between Japan and China.'[58]

Mahendra Pratap's views were diametrically opposed to those of another movement of Indians in China. The Indian Youth League openly denounced him and Japanese Pan-Asianism in meetings in various Chinese cities. The chairman of the League, Jara Singh, declared: 'In view of the fact that certain Indians are working hand in hand with and for the Japanese imperialists against Chinese national aspirations, and that we have often been reproached by our Chinese friends for this shameful behaviour of our countrymen, we have sounded the opinion of all Indians living in China prior to taking action against the unrepresentative elements. . . .' The League also issued a resolution that read:

We Indians living on Chinese soil have full sympathy with the Chinese toiling masses and fully support their heroic resistance to the Japanese imperialist exploitation and aggression in China. We are confident that the brave efforts of the Chinese masses to liberate their country from the yoke of all foreign exploiters who have reduced China to the state of a semi-colonial country would ere long be crowned with success. India herself is a colony of Great Britain and her fighting masses firmly believe that a cooperation between India and China would surely accelerate the emancipation of both countries from foreign yoke. Pratap can be loyal to Japanese imperialism or may have faith in the puppet ruler of Manchukuo, for it pays well, but we denounce this loyalty and faith as a treachery towards China and the Chinese masses whose hospitality and cordial relations towards us have become proverbial. It appears to us that the false servant of many loyalties did not in the least understand the teachings and principles of the late Dr. Sun Yat-sen, otherwise he would not have cited his name in the same breath in which he assures the world of his allegiance to the oppressors of China. Contrary to the advice of Pratap, the Indians not only do not support Japanese militarism and militarists whose intrigues and wire-pulling is responsible for the disintegration of China, but lodge energetic protest against Japanese aggression.[59]

The Japanese aggression against China was strongly denounced also by the Indian National Congress. 'Our attitude is one of complete opposition to Japanese aggression and of sympathy to China', declared Jawaharlal Nehru as President of the Congress.[60] The Congress organized various campaigns to demonstrate Indian solidarity with the war of the Chinese people, including the despatch of an Indian Medical Mission with the legendary Dr. Kotnis to China; Nehru himself visited Chongqing, the wartime capital, in 1939. Acccording to a US Government OSS report (1944) the Indian National Congress was the main political influence on the Indian community in China in the period before World War II.[61] However, from the available records, it is not clear to what extent this influence manifested itself in any organizational form within the Indian community before the War. By all accounts, Anand Mohan Sahay was the Indian nationalist in the Far East with the closest active connection with the Congress, but even he set up his pro-Congress organization in China—the Indian National Association of China—only in 1938. After just three years, when the Indian Independence League was reorganized under Japanese sponsorship, Sahay himself dissolved the Indian National Association and called on its members both in China and Japan to join the League under Rash Behari Bose (who later handed over the leadership to Subhas Chandra Bose in 1943).[62] Thus the trend that turned out to be the most influential and active among Indians in China at this time appears to have been the pro-Japanese trend represented by Subhas Chandra Bose and the Indian Independence League. This was corroborated by the report that the Agent General for India in China sent to the Government of India at New Delhi at the end of the War, in which he analysed that 'the entire Indian community in Shanghai could be called collaborationist.'[63]

Throughout the late 1930s, what the British called 'seditious' activities continued at a somewhat desultory pace. One of the leading activists among Shanghai Indians at this time was Usman Khan, who maintained contacts both with the Ghadar Party in San Francisco and with Rash Behari Bose and Anand Mohan Sahay in Japan, and received anti-British literature for distribution from them. He and some of his comrades were living under Japanese protection at Darroch Road north of Suzhou Creek, according to British intelligence reports. However, during the course of 1940, political activity among Indians seems to have picked up considerably. Sahay is reported to have visited Shanghai from Japan twice, and to have held a 'large meeting of the local Indians' on 4 August. At this stage, though, Sahay seems to have stressed non-violence and non-confrontation as a policy, and to have been interested mainly in recruitment and organizational development.[64]

Developments in the Indian community in China moved with lightning speed with the entry of Japan into the World War in 1941, the revitalization of the Indian Independence League, the fall of one place after another (including the European colonies such as Singapore and Hong Kong) to the Japanese army, and the arrival of Subhas Chandra Bose in Singapore in 1943. With Japanese support, the Indian Independence League in Shanghai and other places quickly assumed a prominent place in the life of the community. It is possible that not all the support it received from the community was entirely voluntary, given the conditions of wartime insecurity and Japanese occupation. A notice in the *Shanghai Times* of 22 January 1944, for instance, read: 'In order to make a complete official list, all Indian nationals who have not yet registered with the Indian Independence League are urgently requested to register before the end of the month, otherwise much inconvenience may arise to the defaulters.'[65] Nevertheless, given the strong army-policeman component within the Indian community, as well as the tradition of support for movements to overthrow the British domination of India by force of arms, it was not surprising that there was also real enthusiasm for the League and its armed wing, the Indian National Army, and for the venture to march on India's borders in the company of the advancing Japanese armies. It was not only the soldiers and policemen, but the merchant and business community as well, that gave strong support to the Indian Independence League and the Indian National Army.

The attitude of the Indians in Shanghai to the League was later described in the following words by Major B. Narayan Singh, the commander of the local branch of the INA.[66]

As there were variety of Indian faces, similarly there had been variety of different public opinion amongst Indians. But the majority—i.e. Sikhs— and a few from other provinces were in favour of joining our Indian Independence Movement. The Parsis at first were against any violent aggression or battle for India's freedom but later on they also started to show their voluntary cooperation and sympathies towards our movement. The Sindhies too opened out their treasuries for generous donations. The Sikhs in particular, including all sections from Majha, Malwa and Dwaba groups got together and offered not only themselves for services under Azad Hind Arzi Hukumat (Provisional Government of Free India) but also sacrificed their all in possession.

The Indian Independence League, which had its headquarters at 157 Peking Road in Shanghai, maintained an active programme. In June 1944 a Military Camp was established in Shanghai where volunteers for the Indian National Army, including the women's Rani Jhansi Regiment, were regularly drilled. An Azad Hind Club was also opened, for the use of all Indians. The League broadcast short-wave and long-wave programmes through two radio stations in Shanghai, and brought out two journals, *On to Delhi* in English, and *Chalo Delhi* in romanized Urdu. Once or twice a month, public meetings or functions were organized. The League also sought to become the main welfare organization among Indians in Shanghai, organizing relief measures, maintaining a record of deaths, organizing the sending of personal radio messages by Indians to their families in India, and so on. 'By such activities', wrote Major Narayan Singh, '. . . we managed to raise not only the moral and social status of all Shanghai settled Indians in general, but we brought about full confidence in our movement in our people and at the same time the status of our Indian brothers and sisters in general was also raised that drew also admiration from Chinese, Japanese, Germans and other then foreign diplomatic circles.'[67]

The functionaries of the League stressed its independence from the Japanese and its reliance on its own resources. Narayan Singh emphasized that Japanese help was slow in coming, and said that 'we were no puppets in the hands of any foreign power'. They insisted that it was financed entirely from the resources of the Indians in China themselves. On this sensitive matter, Harnam Singh, Vice-Chairman and Finance Member of the League in Shanghai, wrote:

Since Netaji's clarion call was sounded to the Indians living in East Asia for organizing themselves in battle lines, the local Indians, though poor and small in number have given over $5,000,000.00 for the Indian war-chest. Most of this money comes from the pockets of those poor people who had saved cent by cent during years of their residence in Shanghai and hard labor as watchmen. Some merchants have also followed their suits [*sic*].

There have been many instances when people have not only given whatever they possessed but have also left their jobs and enrolled as members of the Indian National Army. . . .

Voluntary contribution of such a big amount from such a poor class is not short of a miracle.[68]

In Tianjin, the number of Indians was relatively small, but they were organized with Japanese encouragement in a Tientsin Indian Residents' Association headed by a businessman, A. Bari. Bari later formed the local chapter of the Indian Independence

League, although apparently with some reluctance. At the end of the War he was accused by other Indians who had been interned by the Japanese, of having made good use of his services to the Japanese to benefit his business interests, as well as of having used funds belonging to the Association for lavishly entertaining Japanese military personnel.[69] In Hong Kong, Indians in large numbers are reported to have joined the Indian Independence League after the island was occupied by the Japanese. The local President of the League was Col. Dost Mohammed Khan, while a businessman named P.A. Krishna was its Secretary. Indian policemen in Hong Kong by and large remained on duty under the Japanese.[70]

The Chairman of the China Territorial Committee of the Indian Independence League was Jalal Rahman, formerly with the Indian National Association. The Chairman of the Shanghai branch was Lala Nanak Chand. In September 1944, Anand Mohan Sahay, described as 'Minister without Portfolio and Secretary General to the Government of Free India', visited Shanghai from Japan where he was based, on a fund-raising and recruitment tour. But the fervour among local Indians for the cause reached a crescendo when Subhas Chandra Bose visited Shanghai and Nanjing in December for a whirlwind visit, accompanied by A.C. Chatterjee, Colonel Kiany and H. Rahman Khan. Bose followed a hectic schedule in Shanghai, with his base at the Cathay Hotel on the Bund. He is reported to have held consultations with the local functionaries of the League till 1 a.m. of the day he arrived. On the following day, 2 December, he first inspected cadets of the INA Training Centre and reviewed a parade of INA volunteers. He also received members of the Indian community at his hotel, and held a press conference. That night he was the chief guest at a dinner hosted by the Japanese Consul-General. On 3 December, he took the salute of INA recruits from the terrace of the Pacific Hotel. At a packed gathering of the Indian community at the Grand Theatre, Subhas Chandra Bose spoke for one and a half hours continuously. In his speech, Bose emphasized the importance of the work being done by Indians in Shanghai, a city he described as the nerve-centre of communications in this part of the world. After playing the host at a tea party for Axis officials and some members of the Indian community, he carried on with meetings and discussions with League office-bearers and other Indians until late at night. He left Shanghai a day later than scheduled, on 5 December, due to bad weather which delayed his flight.[71]

Within a few months of Bose's visit, however, it was clear that Japan and the Axis powers were losing the war, and that the projected march into India had been irrevocably halted at Imphal. According to Sahay, Bose at this point sought collaboration with the USSR, and Sahay himself tried to get the help of leaders of the Chinese Communist Party to surrender to Soviet forces in Manchuria, although this did not materialize.[72] Bose was later killed in a plane crash before the formal surrender of Japan. Indians who were accused of collaboration with Japan, particularly League office-bearers and those in the police services, now felt the full force of retaliatory measures on the part of both the British and the Chinese authorities. They were rounded up, and detained in large numbers. The conditions faced by many of them in the jails was considered pitiable enough for the Indian embassy at Nanjing and the Consul at Shanghai to dole out relief in the form of money, food, and clothing. The Government of India Finance Department objected initially, saying that it was the responsibility of the Chinese Government to provide bare maintenance according to prison conventions, but eventually agreed to the provision of just that amount of relief 'as is in the Ambassador's opinion absolutely necessary in order to bring their condition to the same level as that of the prisoners in Indian jails'.[73]

An interesting footnote to the rather dismal end of the nationalist movement among Indians in China, in the midst of arrests and mass repatriations and accusations of collaborationism, is provided by Sahay's account of his own surrender to the Chinese General Lo Han who commanded the Chinese forces occupying Vietnam north of the 17th parallel. Sahay recounts the following exchange having taken place between himself and the General:

GENERAL LO HAN: What have you done to be arrested?

SAHAY: We fought against the British.

GENERAL: Did you fight against the Chinese?

SAHAY: Netaji asked us not to do so.

GENERAL: But you collaborated with our enemies, no?

SAHAY: Yes, that was the tragedy. We collaborated with your enemies and you collaborated with ours. But neither of us fought for them, did we?

The General was silent for a moment and then he laughed and said, 'you may go and live as free men or go away wherever you want. No Britisher can touch you within my territory, unless my Government asks me to hand you over to them.'[74]

NOTES

1. Cited in David Petrie, *Communism in India*, Calcutta, 1927, p. 190.
2. Cited in Sohan Singh Josh, *Hindustan Gadar Party: a Short History*, New Delhi: People's Publishing House, 1977, p. 193.
3. In the same article in the *United States of India*, June 1927, Tagore commented: 'The perpetrators of the tyranny that is doing havoc in China always keep themselves behind while the Indians who are being used as tools in carrying out their nefarious designs have to come in direct contact with the Chinese people. The result is that all their resentment and hatred are directed against the Indians so much that they call us demons.' Cited in Sohan Singh Josh, *Hindustan Ghadar Party*, vol. II, New Delhi: People's Publishing House, 1978, p. 261.
4. A background paper on 'Indian Minorities in South and East Asia: The Background of the Indian Independence Movement Outside India', prepared by the United States Government Office of Strategic Services (OSS) Research and Analysis Branch in September 1944 (R. & A. No. 1595), noted that whereas before World War II, 'there is no indication that the majority of those Indians [i.e. in the countries of South-East and East Asia] took any interest in Indian political problems', the situation in China was 'somewhat different'. Cited in Moti Lal Bhargava, *Netaji Subhas Chandra Bose in South-East Asia and India's Liberation War, 1943-45*, New Delhi: Vishwavidya Publishers, Appendix A, p. 196.
5. Harish K. Puri, *Ghadar Movement: Ideology, Organisation and Strategy*, Amritsar: Guru Nanak Dev University, 1983, p. 15.
6. Puri, *Ghadar Movement*, p. 37.
7. See ibid., pp. 38-59, for an account of their activities.
8. Cited in Horst Kruger, 'Indian Revolutionaries Abroad Before 1914', in *Challenge: A Saga of India's Struggle for Freedom*, New Delhi: People's Publishing House, 1984, p. 399.
9. Don Dignan, *The Indian Revolutionary Problem in British Diplomacy, 1914-1919*, New Delhi: Allied Publishers, 1983, p. 32-3.

10. Foreign & Political/Secret-War/June 1917, NAI, pp. 1-46.

11. Bhai Nahan Singh and Bhai Kirpal Singh, eds., *Struggle for Free Hindustan: Ghadar Directory (Punjab Section)*, vol. 4, *1913-15*, New Delhi: Gobind Sadan Institute for Advanced Studies in Comparative Religion, 1996, pp. 195-9.

12. *CO 129/422*, May 5, 1915, pp. 36-9; *CO 129/428*, 28 June, 1915, pp. 468-70.

13. *CO 129/410*, April 8, 1914, p. 286.

14. *CO 129/418*, March 1914, pp. 202-03.

15. *CO 129/424*, September 21, 1915, pp. 109-16.

16. Raja Mahendra Pratap, *My Life Story of Fifty Five Years (December 1886 to December 1941)*, Dehradun, 1941, p. 99. The following files of the *CO 129* series in the 1914-15 period are devoted to Bhagwan Singh: nos. 410, p. 413; 423, pp. 121-3; 427, pp. 388, 400, 422, 440, 447. See also Bhagwan Singh's own article, 'Two Rebels Meet', in *Rash Behari Basu: His Struggle for India's Independence*, ed. Radhanath Rath and Sabitri Prasanna Chatterjee, Calcutta, 1963, pp. 514-22, as well as references in Puri, *Ghadar Movement*, p. 50, and Sohan Singh Josh, *Hindustan Ghadar Party*, pp. 90-1.

17. *CO 129/410*, 8 April 1914, p. 280.

18. For a full account of the *Komagata Maru* episode, see Hugh Johnston, *The Voyage of the Komagata Maru: The Sikh Challenge to Canada's Colour Bar*, New Delhi: Oxford University Press, 1979.

19. See Sho Kuwajima, *Indian Mutiny in Singapore (1915)*, Calcutta: Ratna Prakashan, 1991, pp. 25-6.

20. Puri, *Ghadar Movement*, p. 92.

21. Dignan, *Indian Revolutionary Problem*, p. 31.

22. Letter from Chakravarty to Berlin, dated 5 September 1916. This letter was produced as evidence at the trial of various Ghadar Party leaders and activists which began at San Francisco in November 1917. It mentioned that Sun Yat-sen, unlike certain other Chinese leaders sympathetic with the Indian revolutionaries' schemes, was reluctant to have China drawn into the War on the German side. Cited in G.T. Brown, 'Hindu Conspiracy and the Neutrality of the U.S.A. (1914-1917)', unpublished M.A. thesis, University of California, Berkeley, California. Microfilm in National Archives of India (NAI), Acc. No. 1241(Part)), pp. 67-9.

23. 'German Indian Scheme in the Far East', Foreign and Political/Secret-War/June 1917, NAI, p. 42.

24. Cited in Dignan, *Indian Revolutionary Problem*, p. 110.

25. *CO 129/429*, 17 July 1915, pp. 374-6.

26. An Indian clerk in the Hong Kong Public Works Department, Inayat Ullah Mirza, was suspected of being in league with the well-known Indian revolutionary Barkatullah, but since the evidence against him was scanty, he was accused of improper financial dealings and compelled to resign his job and go back to India. *CO 129/424*, 3 Sept. 1915, pp. 19-21.

27. *CO 129/*423, 13 Aug. 1915, pp. 486-501.
28. *CO 129/*429, pp. 368-9, 377.
29. *CO 129/*437, 9 Oct. 1916, pp. 599-603; *CO 129/*438, 18 Oct. 1916, pp. 531-3.
30. Petrie, *Communism in India,* p. 190.
31. See Josh, *Hindustan Ghadar Party,* pp. 259-61, for Indian reactions to the 30th May and subsequent events.
32. Petrie, *Communism in India,* p. 191.
33. Cited in Petrie, *Communism in India,* p. 189.
34. Josh, *Hindustan Ghadar Party,* p. 260.
35. Mahendra Pratap, *My Life Story,* pp. 102-3.
36. Petrie, *Communism in India,* pp. 206-7.
37. See Josh, *Hindustan Ghadar Party,* pp. 261-4.
38. Petrie, *Communism in India,* p. 217, 208. The extract from the *China Weekly Review* is cited in the OSS report reproduced in Bhargava, *Netaji Subhas Chandra Bose,* p. 221. See also Josh, *Hindustan Ghadar Party,* p. 268.
39. Raja Mahendra Pratap was one of the prominent Indian nationalists in exile in the period from World War I until his return to India in 1946. Son of a zamindar of Aligarh district, UP, he went abroad in connection with his political activities to Germany in 1914. From there he went on to Turkey and then to Afghanistan. There, with the support of King Amanullah, he set up a 'Provisional Government of Free India' with himself as President and Maulana Barkatullah as Prime Minister. About this step, he later wrote: 'My only idea was that if our Provisional Government of India could reach Delhi at the head of the victorious troops we could call a general meeting of the Congress and ask her to form a regular Government of India.' *My Life Story,* pp. 149-50. He travelled extensively, mainly in the United States and the Far East, engaging in various activities aimed at mobilizing support in those countries for India's freedom from British rule. The British would not let him return to India until 1946. From the 1930s, the idea of building a World Federation occupied as much, or even more, of his time and energies. In the course of his years abroad, he made about 10 visits to China, of duration ranging from a few days to nearly two years in 1931-3. A maverick among political personalities, who constantly stressed the theme of unity among Indians and among Asians, he sometimes chose to style himself as 'M. Peter, Peer, Pratap Singh-Khan (Raja), Servant of Mankind'.
40. Mahendra Pratap, *My Life Story,* p. 122.
41. Ibid., p. 105.
42. Ibid., p. 129.
43. Ibid., pp. 142-8.
44. It is not clear whether this episode had something to do with the growing estrangement between Mahendra Pratap and his former comrades among the Ghadar activists. Given the Raja's eclectic views and his increasing

obsession with his vision of building a 'World Federation', a break between them appears to have been inevitable. Later Mahendra Pratap described the estrangement in the following words: 'We confess we did not understand our own affinities. We all along believed that the most radical sections of our society should be the most generous to us. We met Comrade Lenin. We like him too! Then why do not the communists come forward to help us? But they would not! And in the royal camp where we are nothing short of renegades we find friends! We have decided we shall no longer insist on our connections with the so-called radical element. It appears to us they care little for universal welfare. They have developed too narrow party feelings. We shall henceforth move with those who care to move with us. . . .' Citation from a purported statement of Raja Mahendra Pratap circulated by the Indian Youth League in Shanghai, in *China Press*, Shanghai, of 18 March 1934. Scrapbook no. II, S. No. 33, Raja Mahendra Pratap Collection, NAI.

45. Petrie, *Communism in India*, p. 207.

46. See Mahendra Pratap, *My Life Story*, pp. 198-205, 233.

47. See Ibid., *My Life Story*, p. 209. According to the OSS report of the U.S.Government, 'Expenses of the Indian organization are alleged to have been paid by donations from Chinese friends and members of the Kuomintang. On the whole, the Indians in Shanghai were too poor to contribute large sums to the movement, though they gave what they could afford.' OSS R&A No. 1595, reproduced in Bhargava, *Netaji Subhas Chandra Bose*, p. 222. The OSS report, on p. 221, suggests that Jawaharlal Nehru was a moving force behind the founding of the Eastern Oppressed People's Association. This does not seem to be likely in view of the letter from Nehru to the Secretary of the Association of June 1928, reproduced in vol. II, no. 15 of the *Hindustan Ghadar Dhandora*, in which he wrote: 'Raja Mahendra Pratap writes to us from Nanking mentioning your association. It will give us great pleasure to keep in touch with you and to correspond with you. We have a great deal in common in our subjects and I have no doubt that knowledge of and contact with each other will be of help to both of us. I shall be glad if you will kindly send me full information about your association. I should like to know specially what your objects are, what kind of work you are doing and how long has your association been in existence. A reply giving the information will be greatly appreciated.' Acc. No. 316, S. No. 1, Raja Mahendra Pratap Collection, Newspapers, NAI.

48. Petrie, *Communism in India*, p. 210. OSS, R&A No. 1595, reproduced in Bhargava, *Netaji Subhas Chandra Bose*, p. 222.

49. Petrie, *Communism in India*, pp. 211-12.

50. Ibid., pp. 214, 219.

51. Mahendra Pratap, *My Life Story*, p. 201.

52. Acc. No. 316, S. No. 1, Raja Mahendra Pratap Collection, Newspapers, NAI.

53. OSS, R&A No. 1595, reproduced in Bhargava, *Netaji Subhas Chandra Bose*, p. 223.

54. 'Activities of Indians in China', Foreign and Political/1932/F. No.139-X (Secret), NAI.

55. Letter of 19 June, 1932. Raja Mahendra Pratap Collection, Scrapbook no. 1 (no serial number), NAI.

56. See the references to this episode in Scrapbook I, S. No. 108; Scrapbook II, S. Nos. 23 (i), 33, 26 (i), 26 (ii), 27, Raja Mahendra Pratap Collection, NAI.

57. Scrapbook II, S. No. 79, Raja Mahendra Pratap Collection, NAI.

58. Article in *The Japan Adventurer*, 18 March 1934. Scrapbook II, S. No. 26 (i), Raja Mahendra Pratap Collection, NAI.

59. S. No. 26 (ii), Scrapbook II, Raja Mahendra Pratap Collection, NAI.

60. Cited in Lin Chengjie, 'Friends in Need: Comradeship between Chinese and Indians in their Common Struggle in Modern History', in Tan Chung, ed., *Indian Horizons* Special Issue: India and China, vol. 43, nos. 1-2, 1994, p. 51.

61. OSS, R&A No. 1595, reproduced in Bhargava, *Netaji Subhas Chandra Bose*, pp. 196, 220-1.

62. OSS, R&A No. 1595, reproduced in Bhargava, *Netaji Subhas Chandra Bose*, p. 228. See also Anand Mohan Sahay, *Indian Revolutionaries in Japan*, transcript in Nehru Memorial Museum & Library, New Delhi, pp. 7-10, for his own account of the establishment and dissolution of the Indian National Association in China. Moti Lal Bhargava, in *Indian National Congress and its Affiliates in South and East Asia*, op. cit., also does not give more concrete evidence of any other Congress-sponsored organizational activity among Indians in China before 1941.

63. Cited in Bhargava, *Indian National Congress*, p. 31.

64. The six-monthly report on Indians by the British intelligence in Shanghai for the period ending 31 March 1940 concluded that 'seditious activities have been negligible'. However, the next such report, for the period ending on 30 September assessed that 'during this period there has been considerably greater activity in the Indian community in Shanghai than normal'. External Affairs Dept/External Branch/1940/F. No. 424-X(Secret), NAI.

65. Cited in OSS, R&A No. 1595, reproduced in Bhargava, *Netaji Subhas Chandra Bose*, p. 198.

66. Major B. Narayan Singh, 'Memoirs and INA Activities in Shanghai, China', 10 October 1949. Acc. No. 205, F. No. 10, Indian Independence League Papers, NAI, p. 1. Major Narayan Singh was possibly the same as the erstwhile President of Eastern Oppressed People's Association in 1927-8. See Petrie, *Communism in India*, p. 206.

67. Maj. Narayan Singh, p. 4. See also the corpus of Indian Independence

League Papers relating to activities in China (Acc. No. 205) in the National Archives of India, for an idea of the kinds of activities organized by the League.

68. Harnam Singh in *On to Delhi*, vol. 1, no. 5, December 1944, p. 12, Indian Independence League Papeers, Acc. No. 205, F. No. 8, IIL, NAI. See Claude Markovits, *The Global World*, pp. 228-30, for the involvement of Sindhi merchants overseas with the activities of the INA and the India Independence League. Markovits writes that 'the alignment of some Sindwork merchants with Subhas Bose in the Far East had more to do with preserving their own life and livelihood than with deep-seated pro-Japanese sympathies, though this does not rule out the possibility that some of them had a strong commitment to Indian independence'. At the same time, Sindhi merchants had increasingly close business connections with the Japanese in the inter-war years, with many of them playing a crucial role in the marketing of Japanese textiles in East and South-East Asia.

69. See Bhargava, *Indian National Congress*, pp. 35-7 for an account of Bari's activities and the affairs of Tianjin Indian residents.

70. Bhargava, *Indian National Congress*, pp. 38-40.

71. This account of Bose's visit to Shanghai is based on the report in *On to Delhi*, vol. 1, no. 5, December 1944, op. cit., pp. 1-3.

72. Sahay, *Indian Revolutionaries*, p. 31.

73. Cited in Bhargava, *Indian National Congress*, p. 35.

74. Sahay, *Indian Revolutionaries*, p. 32.

CHAPTER 8

Exodus

Jobless, penniless and friendless in a faraway land of fantastic prices
is a dreadful situation. Viewed from whatever angle, the future looks
dismal. . . .

S. Narain Singh, Nanjing, Sept. 1949[1]

Three major streams of migration—of the merchant in eastern
China, the merchant in Xinjiang, and of the member of the
security services—have been identified as making up the basic
profile of the Indian population in China in the nineteenth and
early twentieth centuries. In their origins, these three streams
were quite distinct. But at the end these separate streams in a
very real sense merged together. War and political turbulence,
along with the shrinking of the economic space which had
nurtured the Indian community in China, led to a mass exodus
of the Indians from the Chinese mainland. Soldiers and shopkeepers, businessmen and watchmen, policemen and moneylenders, clambered on board ships and planes or joined overland
caravans, in a precipitate withdrawal, in many cases pulling up
the roots of a lifetime. The completeness of the exodus was quite
unique in the history of the Indian diaspora.

The exodus began somewhat earlier in western China. The
reasons for this were two-fold. In the first place, the rebellions
and civil war in Xinjiang, which disrupted trade and threatened
the lives and property of Indians, began in the early 1930s.
Second, the governor of the province, as the British were to
complain, was clearly indifferent to Britain's status as an ally of
China during World War II when it came to dealing with the

Indian subjects of the British empire in his own province.[2]

In eastern China, it was the Japanese assault on Shanghai that began in September 1937 which dealt the first major blow to the fortunes of the Indians there. By November, three Indians were reported dead, seven were missing and twenty-one were wounded as a result of the Japanese bombardment and the fighting around the International Settlement.[3] Public opinion in India began to express anxiety over the fate of the Indians in Shanghai, and the Government of India was forced to answer questions on this account in the Legislative Assembly.[4] It made arrangements for the repatriation to Calcutta of a large number of Indians, especially women and children. About 900 persons set sail for India on board the *Elephanta* as early as 10 September 1937. In addition, a refugee camp for Indians was set up at Laichikop in Hong Kong which at that time was still outside the theatre of hostilities.

The position of Indians in Japanese-occupied China, as well as in Hong Kong after it fell to the Japanese, was a paradoxical one. On the one hand, the Japanese professed friendship for the Indians and support for the Indian struggle for freedom and so Indians as a whole were not interned during the War, in contrast to the British and many other nationalities in China and Southeast Asia. Nevertheless, Indian livelihoods were severely affected by the Japanese occupation. Normal trading was completely disrupted. In many cases, the bank assets of these families were frozen, and their goods stockpiled in godowns were confiscated.[5] A news despatch from Hong Kong to the *Statesman* of 25 April 1943, noted that 'Indian merchants are selling out their stock and then prepare to run away. All big business are in Japanese hands under the motto of "East Asia Co-Prosperity" which is shared by Indians and Chinese in name only.'[6] A member of a prominent Indian business family who had been in Hong Kong during the occupation described the Japanese attitude towards Indians at that time as 'honey on the tongue, dagger in the heart'.[7] The business families who remained in the Japanese-occupied territories were able to manage by living off their assets, selling jewellery, and so on. However, the condition of small-time merchants and those dependent on the British establishment for their livelihood was more precarious. Initially, they received some kind of relief payments through the Swiss, who represented the interests of Indians in China on behalf of the British. But in 1944, the Japanese terminated these payments, saying that they did not recognize British authority over India or the Swiss right to make payments to Indians on their behalf. A large number of Indians lived from hand to mouth during the war years. Making a report on the condition of Indians in Shanghai just after the conclusion of the War, the Indian Agent-General in China claimed that 'hundreds of Indians are in dire distress, and many are so emaciated that they cannot stand another Shanghai winter'.[8]

During the War, a certain number of Hong Kong Indians managed to make their way home to India via west and south-west China. These areas remained under the control of the Government of China throughout the War, and the British and Americans also had a diplomatic or military presence there. A British official despatch of January 1943 noted about the Japanese on Hong Kong that 'while they do very little to assist the Indian population in Hong Kong they probably do not do very much to prevent them from getting out'.[9] However U.S. Chellaram, who escaped from Hong Kong with his family members via this route, recalled that they had to resort to subterfuge to get to western China. The family had to pretend that they were leaving Hong Kong just for a holiday in Vietnam, and packed their baggage accordingly. They reached Chongqing after undergoing considerable tension and difficulty, only to find that their troubles were not over. The British embassy denied them assistance to get to India and they had to make their way to Guilin. From there they secured an air passage for their party to Calcutta only with the help of a colonel of the US Army stationed there.[10] British official reports admitted that most of the Indian refugees from Hong Kong were in bad condition, with as many as eighteen out of the twenty-four in Guilin in March 1943 being sick and exhausted from the cold and privations suffered by them.[11] Air transport for non-military personnel was scarce during the War years and many escapees had to undergo a lengthy wait until something could be arranged for them, even though most were willing to pay for their passage. The Sindhi merchants association in Hyderabad, Sindh, complained that the delay in repatriation was largely responsible for the 'extremely miserable' conditions of their compatriots stranded in China. The British military authorities in Chongqing, however, claimed that they were doing all they could and that they had spent 4,00,000 Chinese Nationalist dollars for the maintenance and transport of 230 Indian civilian refugees in 1943. By the end of March 1944, they were able to claim with some relief that only six Indian refugees remained to be airlifted from Kunming.

The major exodus of Indians from China, however, took place just after the conclusion of the War. While the condition of the large number of Indians in Chinese jails awaiting trial as 'collaborationists' was wretched, that of the majority of other Indians in Shanghai and other places was not much better. With the winding up of the International Settlement at Shanghai and the taking over of its functions by the Shanghai Municipality, most of the Indian policemen and watchmen found themselves with no jobs and with virtually no prospects of finding any. 'Apart from Chinese nationalism', reads the report sent to the External Affairs Department at Delhi on their conditions, 'the methods employed by the Sikhs, however efficient, and their money-lending propensities, have rendered them odious to the Chinese.'[12] Several hundred Indians who had earlier been employed in the International Settlement had, during the War, managed to secure employment in the US Army and its Auxiliary Military Police. However, by the end of 1946, most of these persons too had been discharged.[13] The Government of India sanctioned a sum of Rs. 50 per head as relief to needy Indians in China, about a third of the amount sanctioned for British nationals. Attempts to distribute it through a committee of the Indians themselves proved to be immensely difficult on account of the sharp political polarization that had taken place during the War and the atmosphere of mutual recriminations among Indians. 'It is difficult to imagine a community more divided against itself', commented the Indian envoy K.P.S. Menon during his visit to Shanghai.[14]

Claiming that it was necessary in order to avoid mass destitution, the Government of India embarked on a programme of mass repatriation of Indians from China, starting at the end of 1945. Repatriation was to be voluntary, but the Indians were made to understand in clear terms that the offer to provide free passage back to India would not be open indefinitely, and that if they failed to take advantage of it, the Government of India would not assume further responsibility for their condition. Accordingly, hundreds of families in great haste gathered up whatever they could of their belongings, many acquired after a lifetime in China, and boarded ships bound for an India where too an uncertain future awaited them—an altogether 'pathetic sight', as K.P.S. Menon described it in his diary.[15]

Between November and December 1945, 1,159 Indians were repatriated from Shanghai, in batches averaging between 100 and 200 per ship. Some of those repatriated were under a cloud for being 'collaborationists' and were put under close watch. There was a fair amount of chaos involved in the entire process of getting the repatriates back to their homes. The passengers frequently showed their resentment about inadequate arrangements, especially regarding food. Moreover, a multiplicity of authorities in China and India, ill-prepared to deal with an exodus of this kind, often ended up working at cross-purposes.[16] The process of repatriation continued at a feverish pace through to the end of 1946.

The panic-stricken manner in which the Indians departed from China, which was due in no small measure to the way in which the British organized repatriation, amounted to a sort of burning of bridges, effectively cutting off the possibility of return. Later, the reorganization of the Chinese economy under the leadership of the communists, which greatly restricted the scope for private enterprise particularly on the part of foreigners, offered little inducement to those businessmen who had uprooted themselves to consider returning. A few Indians stayed back, but after 1949, virtually nothing remained on the Chinese mainland of the community that traced its origins back to the late eighteenth century.[17]

NOTES

1. Narain Singh had been in charge of the security guards at the Indian Embassy at Nanjing. This is an excerpt from his letter to K.P.S. Menon, then Foreign Secretary of the Government of India, dated 9 September 1949. MEA/1949/ F. No. 826-CJK/49 (Sec.), National Archives of India (NAI).
2. See Chapter 4 for an account of the exodus and deportation of Indians in Xinjiang.
3. EAD/1937/146(3)-X (Secret), NAI.

4. Among the legislators who raised questions on this subject were M. Ananthasayanam Ayyangar, T.S. Avinashilingam Chettiar, Seth Govind Das, G.S. Motilal, Mohan Lal Saksena and S. Satyamurti.

5. Interview with Ruby Master, formerly of the firm Pavri & Sons, Hong Kong, April 1997.

6. EAD/Extl Branch/1943/452-X, NAI.

7. Interview with U.S. Chellaram, Hong Kong, 9 April 1997.

8. Report of K.P.S. Menon to Secretary, External Affairs Department of the Government of India, 8 October 1945. EAD/Far Eastern Branch/1945/ F. No. 762(62)-F.E. /45, NAI.

9. EAD/Extl Branch/452-X, NAI.

10. Interview with U.S. Chellaram, Hong Kong, April 1997.

11. EAD/1943/452-X, NAI.

12. EAD/Far Eastern Branch/1945/F. No. 762(62)-F.E. /45, NAI.

13. EAD/1946/573-CA/46(Secret), NAI.

14. EAD/Far Eastern Branch/1945/F. No.762(62)-F.E./45, NAI.

15. K.P.S. Menon's personal diary for 1945, entry dated 5 December, K.P.S. Menon Papers, deposited at the Nehru Memorial Museum & Library, New Delhi.

16. See EAD/1946/573-CA/46(Secret), NAI.

17. A few Indians, some of them with Chinese wives and families, stayed on in Shanghai, but the events of the Cultural Revolution impelled even these survivors to leave the mainland. The last Indian in Shanghai left in 1971. The last three Indian traders left Xinjiang in 1951. I am grateful to T.C.A. Rangachari of the Ministry of External Affairs and R.D. Sathe, former Consul-General of India at Kashgar, for this information.

CHAPTER 9

Conclusion

This study arose from a sense of dissatisfaction with the generally prevalent portrayal of the history of Sino-Indian relations as an inexplicable plunge from the 'golden age' of peaceful relations based on Buddhism to the dark days of tension and war in the recent past. That version left too many gaps and too many un-answered questions, and what exactly happened between India and China in the colonial era appeared particularly to be a blind spot among scholars and historians. The lack of interest in the fact that there were Indian résidents in China in this period seemed to me to be symptomatic of the problem. It was felt that an investigation into this community and its experiences could help to throw light on certain obscured but perhaps significant aspects of the Sino-Indian relationship.

One of the most important developments in the nineteenth century was the gradual transformation in the image or per-ception of India among the Chinese, and the activities of Indians in China without doubt contributed to this. Until that time, all the evidence goes to show that Chinese continued to have a generally positive if somewhat nebulous image of India, as the so-called 'Heavenly Kingdom' of ancient times. However thereafter, as the Chinese became familiar with the progress of the British conquest of India, the image began to change to that of a subjugated, ruined, country (*wangguo*)—a country, moreover, whose people were either being used as pawns by their foreign rulers against other countries and peoples, or else who cynically used the protection afforded by the British connection to further their own interests at the expense of other peoples.[1]

This image (the 'ugly Indian') is not unique to Indians in China, but has equally dogged the perception of Indians in several other countries where Indian communities were established under colonial auspices. It has been commented upon, not without some despair, by several scholars and analysts of the Indian diaspora. I.J. Bahadur Singh trenchantly characterized the Indian emigrants of the colonial period in the following words:

As menials or camp followers of a colonial power, the Indians did not endear themselves to the indigenous peoples. . . . The overseas Indian of the colonial era stood in marked contrast to the Indian immigrant of yore. He was no longer a member of a master race constantly extending the frontier of its political and cultural domain. He was, on the other hand, an indentured labourer (a virtual slave), or a petty trader, a government clerk or a policeman. He maintained his exclusiveness and had little more than formal or business-like dealings with the native peoples. A member of a subject race, he was manipulated by his colonial master and his own primary interest lay in his own sustenance and economic mobility within the constraints of the colonial system.[2]

Niharranjan Roy elaborated on this image of the Indian expatriate when he wrote, 'Where Indians went as traders and professionals, they minted money but did little to promote native welfare and advancement. Unlike the Chinese traders, Indian traders did not plough back their profits into their trade or invest in industry, but repatriated them to India.'[3]

The study of Indians in China in the colonial period confirms the conclusions of these and other scholars and observers of the Indian diaspora in some major respects. Nevertheless, it also suggests that the picture was not so clear-cut, that the character and complexion of this community was much more complex than the widely accepted image would suggest. At the very least, one could say that this image was not true of all sections of Indians in all parts of China throughout the period under review.

In the first place, it would not be correct to view the trade between India and China in this period as a mere offshoot of the British economic presence in China. Trade-based direct interaction between Indians and Chinese was not new to the colonial period. There had been a long tradition of Indian traders travelling to China and conducting their business there. There was, it is true, a hiatus in this form of commercial interaction for a couple of centuries due to various historical developments. Nevertheless, it showed signs of reviving from the earlier part of the eighteenth century, well before opium became an item of consequence in the trade and before the British began their efforts to systematically demolish the foreign trading system of the Chinese empire and to recast it on their own terms. Keeping this in mind, it can perhaps be said that Indian trade with China in the colonial period, while undergoing a metamorphosis and becoming subordinated to the mechanism of Britain's 'unequal' trade with China, had nevertheless an independent origin and basis of its own.

This was best seen in the trade with Xinjiang. In the nineteenth century, this was still the traditional trade—based on largely traditional items and forms of exchange—continuing even under conditions of colonial rule in India. This is not to say that the traditional trade was an entirely smooth affair with no friction between the Indians and the people they had to deal with in Xinjiang. Yet it is obvious that the status of Indian merchants, and their image in Chinese eyes, underwent a transformation once they became the subjects of a belligerent Britannia. As the experience of the Indian traders in Xinjiang in the later nineteenth and early twentieth centuries shows, once they became factors in the British political and diplomatic forward thrust in this part of the world, it was hard for the Chinese to regard them as just carriers of exotic commodities dependent on the goodwill shown to them by their hosts. Moreover, the traditional institutional arrangements that had facilitated the conduct of trade and the resolution of minor problems that arose in the course of this trade, began to break down under British pressure. The Chinese authorities in Xinjiang did not yield without a fight, but eventually they had to agree to the relinquishment of their authority in vital respects over the Indian traders in their midst.

It is true that many Indian traders actively sought the 'benefit' of British imperial protection. However, when it was extended to them, this protection turned out to be a double-edged sword. It did not substantially help them in their trade, particularly in the face of Russian competition. What is more, it prejudiced the local authorities against them, particularly in the twentieth century when resurgent Chinese national pride made anything with the smell of extra-territoriality unpalatable to the Chinese. The relative harshness with which they were treated there in the 1930s and 1940s was at least partially a reaction to their redefined roles in modern times.

The situation was different in eastern China. Here the British commercial and political-military presence was undoubtedly beneficial, even crucial. The kind of fortunes made by the Bombay-based China traders and the Hong Kong-based tycoons would have been unthinkable without it. However in the long run this association harmed the prospects of these Indian businessmen in China. So great was their dependence on the British imperialist presence that the possibility of Indians maintaining a presence in mainland China on their own strength and doing business with the Chinese once the British had to wind up their affairs, was not seriously considered.[4]

The image of the overseas Indian businessmen in this period as 'petty traders' who repatriated all their profits, failed to reinvest their profits in trade and industry, and did not give anything back to the host society, is rather easily contradicted in the case of some of the more prominent Indian business families in Hong Kong. On the other hand, for those at the other end of the commercial spectrum—the small shopkeepers, retail merchants and service-providers, who constituted the majority—earning a livelihood was the main issue, and they probably did not make enough profit to think in terms either of investing in larger enterprises or of philanthrophy. At the same time, unlike their counterparts in parts of East Africa and South-East Asia in this period, the Indians in China did not have a monopoly or anything near a monopoly in the trade and distribution networks of the areas in which they operated. Hence, they did not pose a significant threat or obstacle to the livelihood of the local people or incur resentment on that account. A possible exception would be the case of the Indian moneylenders in southern Xinjiang, against whom there was considerable resentment. At the same time, in Xinjiang, the pattern of Indian social exclusivity or aloofness from the local population—which appears to have been pronounced in eastern China—was not so apparent. A significant proportion of Indians who went to Xinjiang appear to have settled down there, married local women and adapted to Turki language and customs. Many became landowners, even accepting Chinese nationality in the process.

Perhaps the most dramatic way in which Indians in China were an exception to the general pattern of overseas Indians was in the extent and manner of their politicization—specifically, of their mobilization in the fight against British imperialism. Although Indians in China fell into the category of economic migrants rather than political exiles or refugees, their story highlights the need to guard against taking these labels too literally. It shows that it is wrong to assume *a priori* that economic migrants can be moved only by economic considerations and are hence, by derivation, apolitical in character.

If this story of Indians in China is in one sense a study of how colonialism and imperialism affected the relations between India and China, it also provides an illustration of how nationalism conditioned and moulded these relations. Personally, one of the more exciting aspects of my investigations into the Indian community in China was discovering how actively it responded to and participated in the currents of nationalism and anti-imperialism that swept India, China, and Asia in general in the twentieth century. As a community of largely economic migrants, small in size and very dependent for their livelihood and status on the imperialist presence in China, the Indian community in China was politically active and anti-imperialist to a surprising degree. Here we are not talking of the activities of a few political exiles, but of the involvement of a substantial section of the community as a whole, and particularly of the ordinary soldier and policeman—that pillar of British interests in China. Beginning with the soldiers that were sent out to crush the Taiping rebels, Indians exhibited again and again a tendency to turn against the colonial master. There are few parallels in the history of the Indian overseas communities to the repeated challenge offered by Indians in China in the twentieth century to British authority. The real danger to British authority from the nationalism manifest among these Indians came from the fact that it was mass-based and rooted chiefly in the personnel of the army and police forces, of which there was a much higher proportion in China than among overseas Indians in any other country. This meant, first, that a major prop of British interests in China—the Indian soldiers and policemen—was rendered unreliable in crucial periods; second, that guns meant for use against enemies of the British Empire could be and were turned against the British themselves; and third, that disaffection could and did spread like lightning along lines of kinship and social ties, as well as along the network fostered by the military organization itself, all the way from North America to China to South-East Asia to India, and in the reverse direction.

The story of the nationalist and anti-imperialist activities of Indians in China is significant because to some extent it redeemed the Indians in Chinese eyes and belied their image as 'slaves' doing the bidding of their imperialist masters. It also shows that the bonds between the Indian and Chinese national movements were not limited to the declarations of goodwill and friendship of a few leaders. They also took the form of comradeship in the field, as Indian soldiers and policemen refused to fire on the Chinese, and Chinese political figures afforded protection and support to Indian nationalists hounded by the British authorities. The participation of Indians in China, and particularly those of the security forces, in the struggle against British imperialism—often in direct collaboration with Chinese nationalists—opened up very real possibilities for reversing the stereotype of the Indian emigrant as a tool of imperialist interests who had no place in a China free from imperialist domination. It could have served them as a protective shield when triumphant Chinese nationalism after the revolution of 1949 led to the expulsion of the interests of Britain and other imperialist powers. However, this was not to be. In the complicated politics of World War II, it was Britain that was an ally of China. Indian nationalists in China, even if not all of them, sought the patronage of Japan, the enemy of China. The end of the War found the Indians divided, demoralized and unwelcome as 'collaborationists'. Thus nationalism, which had helped to offset some of the negative image of Indians as servants of imperialism, found Indians and Chinese once more on opposite sides of the fence in the last years of the period under review, just when the new states of post-colonial India and post-Revolution China were about to emerge. The consequences of this are worth pondering over.

Thus, one legacy of the Indian community in China, certainly, was its impact on the Chinese image or perception of India and the Indians. It is also worthwhile to consider the impact of these Indians on *India*. Markovits has observed with great insight that the movement of Indians outside India in the modern era is better understood as circulation rather than migration.[5] In other words, particularly in the period under consideration, the great majority of Indians who went abroad returned to their homeland after a term abroad. Even though a certain number did settle down overseas, the majority went with the aim not of making a new life for themselves in a different country, but of improving the conditions of their kin at home. From this it follows that the question of how they contributed to, or integrated with, their host society may not be as appropriate as the question of how their sojourn abroad affected their own families, their own localities or regions in India. In this context, what is surprising is that, despite their small number in proportion to the population as a whole, the China-based or China-returned Indians did leave some imprint on their own country.

Jacques Downs has explained this phenomenon in general terms:

Under almost any circumstances people far from their homes behave differently from more sedentary folk. They also are changed by their experience. When they return to their place of origin, they often carry back in their luggage strange ideas, tastes and perspectives. They are marginal, not quite fully integrated into any culture, but they sometimes show great capacity for changing things, both at home and abroad.[6]

We have already seen how Indians in China were distinguished by their involvement in radical nationalist politics. It could be argued that it was the experience of racial discrimination in the US, Canada and other 'white' countries, rather than anything particular in their experience in China, that turned so many of the Indians in China around the time of the first World War into supporters of the Ghadar Party. It could also be argued that they were just carried along by the prevailing currents of opinion in India in their times, and did not influence them in any significant way. Nevertheless, both at the time of World War I and during World War II, the existence of a strong base of 'sedition' and armed revolt among Indians in China caused the British no little anxiety. The heightened political activity within the Indian community in the late 1920s in particular could be attributed to the effect of the heady climate of anti-imperialism in China in those years, over and above the effect of any developments within the nationalist movement in India.

Yet perhaps the most lasting impact of the Indians in China on their home country could be seen in the growth and development of Bombay.[7] Bombay grew as the premier commercial city of India in the nineteenth century, displacing Calcutta from this position, largely on the basis of the trade with China. It is no coincidence that in this period the wealthiest and most prominent business families of Bombay were almost all connected with this trade and counted several 'old China hands' among their members. Jamsetjee Jejeebhoy, the Tatas, the Petits, the Camas, the Sassoons and many others, were not only prominent China merchants, but their names are intimately linked with the building of Bombay, as reflected in the numerous buildings, roads and institutions in that city that bear their names. The capital accumulated by these 'merchant princes' through the China trade was moreover instrumental in establishing the earliest textile mills in the country, which in turn marked the beginnings of modern industry, indigenously owned and promoted, in India. When the cotton cloth the early millowners produced could not compete with the imported British cloth, it was but natural, given their background and familiarity with the China market, that they switched over mainly to the production of cotton yarn for which there was a demand in China. By the 1880s, as much as 80 per cent of the output of this industry was absorbed by the Chinese market. It is only with the gradual displacement of Indian cotton yarn in the Chinese market first by the Japanese in the early twentieth century, and later by the Chinese manufactured product, that the vital connection between the economy of Bombay and China, that had begun with the trade in raw cotton and opium, weakened. Yet it would come as a surprise to most Indians, even to most Mumbaikars, to learn that the growth of Bombay was so intimately linked with China, and with those who set out from its shores to make their fortune in China.

International relations as a field of study is yet to take due cognizance of the role played by the movement of ordinary people across national boundaries in the relations between countries. In its obsession with war, diplomacy and geopolitics, it rarely pauses to analyse the impact of migratory peoples, their potential for giving rise to either friction and tension on the one hand or to sympathy and friendship on the other hand between different countries. At the same time, what may be called migration studies also tend to overlook the significance of immigrant communities for the relations between countries. Most of these studies tend to view the impact of such communities from the point of view of race or ethnic relations *within* the host society, rather than from the standpoint of international relations.

Relations between China and India are peculiar in the sense that, despite being neighbours sharing a lengthy boundary line, the physical and geographical barriers between the two are immense and have tended to inhibit intercourse on a scale commensurate with the size of their populations. Even the wondrous technological advances in transport and communication in the modern era have done little to actually facilitate interaction among their peoples in practical terms. It is common to pin the responsibility for the problems in Sino-Indian relations in modern times on a tricky border question and on the shortcomings of diplomacy, and to leave it at that. But this is perhaps only part of the problem. If one looks beyond, a part of the problem in Sino-Indian relations in the modern era could be that these relations have rested on a paucity of direct interaction between the two countries and peoples. This has meant that Sino-Indian relations have had a narrow base, leading to a certain element of unreality and excessive dependence on the perceptions and interests of a few individuals. Because the Chinese and Indian perceptions of each other have not been deep-rooted, they could change radically and repeatedly, swinging from the highs of friendship and brotherhood to the lows of sharp hostility in an alarming fashion, according to passing political compulsions.

The passage of thousands of ordinary Indians to China over the course of the nineteenth and first half of the twentieth centuries is one of the few, and certainly one of the major, forms of direct, mass, interaction between Chinese and Indian peoples in the modern era. It is for this reason that their experience needs to be analysed objectively and in all its complexity, for the impressions it may have left on the perceptions of Indians and Chinese about each other, for what it may tell us about how colonialism and imperialism affected the relations between Indians and Chinese. The story of these Indians is no doubt a disturbing one in many respects. It is not easy for the Indian to live down the legacy of having been a peddlar of opium or, an auxiliary of imperialist interests in China. Nevertheless, the story also shows that Indians have not been strangers to China; that a number of them have in fact lived and worked in Chinese cities and towns, interacted and forged relationships with Chinese people, and have to that extent at least, been a part of the lives and times of the Chinese people in their recent history.

NOTES

1. Guo Deyan's dissertation on the Parsis at Canton gives plenty of examples of this perception of Indians in Chinese documents. 'Qingdai Guangzhoude Pasi Shangren', unpublished Ph.D. thesis, Zhongshan University, Guangzhou, China, 2001.

2. From the introduction to I.J. Bahadur Singh, ed., *The Other India: The Overseas Indians and their Relationship with India*, New Delhi: Arnold-Heinemann, 1979, p. 2.

3. Niharranjan Roy, 'A Cultural History of the Overseas Indian', in *The Other India*, ed. I.J. Bahadur Singh, p. 41.

4. There were a few exceptions. One of the few Indians who appeared to be enthusiastic about the prospects of continuing and further expanding Indian business ties with China in the turbulent post-war period was one K.B. Vaidya, a businessman in China. His books, *And Now China* (1945) and *India and the Far East* (1946), detailed the areas in which India-China business cooperation could be extended, and made a forceful plea in its favour.

5. Claude Markovits, *The Global World of Indian Merchants, 1750-1947: Traders of Sind from Bukhara to Panama*, Cambridge: Cambridge University Press, 2000, pp. 5-6.

6. Jacques M. Downs, *The Golden Ghetto: the American Commercial Community at Canton and the Shaping of American China Policy, 1784-1844*, Bethlehem: Lehigh University Press, 1997, p. 238.

7. This subject is being explored more fully in a research project which the author is undertaking in collaboration with Shalini Saksena, entitled 'China in the making of Bombay'.

Appendix A

A NOTE ON THE INDIAN POPULATION IN CHINA[1]

Arriving at an accurate assessment of the total number of Indians in China at any given point in the period under review poses several difficulties. In the first place, different authorities were responsible for the Indians in different parts of China. Hong Kong Indians were the responsibility of the colonial authorities on the island; Shanghai Indians came under the jurisdiction of the Municipal Council of the International Settlement of Shanghai; Indians in Xinjiang were covered by the British Consulate General at Kashgar and its predecessors. These authorities for the most part carried out surveys to suit their own purposes at irregular intervals. For much of the period in question, a regular census of the Indian population was not conducted even in the more important centres of Hong Kong and Shanghai. As for the Indians who managed to find their way to the smaller towns, there is practically no way of accounting for them.

Nevertheless, for Shanghai, we have a regular quinquennial estimate of the total number of Indians carried out by the authorities of the International Settlement for the period from 1880 to 1935. In Hong Kong, Indians began to figure in the census reports from 1872. However, the varying categories under which they have been listed, and the lack of consistency in the kinds of information presented from one census report to the next, make it difficult to give an accurate picture of the growth and development of the community. In the early reports, Indians are included in the category of 'Goa, Manila, Indian and others of

Mixed Blood'. Even after Indians begin to be listed separately, the listings are sometimes those of 'civilians' and sometimes those of 'residents' (a smaller category, which excludes members of the merchant marine in Hong Kong at the time of the census). Military and police personnel are sometimes listed separately, but at other times it is not specified, while in some cases family members of these personnel are listed along with them. The movement of troops in and out of Hong Kong, as well as of Indian migrants passing through Hong Kong on their way to other countries, accounts for considerable fluctuation at certain times in the number of Indians in Hong Kong.

A peculiar problem arises from the listing of Indians from time to time under the general category of 'British subjects', in the surveys carried out by the authorities both in Hong Kong and in Xinjiang. Where this is followed by a list according to birthplace, it is fairly simple to identify which of this category were Indians. However, this would not have accounted for all the Indians, because those second and third-generation Indians born in Hong Kong and China would not be identifiable as Indians by their place of birth. The propensity of the British authorities to sometimes list Indians not according to nationality, but according to religious denomination, also clouds the picture. Whereas 'Hindus' and 'Parsis' are easily identifiable as Indians, the same is not true of those listed as 'Muslims', 'Christians' or 'Jews'.

In the following account of the Indian population, statistics based on official surveys consulted by me have had to be supplemented wherever necessary by figures recorded in other secondary sources, or by approximate estimates given by contemporary writers and officials.

MACAO, CANTON AND HONG KONG

The earliest Indians to arrive in eastern China in the period under review were based at Macao, since the regulations of the Chinese Empire at that time permitted them to come to Canton only for the duration of the trading season. The number of Parsi traders in Macao in 1831 and 1833 were forty-one and fifty-two respectively. At this stage they actually outnumbered the numbered the English traders there. Although in the aftermath of the Opium War, many Indian firms shifted to Hong Kong and the other treaty ports, Canton continued to be a major base of operations for a while. The 1848 Hong Kong Almanack and Directory shows a figure of thirty-one Parsi firms in Canton, with 117 resident partners and assistants.

When the British took possession of Hong Kong in January 1841, there were about 2,700 Indian troops and at least four Indian merchants present. By 1845, the number of merchants had reached 368. There seems to have been a drop-off in their number in the following years. In 1855, there was an actual decrease in the number of merchants to just 193, probably because of the departure for India of those merchants who had been staying on in Hong Kong only to press their claims for compensation for opium surrendered during the War of 1840-2. However, there was an increase in the number of women and children (79 and 99 respectively), indicating a more permanent settlement. In the early 1870s, there was another drop in the size of the civilian Indian population on the island, as the first batch of administrative personnel retired and left for home. Thereafter, the rise in the number of Indians remained fairly steady. In 1876, the total number of Indians was 639, in 1881 it was 754, in 1897 it was 1348, and in 1901 it had risen to 1548. In 1897 the ratio of Indian males to females was 977:371, while in 1901 it was 1203:345.

By 1906 the number of Indians had increased significantly, to a total of 2,068, mainly because of the arrival of coolies to work on the Kowloon-Canton Railway and because of the presence of a number of migrants passing through on their way to North America. The 1911 census, conducted by P.P.J. Wodehouse, contained the most complete survey and analysis of the Indian population. This census listed the total number of Indians as 3,049. About 700 of these were considered permanent residents. A new phenomenon—that of Hong Kong-born Indians—was also recorded in this census. 264 Indian males and 279 Indian females belonged to this category. The report also mentioned that 115 Punjabi males described themselves as unemployed, most probably because they were awaiting passage to North America. Occupation-wise categorization of the Indian population showed that 375 were policemen, 50 were gaolers, 388 were private watchmen, and 233 were in the commercial sector (mainly drapers and silk dealers), while only a handful were professionals.

The bulk of the population were Punjabi Sikhs and Muslims and non-Punjabi Muslims, while Hindus and Parsis numbered only 64 and 66 respectively. Of the Punjabis on Hong Kong, the overwhelming majority hailed from the three districts of Amritsar, Ludhiana and Lahore.

The 1921 census went back to the practice of including Indians under a larger, more general, category—that of 'British subjects'. It mentioned, however, that a large number of those Indians born outside India (628 altogether) were of mixed race. It also noted that 85 per cent of the Indians were policemen, watchmen or in government service. However the next census, of 1931, showed that of the 3475 Indians in Hong Kong, as many as 1,294 were connected with trade and commerce. The increase in the proportion of those in this sector may have been due to the increase in the number of Sindhi merchants and their families arriving in this region, as well as the declining percentage of policemen who were Indians due to the conscious policy of increasing the proportion of Chinese in the force.

The total number of Indians registered for the year 1941 was a high 7,379, but this was an abnormal figure accounted for by the presence of a number of Indian refugees from other parts of the region who fled to Hong Kong during the War.

SHANGHAI

The following table shows the steady growth of the Indian population in Shanghai:

Year	No. of Indians	Year	No. of Indians
1880	4	1910	804
1885	58	1915	1,009
1890	89	1920	1,954
1895	119	1925	2,154
1900	296	1930	1,842
1905	568	1935	2,341

From the above table, we can see that the number of Indians in Shanghai began to pick up only around the turn of the century. A particularly big leap took place in the years from 1915 to 1920. The slight drop in the figures between 1925 to 1930 (the only exception to the pattern of growth in numbers) could be due to political turbulence in Shanghai and southern and central China in general in that period. One source gives an approximate estimate of 3500 Indians in Shanghai in 1937, at the outbreak of the Sino-Japanese War. Various official sources give an estimate of about 2,000 to 2,500 Indians in Shanghai in 1945, at the end of the War and before mass repatriation commenced.

According to one source, there were fourteen Indian traders out of a total of seventy-six foreign traders in Shanghai before 1859,[2] but little is known about what became of them, and why the Yearbooks of the Shanghai Municipal Council should list only four Indians in 1880. The fact is that after the 1880s, the overwhelming majority of Indians in Shanghai belonged to the group of policemen, jailers and watchmen. In this sense, the community had a different socio-economic composition from that in Canton and Hong Kong. For instance, in 1903, 181 were policemen and 180 were watchmen; and in 1912, 449 were policemen, 400 were watchmen and 76 were jailers. The arrival of families to join these men probably accounted for a significant proportion of the increase in the number of Indians in the last few decades. For example, of the total number in 1935, 1655 were men, while 325 were women, 188 were boys and 173 were girls. Nevertheless, in 1938 the number of Indian companies operating in Shanghai was as many as forty-five, and in 1939 this increased to forty-nine. Even as late as 1950, there were fifteen Indian enterprises in Shanghai, all in the import-export business.

OTHER PARTS OF EASTERN CHINA

There is evidence of Indians in Hankou, Nanjing, Chefoo, Swatow, Tianjin, Beijing, Mukden, Harbin and other places among the numerous 'treaty ports' that were opened to foreign trade and commerce from the later nineteenth century. However, there are few estimates of their number. Hankou had by far the largest concentration of Indians in eastern China apart from Shanghai and Hong Kong. In the twentieth century, before the outbreak of the Sino-Japanese War, there appear to have been between 100 and 200 Indians there, mostly working as employees of the foreign concessions in these places. None of the other towns and cities appear to have had more than twenty to forty Indians at most, although in 1908, Tianjin is supposed to have had more than seventy Indians, of whom about thirty were policemen. In 1910, four Indians were recorded as being in Yunnan and Guizhou.

XINJIANG

Surveys of Indians in Xinjiang were not conducted on a systematic basis, and even when they were undertaken from time to time, political considerations led to varied interpretations of who exactly constituted an Indian. A number of Indian Muslim settlers in the region, who originally came from north Kashmir, Ladakh, etc, were virtually indistinguishable from the local population in Xinjiang. Official British sources in 1900 estimated that there were about 150 Indian traders and moneylenders in the towns of southern Xinjiang. Another source estimates that by 1913, the number of Punjabi traders had come down to about twenty, but this number increased during the boom of the early 1920s to reach a figure of about 100-50 Hindu traders, in addition to an unspecified number of moneylenders, Muslim merchants and settlers. A British journalist, Peter Fleming, who travelled through Xinjiang in 1936, referred to a total of about 500 British Indians in the province at that time.

NOTES

1. The information presented in this appendix is based on the following sources: for Shanghai, the *Yearbooks of the Municipal Council of the International Settlement of Shanghai, Jiu Shanghai renkou bianqian de yanjiu,* Shanghai: Shanghai renmin chubanshe, 1980; and Chen Zhilong, 'Shanghai: A Window for Studying the Sino-Indian Relations in the Era of Colonialism and Imperialism' (draft paper submitted to the seminar on 'Interactions between India and China in the era of colonialism and imperialism', New Delhi, 6-7 November, 2000; for Hong Kong, the *Hong Kong Census Reports, 1841-1941,* Hong Kong, 1965; K.N. Vaid, *The Overseas Indian Community in Hong Kong,* Hong Kong: Centre of Asian Studies, University of Hong Kong, 1972; and Barbara-Sue White, *Turbans and Traders: Hong Kong's Indian Communities,* New York: Oxford

University Press, 1994; for Macao and Canton, H.B. Morse, *Chronicles of the East India Company Trading to China,* vol. 3, Oxford: the Clarendon Press, 1926; and the collection of notes of the Rev. Carl T. Smith which he was kind enough to share with me; for Xinjiang, proceedings of the Foreign Department, the Foreign and Political Department and the External Affairs Department at the National Archives of India, New Delhi; C.P. Skrine and Pamela Nightingale, *Macartney at Kashgar: New Light on British, Chinese and Russian Activities in Sinkiang, 1890-1918,* U.K. Methuen & Co. Ltd, 1973, C.P. Skrine, *Chinese Central Asia: an Account of Travels in Northern Kashmir and Chinese Turkestan,* Hong Kong: Oxford University Press, 1986; and Peter Fleming, *News from Tartary: a Journey from Peking to Kashmir,* London: Macdonald & Co., 1936, rpt. 1980; for the estimates of Indians in other parts of China, relevant files in the above-mentioned proceedings at the National Archives of India.

2. Guo Deyan, 'Qingdai Guangzhoude Pasi Shangren', unpublished Ph.D. thesis, Zhongshan University, Guangzhou, China, 2001, p. 84. Guo refers to them as 'Parsi' merchants, but in fact a number of those listed were clearly Ismaili and not Parsi.

Appendix B

INDIAN ARMED FORCES DEPLOYED IN CHINA, 1800-1949[1]

The earliest involvement of Indian armed forces in China was the despatch of 600 sepoys of the Bengal army under Rear Admiral Drury to Macao during the Napoleonic Wars. The contingent arrived in Macao on 11 Sept. 1808 and departed for India on 23 December of the same year.

FIRST OPIUM WAR, 1840-1842

Name of Unit	Arrival in China	Departure	Places deployed/ Campaigns fought
1. Madras Sappers & Miners			Dinghai, July 1840; Amoy, Aug. 1841; Dinghai, Zhenhai, Ningbo, Oct. 1841-winter 1842; Shanghai, June 1842
2. 2nd Regiment, Madras Native Infantry (MNI)		June 1845 (arr. Madras)	Yangzi exped. force; Shanghai, June 1842; Zhenjiang, July 1842; Zhoushan Field Force.
3. 6th, MNI		Nov. 1842	Zhenjiang, July 1842

4. 14th, MNI	June 1842	Dec. 1842	Zhenjiang, July 1842
5. 36th, MNI			Ningbo, winter 1841-2
6. 37th, MNI	Dec.1840		Chuanbi, Jan. 1841; the Bogue defences, Feb. 1841; Canton, Sanyuanli, May 1841
7. 41st, MNI			Zhoushan garrison, from July 1840
8. Madras Rifles			Dinghai, Zhenhai, Ningbo, Oct. 1841; Zhapu, May 1842; Yangzi exped. Force
9. Madras Artillery			Dinghai, July 1840; Chuanbi, Jan. 1841, Bogue defences, Feb. 1841; Dinghai, Zhenhai, Ningbo, Oct. 1841; Zhapu, May 1842; Shanghai, Zhenjiang, June-July 1842

(Contd.)

Name of Unit	Arrival in China	Departure	Places deployed/ Campaigns fought
10. 18th, MNI			Zhoushan; Chuanbi, Jan. 1841; Amoy, Aug. 1841; Dinghai, Zhenhai, Ningbo, Oct. 1841; Zhapu, May 1842; Shanghai, Zhenjiang, June-July 1842
11. 26th, MNI			Zhoushan; Chuanbi, Jan. 1841; Amoy, Aug. 1841; Dinghai, Zhenhai, Ningbo, Oct. 1841; Zhapu, May 1842; Shanghai, Zhenjiang, June-July 1842
12. 49th, MNI			Zhoushan; Chuanbi, Jan. 1841; Amoy, Aug. 1841; Dinghai, Zhenhai, Ningbo, Oct. 1841; Zhapu, May 1842; Shanghai, Zhenjiang, June-July 1842.

13. Madras Gun Lascars

14. Bengal Volunteers	1840 (1st contingent); 1842 (2nd contingent)	Yangzi exped. force
		Macao; Chuanbi, Jan.1841; Zhenjiang. July 1842

Barring a force of about 1,250 men, including men from the 41st MNI, one company of gun lascars and one company of Madras Sappers & Miners, the rest of the force were withdrawn from China on 20 December 1842.

SECOND OPIUM WAR, 1857-60

Name of unit	Arrival in China	Departure	Places deployed/Campaigns fought
1. 47th, Bengal Native Infantry (BNI)	June 1858	1859	
2. 65th, BNI	June 1858	1859	Shek-tsin, Jan. 1859
3. 70th, BNI	Feb. 1858	1859	Baiyunshan
4. 38th, MNI			Canton, Dec. 1857
5. 3rd Bombay Native Infantry (ByNI)	1859		Hong Kong, Canton
6. 5th, ByNI	1859		Hong Kong, Canton
7. 21st, MNI		May 1861 (arr. India)	Hong Kong, Canton

Name of unit	Arrival in China	Departure	Places deployed/Campaigns fought
8. 1st Sikh Irregular Cavalry (Probyn's Horse)	Apr. 1860		Dagu; Matou
9. 2nd Sikh Cavalry (Fane's Horse)			Zhangjiawan, Dangzhou, Tianjin
10. Madras Sappers & Miners, A & K companies			
11. 8th, Punjab infantry	Apr. 1860		
12. 11th, Punjab infantry	July 1860		Canton
13. 19th, Punjab infantry	Apr. 1860		
14. Ludhiana Sikh Reg.	Apr. 1860		
15. 15th, Punjab infantry	Apr. 1860		
16. 2nd, MNI			
17. 12th, MNI			
18. 1st Light infantry			
19. Madras Mountain Train			

TAIPING SUPPRESSION CAMPAIGN, 1860-1864

Name of unit	Places deployed/ Campaigns fought
1. Ludhiana regiment	Shanghai
2. 11th, Punjab infantry	Shanghai (till May 1862)
3. 19th, Punjab infantry	
4. 5th, Bombay light infantry	
5. Madras Artillery	
6. Baluchi regiment	
7. 22nd Regiment (?)	
8. Agra troops (?)	

SUPPRESSION OF BOXER REBELLION (YI HE TUAN UPRISING), 1900

Name of unit	Places deployed/ Campaigns fought	Name of unit	Places deployed/ Campaigns fought
1. 1st Bengal Lancers (Skinner's Horse)	Beizang, Yangzun, Beijing, Baoding	18. 5th Infantry, Hyderabad contingent	
2. 16th Bengal Lancers		19. 3rd Punjab Light Infantry	
3. 7th Rajputs	Dagu, Beijing	20. 4th Punjab Infantry	
4. 24th Bengal Infantry		21. 20th Punjab Infantry	
5. 2nd Bengal Infantry	Shanghai	22. 28th Madras Infantry	
6. 6th Bengal Infantry		23. 3rd Bombay Light Cavalry (later Poona Horse)	
7. Bengal Sappers & Miners		24. 1st Sikh Regiment	Beijing, Baoding
8. 51st Sikhs		25. 14th Sikhs	
9. Bombay Sappers & Miners		26. 14th Gurkha Rifles	

No.	Unit	Location
10.	26th Bombay Infantry	Baoding
11.	30th Bombay Infantry	Shanghai
12.	22nd Bombay Infantry	
13.	3rd Madras Infantry	
14.	1st Madras Infantry (Pioneers)	Weihaiwei
15.	28th Madras Infantry	Weihaiwei
16.	31st Madras Infantry	
17.	Madras Sappers & Miners	Baoding
27.	24th Punjab Infantry	Beijing, Baoding
28.	Hong Kong Regiment	Tianjin, Beijing
29.	Hong Kong & Singapore Batallion Royal Artillery	
30.	Jodhpur Sardar Risala*	
31.	Alwar infantry regiment*	
32.	Bikaner Camel Corps*	
33.	Malerkotla Sappers*	

* Imperial service troops, who did not participate in the actual fighting, but did garrison duties, patrolled railway lines, etc.
A total of 18,000 Indian troops formed part of the Allied Expeditionary Force.

POST-BOXER OCCUPATION OF CHINA BY ALLIED FORCES

Name of unit	Period of deployment	Area of deployment
21st Punjab Infantry	Jan. 1904	North China
30th Punjab Infantry	Jan. 1904	North China
10th Bombay Infantry	Jan. 1904	South China
14th Bombay Infantry	Jan. 1904	South China
41st Dogra	1907	North China
47th Sikhs	1907	North China
119th Infantry	1907	South China
129th Baluchis	1907	
76th Punjabis	1908	North China
13th Rajputs	1908	South China
105th Mahrattas	1908	
124th Infantry	World War I	North China
8th Rajputs	World War I	South China
126th Infantry	World War I	South China

THE GARRISON OF HONG KONG

Name of unit	Period of deployment	Name of unit	Period of deployment
37th MNI	1842	34th Pioneers	Boxer Rebellion
Bengal Volunteers	1842	25th Punjabis	1912
Madras Sappers & Miners	1842	26th Punjabis	1912
39th MNI	1842	24th Hazara Mountain Battery	1912
'Gun lascars'	1845-1946*	2nd Punjab, 5th Battalion	1926
42nd MNI	1847	15th Punjab, 3rd Battalion	1929
12th MNI	1857	9th Jat, 3rd Battalion	1931
21st MNI	1860	1st Kumaon Rifles	1938
29th MNI	1870-72	7th Rajputs, 5th Battalion	1941
13th MNI	1872	14th Punjabis, 2nd Battalion	1941
Hong Kong Regiment	1892-1902		

* From 1892, the 'gun lascars' came to be known as the Asiatic Artillery Company. In 1898, they were renamed the Hong Kong and Singapore Battalion Royal Artillery and in 1899, the Hong Kong and Singapore Royal Garrison Artillery. From November 1946 commenced the gradual withdrawal of all Indian garrison troops from Hong Kong, except for the Gorkha troops.

Bibliography

PRIMARY SOURCES

DOCUMENTS:

National Archives of India, New Delhi

Proceedings of the Foreign Department, Foreign and Political Department and External Affairs Department.
Indian Independence League Papers.
Raja Mahendra Pratap Papers.

Nehru Memorial Museum & Library, New Delhi

K.P.S. Menon Papers

Maharashtra State Archives, Mumbai

Select files pertaining to China from the proceedings of the Secret and Political Department, Political Department, General Department and Revenue Department.

University of Bombay Library

Jamsetjee Jejeebhoy Papers

University of Hong Kong Library, Hong Kong

Great Britain Colonial Office—Hong Kong: Original Correspondence (C.O. 129 series) (microfilm).

PUBLISHED COLLECTIONS

Qingdai Chouban Yiwu Shimo (Daoguang, Xianfeng and Tongzhi
        Periods), Beijing: Palace Museum, photolithograph of original
        compilation, 1930; rpt., Shanghai: Zhonghua Shuju, 1964.
Yapian Zhanzheng Ziliao Congkan, vols. 3, 4, Shanghai, 1954.
Hong Kong Census Reports, 1841-1941, Hong Kong, 1965.
Yearbooks of the Municipal Council of the International Settlement of Shanghai,
        1935-42.

PERIODICALS

The Canton Register, Canton, 1827-43.

Friend of China, Hong Kong, 1842-59.

SECONDARY SOURCES

Ali, Imran, *The Punjab Under Imperialism, 1885-1947,* New Delhi: Oxford
        University Press, 1989.
Amba Bai, *Indian Views of China Before the Communist Revolution,*
        Cambridge, Mass.: M.I.T. Centre for International Studies,
        1955.
Bagchi, Prabodh Chandra, *India and China: A Thousand Years of Cultural
        Relations,* Bombay: Hind Kitabs, 2nd edn., 1950.
Bard, Solomon, *Traders of Hong Kong: Some Foreign Merchant Houses, 1841-
        99,* Hong Kong: Hong Kong Urban Council, 1993.
Barrier, N. Gerald and Verne A. Dusenbery, *The Sikh Diaspora: Migration
        and the Experience Beyond Punjab,* Delhi: Chanakya Publishers,
        1989.
Barstow, A.E., *Handbooks for the Indian Army—the Sikhs,* New Delhi:
        Government of India, rpt., 1941.
Benjamin, N., 'Bombay's "Country Trade" with China (1765-1865)',
        Indian Historical Review, vol. 1, no. 2, Sept. 1974, pp. 295-303.
Betham, Geoffrey, and H.V.R. Geary, *The Golden Galley: The Story of the
        Second Punjab Regiment, 1761-1947,* New Delhi: Oxford
        University Press, 1956.
Betta, Chiara, 'Myth and Memory: Chinese Portrayal of Silas Aaron
        Hardoon, Luo Jialing and the Aili Garden between 1924 and
        1995', in *From Kaifeng . . . to Shanghai: Jews in China,* ed. Roman
        Malek, Nettetal: Steyler Verl., 2000.
Bhargava, Moti Lal, *Indian National Congress—Its Affiliates in South and
        East Asia,* New Delhi: Reliance Publishing House, 1986.
———, *Netaji Subhas Chandra Bose in South East Asia and India's Liberation
        War, 1943-5,* New Delhi: Vishwavidya Publishers, 1982.

Bhatia, Prem, *Indian Ordeal in Africa*, New Delhi: Vikas, 1973.

Bhatia, Shyamala, *Social Change and Politics in Punjab, 1898-1910*, New Delhi: Enkay Publishers, 1987.

Bose, Arun, 'Indian Revolutionaries in Thailand till 1941', in *Challenge: A Saga of India's Struggle for Freedom*, New Delhi: People's Publishing House, 1984.

Brown, G.T. 'Hindu Conspiracy and the Neutrality of the U.S.A. (1914-17)', unpublished M.A. thesis, University of California, Berkeley, California. Microfilm, National Archives of India, Acc. No. 1241 (Part).

Bulley, Anne, *The Bombay Country Ships, 1790-1883*, Richmond: Curzon Press, 2000.

Cardew, Lt. F.G., *A Sketch of the Services of the Bengal Native Army to the Year 1895*, New Delhi: Today and Tomorrow's Printers and Publishers, 1971.

Chakrabarti, Dilip K. and Nayanjot Lahiri, 'The Assam-Burma Route to China', *Man and Environment*, vol. 10, 1986, pp. 123-34.

Chang, Hsin-pao, *Commissioner Lin and the Opium War*, New York: W.W. Norton, 1964.

Chaturvedi, Gyaneshwar, *India-China Relations: 1947 to Present Day*, Agra: MG Publishers, 1991.

Chaudhuri, K.N., *Trade and Civilization in the Indian Ocean: An Economic History from the Rise of Islam to 1750*, Cambridge: Cambridge University Press, 1985.

Chen Dasheng and Denys Lombard, 'Foreign Merchants in Maritime Trade in Quanzhou ("Zaitun"): Thirteenth and Fourteenth Centuries', in *Asian Merchants and Businessmen in the Indian Ocean and the China Sea*, ed. Denys Lombard and Jean Aubin, New Delhi: Oxford University Press, 2000.

Chen Qilu, 'Xin Shasun Yanghang Pianduan', in *Jiu Shanghai de Waishang yu Maiban*, Shanghai: Shanghai Renmin Chubanshe, 1987.

Chen Zhilong, 'Shanghai: A Window for Studying the Sino-Indian Relations in the Era of Colonialism and Imperialism', draft paper submitted to the seminar on 'Interactions between India and China in the Era of Colonialism and Imperialism', New Delhi, 6-7 November, 2000.

Cheong, Wang Eang, *The Hong Merchants of Canton: Chinese Merchants in Sino-Western Trade*, Richmond, Surrey: Curzon Press, 1997.

Chhabra, G.S., *Social and Economic History of the Panjab (1849-1901)*, New Delhi: Sterling, 1962.

Chin Keh-mu, *A Short History of Sino-Indian Friendship*, Calcutta: New Book Centre, 1981.

Clarke, Colin, Ceri Peach and Steven Vertovec, eds., *South Asians Overseas: Migration and Ethnicity*, Cambridge: Cambridge University Press, 1990.

Coates, William Herbert, *The Old Country Trade of the East Indies*, London: Corn Market Press, 1911, 1969.

Cohen, Robin, ed., *The Cambridge Survey of World Migration*, Cambridge: Cambridge University Press, 1995.

Cohen, Stephen P., *The Indian Army: Its Contribution to the Development of a Nation*, Bombay: Oxford University Press, 1971.

Crisswell, Colin N., *The Taipans: Hong Kong's Merchant Princes*, Hong Kong: Oxford University Press, 1981.

Crisswell, Colin N. and Mike Watson, *The Royal Hong Kong Police (1841-1941)*, Hong Kong,: Macmillan, 1982.

Curtin, Philip, *Cross-Cultural Trade in World History*, Cambridge: Cambridge University Press, 1984.

Dale, Stephen Frederick, *Indian Merchants and Eurasian Trade, 1600-1750*, New Delhi: Foundation Books, 1994.

Darling, Malcolm, *The Punjab Peasant in Prosperity and Debt*, London: Oxford University Press, 1925.

———, *Wisdom and Waste in the Punjab Village*, London: Oxford University Press, 1934.

Darukhanawala, H.D., *Parsi Lustre on Indian Soil*, 2 vols., Bombay: G. Claridge, 1939.

Das, Rup Narayan, 'A Nationality Issue: Ethnic Indians in Hong Kong', in *The Other Hong Kong Report*, ed. Richard Y.C. Wong and Joseph Y.S. Cheng, Hong Kong: The Chinese University Press, 1990, pp. 147-57.

Das Gupta, Ashin, *Merchants of Maritime India, 1500-1800*, U.K., Variorum, 1994.

———, *Indian Merchants and the Decline of Surat, 1700-1750*, New Delhi: Manohar, 1994.

———, 'Indian Merchants and the Trade in the Indian Ocean', in *The Cambridge Economic History of India*, vol. 1, ed. T. Raychaudhuri and I. Habib, Cambridge: Cambridge University Press, 1982, pp. 407-33.

Datar, Kiran, 'The Traders of Punjab and Asian Trade (seventeenth to nineteenth centuries)', *Panjab Past and Present*, vol. 20, Oct. 1986, pp. 75-87.

Desai, Ashok V., 'The Origins of Parsi Enterprise', *Indian Economic and Social History Review*, vol. 5, no. 4, Dec. 1968.

Digby, Simon, 'The Maritime Trade of Asia', in *The Cambridge Economic History of India, 1200-1710*, vol. 1, ed. T. Raychaudhuri and I. Habib, Cambridge: Cambridge University Press, 1982.

Dignan, Don, *The Indian Revolutionary Problem in British Diplomacy, 1914-1919*, New Delhi: Allied Publishers, 1983.

Dodwell, H.H., *Sepoy Recruitment in the Old Madras Army*, Calcutta: Government Printer, 1922.

Downing, C. Toogood, *The Fan-Qui in China in 1836-37*, 3 vols., London: Henry Colburn Publisher, 1838.

Downs, Jacques M., *The Golden Ghetto: the American Commercial Community at Canton and the Shaping of American China Policy, 1784-1844*, Bethlehem, USA: Lehigh University Press, 1997.

Endacott, G.B., *Biographical Sketches of Early Hong Kong*, Singapore: Eastern Universities Press, 1962.

Famous Parsis: Biographical and Critical Sketches, Madras: G.A. Natesan & Co., 1930.

Farwell, Byron, *Armies of the Raj: From the Mutiny to Independence, 1858-1947*, London: Viking Press, 1990.

Fleming, Peter, *News from Tartary: A Journey from Peking to Kashmir*, London: Macdonald & Co., 1936, rpt. 1980.

Fok, K.C., comp., *Hong Kong and the Asian Pacific: An Index of Source Materials (1840-1900)*, Hong Kong: Joint Publishing (H.K.) Co. Ltd., 1993.

Frontier and Overseas Expeditions from India, vol.6, compiled in the Intelligence Branch, Army Headquarters, India, Simla, 1907-1913.

Fu Lo-shu, *A Documentary Chronicle of Sino-Western Relations, 1644-1820*, Tuscon, Ariz.: University of Arizona Press, 1966.

Gaborieau, Marc, 'Kashmiri Muslim Merchants in Tibet, Nepal and Northern India', in *Asian Merchants and Businessmen in the Indian Ocean and the China Sea*, ed. D. Lombard and J. Aubin, New Delhi: Oxford University Press, 2000.

Gadgil, D.R., *Origins of the Modern Indian Business Class: An Interim Report*, New York: Institute of Pacific Relations, 1959.

Gill, Bir Good, 'Trade of the Punjab with East Turkistan: Its Ramifications, 1865-1877', *Proceedings of Punjab History Conference*, nineteenth session, 22-4 March 1985.

Gopal, Surendra, *Indians in Russia in the 17th and 18th Centuries*, New Delhi: Indian Council of Historical Research, 1988.

Greenberg, Michael, *British Trade and the Opening of China, 1800-42*, Cambridge: Cambridge University Press, 1951.

Gregory, Robert, *India and East Africa: A History of Race Relations within the British Empire, 1830-1939*, Oxford: Clarendon Press, 1971.

Guha, Amalendu, 'Parsi Seths as Entrepreneurs, 1750-1850', *Economic and Political Weekly*, Aug. 1970, pp. M-107-15.

Guo Deyan, 'Qingdai Guangzhoude Pasi Shangren', unpublished Ph.D. thesis, Zhongshan University, Guangzhou, China, 2001.

Gyani, Bhagawan Singh, 'Two Rebels Meet', in *Rash Behari Basu: His Struggle for India's Independence*, ed. R. Rath and S.P. Chatterjee, Calcutta, 1963.

Harfield, Alan, *British and Indian Armies on the China Coast*, Farnham, Surrey: A. & J. Partnership, 1990.

Harris, F.R., *Jamsetji Nusserwanji Tata: a Chronicle of his Life*, Bombay: Blackie & Son (India) Ltd., 2nd edn., 1958.

Hay, Stephen N., *Asian Ideas of East and West: Tagore and his Critics in Japan, China and India*, Cambridge, Mass.: Harvard University Press, 1970.

Hirth, Frederick and W.W. Rockhill, trans., *Chau Ju-kua: His Work on the Chinese and Arab Trade in the 12th and 13th Centuries, Entitled Chu-fan-chi*, New York: Paragon Book Reprint Corp., 1966.

Hunter, William C., *The 'Fan Kwae' at Canton before Treaty Days, 1825-44*, Shanghai: The Oriental Affairs, 1882, 1938.

———, *Bits of Old China*, Shanghai: Kelly and Walsh Ltd., 1911.

Jackson, Stanley, *The Sassoons*, London: Heinemann, 1968.

Jain, Ravindra K., *Indian Communities Abroad: Themes and Literature*, New Delhi: Manohar, 1993.

Jhabvala, S.H., *Framji Cowasji Banaji: A Great Parsi*, Bombay, 1920.

Johnston, Hugh, *The Voyage of the Komagata Maru: The Sikh Challenge to Canada's Colour Bar*, New Delhi: Oxford University Press, 1979.

Josh, Sohan Singh, *Tragedy of Komagata Maru*, New Delhi, 1975.

———, *Hindustan Ghadar Party: a Short History*, vol. II, New Delhi: People's Publishing House, 1978.

Karaka, D.F., *History of the Parsees*, 2 vols., London, 1884.

Karmerkar, Mani P., 'Parsis in Maritime Trade on the Western Coast of India from the Seventeenth to the Nineteenth Century', in *The Parsis in Western India: 1818 to 1920*, ed. Nawaz Mody, Bombay: Allied Publishers, 1998.

Kessinger, T.B., *Vilayatpur, 1848-1968*, Berkeley: University of California Press, 1974.

Koh, Sung-jae, *Stages of Industrial Development in Asia: A Comparative History of the Cotton Industry in Japan, India, China and Korea*, Philadelphia: University of Pennsylvania Press, 1966.

Kondapi, C., *Indians Overseas*, New Delhi: Indian Council of World Affairs, 1951.

Kruger, Horst, 'Indian Revolutionaries Abroad Before 1914', in Nitish Ranjan Ray et al., *Challenge: A Saga of India's Struggle for Freedom*, New Delhi: People's Publishing House, 1984.

Kulke, Eckehard, *The Parsees in India: A Minority as Agent of Social Change*, New Delhi: Vikas, 1974.

Kuwajima, Sho, *Indian Mutiny in Singapore (1915)*, Calcutta: Ratna Prakashan, 1991.

Lal, Shiv, *India's Freedom-Fighters in South East Asia*, New Delhi: Archives Publishers, 1985.

Lattimore, Owen, *Pivot of Asia: Sinkiang and the Inner Asian Frontiers of China and Russia*, Boston: Little, Brown & Co., 1950.

Layton, Thomas N., *The Voyage of the 'Frolic': New England Merchants and the Opium Trade*, Stanford: Stanford University Press, 1997.

Lepervanche, Marie M. de, *Indians in a White Australia*, London: George Allen & Unwin, 1984.

Lethbridge, Henry, *Hong Kong: Stability and Change*, Hong Kong: Oxford University Press, 1978.

Lin Chengjie, *Zhongyin Renmin Youhao Guanxi Shi*, Beijing: Beijing Daxue Chubanshe, 1993.

Linley, A.F., *Ti-ping Tien-kwoh*, 2 vols., London: Day & Son Ltd., 1866.

Liu Xinru, *Ancient India and Ancient China: Trade and Religious Exchanges, AD 1-600*, New Delhi: Oxford University Press, 1988.

Mahajani, Usha, *The Role of Indian Minorities in Burma and Malaya*, Bombay: Vora & Co., 1960.

Mansingh, Surjit, 'An Overview of India - China Relations: From When to Where?', New Delhi: Nehru Memorial Museum & Library Occasional Papers on History and Society, Second Series, no. LVII, 1992.

Markovits, Claude, *The Global World of Indian Merchants, 1750-1947: Traders of Sind from Bukhara to Panama*, Cambridge: Cambridge University Press, 2000.

———, 'Indian communities in China, 1842-1949', in *New Frontiers: Imperialism's New Communities in East Asia, 1842-1953*, ed. Robert Bickers and Christian Henriot, Manchester: Manchester University Press, 2000.

———, 'Bombay as a Business Centre in the Colonial Period: a Comparison with Calcutta', in *Bombay: Metaphor for Modern India*, ed. Sujata Patel and Alice Thorner, Bombay: Oxford University Press, 1995.

McLeod, W.H., *Punjabis in New Zealand*, Amritsar: Guru Nanak Dev University, 1986.

Menon, K.P.S., *Delhi-Chunking*, New Delhi: Oxford University Press, 1947.

———, *Twilight in China*, Bombay: Bharatiya Vidya Bhavan, 1972.

Meyer, Maisie, 'The Sephardi Jewish Community of Shanghai and the Question of Identity', in *From Kaifeng . . . to Shanghai: Jews in China*, ed. Roman Malek, Nettetal: Steyler Verl., 2000.

Mitchell, John, *International Cultural Relations*, London: George Allen & Unwin, 1986.

Mody, Jehangir R.P., *Jamsetjee Jejeebhoy: The First Indian Knight and Baronet (1783-1859)*, Bombay: the author, 1959.

Moharir, Brig. V.J., *History of the Army Service Corps*, vol. 2 (*1858-1913*), New Delhi: Sterling Publishers, 1984.

Mollo, Boris, *The Indian Army*, U.K.: Blandford Press, 1981.

Morse, H.B., *Chronicles of the East India Company Trading to China, 1635-1834*, 3 vols., Oxford: The Clarendon Press, 1926.

Mukherjee, B.N., *External Trade of Early Northeastern India*, New Delhi: Har-Anand Publications, 1992.

Mukhopadhyaya, Sujit Kr. and Hsiao Ling Wu, 'Political Intercourse Between Bengal and China (Translated from Chinese Records)', *The Modern Review*, March 1945, pp. 121-2.

Nag, S.P., *Asian Relations Conference: March-April 1947*, New Delhi: Indian Council of World Affairs.

Nair, A.M., *An Indian Freedom Fighter in Japan*, Madras: Orient Longman, 1982.

Nightingale, Pamela, *Trade and Empire in Western India, 1784-1806*, Cambridge: Cambridge University Press, 1970.

Omissi, David, *The Sepoy and the Raj*, London: Macmillan, 1994.

Ouchterlony, John, *Chinese War: an account of all the operations of the British forces, from the commencement, to the Treaty of Nanking*, New York: Praeger Publishers, 1970 reprint.

Pan Guang and Li Peidong, eds., *Shanghai Jews' Memoirs*, Shanghai: Shanghaishi Zhengxie Wenshi Ziliao Bianjibu, 1995.

Pandian, M.S., 'Bohar (1550-1625): Record of his Visits to China', *Proceedings of the Indian History Congress*, 54th session, Mysore, 1993, pp. 757-8.

Panikkar, K.M., *India and China*, New Delhi: Asia Publishing House, 1957.

Petrie, David, *Communism in India, 1924-7*, Calcutta: Editions Indian, 1972.

Pettigrew, Joyce, 'Socio-Economic Background to the Emigration of Sikhs from Doaba', *Punjab Journal of Politics*, vol. 1, 1971, pp. 18-81.

Pratap, Raja Mahendra, *Reminiscences of a Revolutionary*, New Delhi: Raja Mahendra Pratap Birth Centenary Celebration National Committee, 1986.

———, *My Life Story of Fifty Five Years (Dec. 1886 to Dec. 1941)*, Dehradun, 1947.

Ptak, Roderich, 'China and Calicut in the early Ming period: Envoys and Tribute Embassies', *Journal of the Royal Asiatic Society of Great Britain and Ireland*, no. 1, 1989, pp. 81-111.

Puri, Harish K., *Ghadar Movement: Ideology, Organisation, Strategy*, Amritsar: Guru Nanak Dev University, 1983.

Pythian-Adams, E.G., *Madras Regiment, 1758-1958*, Wellington: The Defence Services Staff College Press, 1958.

Radhakrishnan, S. *India and China*, Bombay: Hind Kitabs, 1954.

Raghava Varier, M.S., 'Trade Relations Between Kerala and China, 1200-1500', *Proceedings of the Indian History Congress*, 51st session, Calcutta, 1990, pp. 690-8.

Ray, Haraprasad, *Trade and Diplomacy in India-China Relations: A Study of*

Bengal during the 15th Century, New Delhi: Radiant Publishers, 1993.

———, 'Nature of Trade and Diplomacy Between India and China During Ancient and Medieval Periods', *Journal of the Indian Congress of Asia-Pacific Studies*, vol. 1, no.1, Jan. 1995, pp. 32-40.

———, 'The Southern Silk Route from China to India—an Approach from India', *China Report*, vol. 31, no. 2, April-June 1995, pp. 177-96.

———, 'An Enquiry into the Presence of the Chinese in South and South-East Asia after the Voyages of Zheng He in Early Fifteenth Century', in *Mariners, Merchants and Oceans*, ed. K.S. Mathew, New Delhi: Manohar, 1995.

Ray, Indrani, 'India in Asian Trade in the 1730s—an 18th Century Memoir', in *Essays in Medieval Indian Economic History*, ed. Satish Chandra, New Delhi: Indian History Congress Publication, 1987.

Ray, Rajat Kanta, ed., *Entrepreneurship and Industry in India, 1800-1947*, New Delhi: Oxford University Press, 1992.

Ray, Sibanarayan, ed., *Selected Works of M.N. Roy*, vol. II *(1923-27)*, New Delhi, Oxford University Press, 1988.

Rizvi, Janet, *Trans-Himalayan Caravans: Merchant Princes and Peasant Traders in Ladakh*, New Delhi: Oxford University Press, 1999.

———, 'The Trans-Karakoram Trade in the Nineteenth and Twentieth Centuries', *Indian Economic and Social History Review*, vol. 31, no. 1, 1994.

Roth, Cecil, *The Sassoon Dynasty*, London: Robert Hale Ltd., 1941.

Rowe, David Nelson, ed., *Index to Ch'ing Tai Ch'ou Pan I Wu Shih Mo*, Hamden, Ct.: The Shoe String Press, Inc., 1960.

Roy, M.N., *M.N. Roy's Memoirs*, Bombay: Allied Publishers, 1964.

Sahay, Anand Mohan, *Indian Revolutionaries in Japan*, transcript in Nehru Memorial Museum & Library, n.d.

Saklatvala, B.Sh., *Jamsetji Tata*, New Delhi: Publications Division, Ministry of Information and Broadcasting, Government of India, 1970.

Sandhu, Maj-Gen. G.S., *The Indian Cavalry: History of the Indian Armoured Crops*, vol.1, New Delhi: Vision Books, 1981.

Sandhu, K.S., 'Sikh Immigration into Malaya During the Period of British Rule.', in *Studies in the Social History of China and South East Asia*, ed. Jerome Ch'en and Nicholas Tarling, Cambridge: Cambridge University Press, 1970.

Sandhu, K.S., and A. Mani, eds., *Indian Communities in Southeast Asia*, Singapore: ISEAS Times Academic Press, 1993.

Sangal, O.P., 'An Indian Soldier Indicts War', in *New Age*, Jan. 1953.

Sanyuanli Renmin Kangying Douzheng, Guangdongsheng Wenshi Yanjiu Guanbian: Zhonghua Shuju, 1978.

Sastry, K.A.N., 'The Beginning of Intercourse Between India and China', *The Indian Historical Quarterly*, vol. 14, 1938, pp. 380-7.

Sen, Tansen, *Buddhism, Diplomacy and Trade: The Realignment of Sino-Indian Relations, 600-1400*, Honolulu: Association of Asian Studies and University of Hawaii Press, 2003, rept. 2004.

———, 'Gautama Zhuan: An Indian Astronomer at the Tang Court', in *China Report* vol. 31, no. 2, April-June 1995, pp. 197-208.

———, 'Maritime Contacts between China and the Cola Kingdom (AD 850-1279)', in *Mariners, Merchants and Oceans*, ed. K.S. Mathew, New Delhi: Manohar, 1995.

Shanghai Gongong Zujie Shigao, Shanghai: Shanghaishi Ziliao Congkan, Shanghai Renmin Chubanshe, 1980.

Shanghai Yanjiu Ziliao, Shanghai, 1935, rpt. 1984.

Shaw, Robert, *Visits to High Tartary, Yarkand and Kashgar*, London: John Murray, 1871.

Siddiqi, Asiya, ed. *Trade and Finance in Colonial India*, New Delhi, Oxford University Press, 1995.

———, 'The Business World of Jamsetjee Jejeebhoy', *Indian Economic and Social History Review*, vol. 19, nos. 3-4, July-Dec. 1982, pp. 301-24.

———, 'Some Aspects of Indian Business under the East India Company', in *State and Business in India: A Historical Perspective*, ed. Dwijendra Tripathi, New Delhi: Manohar, 1987.

Simkin, C.G.F., *The Traditional Trade of Asia*, London: Oxford University Press, 1968.

Sinclair, Kevin, *Asia's Finest: an Illustrated Account of the Royal Hong Kong Police*, Hong Kong: Unicorn Books Ltd., 1983.

Singh, Baba Gurdit, *Voyage of Komagata Maru or India's Slavery Abroad*, Calcutta: Gurdit Singh, n.d.

Singh, Bhai Nahan and Bhai Kirpal Singh, eds., *Struggle for Free Hindustan: Ghadar Directory (Punjab Section)*, vol. IV, *1913-1915*, New Delhi: Gobind Sadan Institute for Advanced Studies in Comparative Religion, 1996.

Singh, Hari, *Agrarian Scene in British Punjab*, vol. 1, New Delhi: People's Publishing House, 1983.

Singh, I.J. Bahadur, *The Other India: The Overseas Indians and their Relationship with India*, New Delhi: Arnold-Heinemann, 1979.

Singh, Navtej, *Starvation and Colonialism: A Study of Famines in 19th Century British Punjab, 1858-1901*, New Delhi: National Book Organisation, 1996.

Singh, Brig. Rajendra, *History of the Indian Army*, New Delhi: Sardar Attar Singh, Army Educational Stores, 1983.

Skrine, C.P., *Chinese Central Asia: An Account of Travels in Northern Kashmir and Chinese Turkestan,* Hong Kong: Oxford University Press, rpt. 1986.

Skrine, C.P. and Pamela Nightingale, *Macartney at Kashgar: New Light on British, Chinese and Russian Activities in Sinkiang, 1890-1918,* London: Methuen, 1973.

Smith, Carl T., *A Sense of History: Studies in the Social and Urban History of Hong Kong,* Hong Kong: Hong Kong Educational Publishing Co., 1995.

Subrahmanyam, Sanjay. 'Iranians Abroad: Intra-Asian Elite Migration and Early Modern State Formation', *Journal of Asian Studies* vol. 51, no. 2, May 1992, pp. 340-61.

Swisher, Earl, *China's Management of the American Barbarians: a Study of Sino-American Relations, 1841-1861, with Documents,* New York: Octagon Books, 1953, 1972.

Tan Chung, ed., *Indian Horizons Special Issue: India and China,* vol. 43, nos. 1-2, 1994.

———, 'Ageless Neighbourliness Between India and China', *China Report,* vol. 15, no. 2, March-April 1979.

Tan Yun-shan, *Cultural Interchange Between India and China: an Address,* Santiniketan: Sino-Indian Cultural Society, 1940.

Thomas, Timothy N., *Indians Overseas: a guide to source materials in the India Office Records for the study of Indian emigration, 1830-1950,* London: The British Library, 1985.

Timberg, T.A., *The Marwaris: From Traders to Industrialists,* New Delhi: Vikas, 1978.

Tinker, Hugh, *The Banyan Tree: Overseas Emigrants from India, Pakistan and Bangladesh,* New York: Oxford University Press, 1977.

———, *A New System of Slavery: The Export of Indian Labour Overseas, 1830-1920,* London and New York: Oxford University Press, 1974.

Tripathi, Dwijendra, *Business Communities of India: An Historical Perspective,* New Delhi: Manohar, 1984.

Vaid, K.N., *The Overseas Indian Community in Hong Kong,* Hong Kong: Centre of Asian Studies, University of Hong Kong, 1972.

Vaidya, K.B., *India and the Far East,* Bombay, 1946.

Wadia, Ruttonjee Ardeshir, *Scions of Lowjee Wadia,* Bombay: R.A. Wadia, 1964.

Wakeman, Frederick Jr., *Policing Shanghai, 1927-37,* Berkeley: University of California Press, 1995.

———, *Strangers at the Gate: Social Disorder in South China, 1839-1861,* Berkeley and Los Angeles: University of California Press, 1966.

———, '1920-1937 Nian de Shanghai Jingcha' (the Shanghai police,

1920-37), in *Shanghai Tongwang Shijie Zhi Qiao*, vol. 1, Shanghai: Shanghai Shehui Kexueyuan Chubanshe, 1989, pp. 73-110.

Waley, Arthur, *The Opium War through Chinese Eyes*, London: George Allen & Unwin, 1958.

Warikoo, K., *Central Asia and Kashmir: a Study in the Context of Anglo-Russian Rivalry*, New Delhi: Gian Publishing House, 1989.

White, Barbara-Sue, *Turbans and Traders: Hong Kong's Indian Communities*, New York: Oxford University Press, 1994.

Yamamoto, T., 'International Relations Between China and the Countries Along the Ganga in the Early Ming Period', *Indian Historical Review*, vol. 4, no. 1, 1977, pp. 13-19.

Yu Sheng-wu and Chang Chen-kun, 'China and India in the Mid-Nineteenth Century', in *Rebellion 1857: A Symposium*, ed. Yu Sheng-wu and Chang Chen-kun, Calcutta: K.P. Bagchi & Co., 1986.

Zhang Zhongli and Chen Zengnian, *Shasun Jituan Zai Jiuzhongguo*, Beijing: Renmin Chubanshe, 1985.

Zhou Yiren, ed., *Jiu Shanghai Renkou Bianqian de Yanjiu*, Shanghai: Shanghai Renmin Chubanshe, 1980.

Index